To Clear Horizons

DOCTOR · WHO

THE TIME TRAVELLER'S ALMANAC

THE ULTIMATE INTERGALACTIC FACT-FINDER

Steve Tribe

BBC
BOOKS

1 3 5 7 9 10 8 6 4 2

Published in 2008 by BBC Books, an imprint of Ebury Publishing
A Random House Group Company

Doctor Who is a BBC Wales production for BBC One. Executive Producers: Russell T Davies and Julie Gardner. Series Producer: Phil Collinson.

The Random House Group Limited Reg. No. 954009

Addresses for companies within the Random House Group can be found at www.randomhouse.co.uk

A CIP catalogue record for this book is available from the British Library.

ISBN 978 1 846 07572 8

The Random House Group Limited supports The Forest Stewardship Council (FSC), the leading international forest certification organisation. All our titles that are printed on Greenpeace approved FSC certified paper carry the FSC logo. Our paper procurement policy can be found at www.rbooks.co.uk/environment.

Commissioning editor: Albert DePetrillo
Project editor: Kari Speers
Designer: Paul Lang
Production controller: Phil Spencer

Printed and bound by Firmengruppe APPL,
aprinta druck, Wemding, Germany

CONTENTS

KEY TO THE ALMANAC

The Time Traveller's Almanac is arranged chronologically from the beginning of time to the end of the universe, and covers a range of subjects and themes. These are colour-coded as follows:

MAJOR EVENTS

SIGNIFICANT PEOPLE

TRAVEL AND PLACES OF INTEREST

PLANETS, STAR SYSTEMS AND GALAXIES OF THE UNIVERSE

SPECIES OF THE UNIVERSE

SOCIAL AND ECONOMIC LIFE

SCIENCE AND TECHNOLOGY

MEDIA, CULTURE AND THE ARTS

SECRET ORGANISATIONS

MISCELLANEOUS

THE DAWN OF TIME

THE TIME LORDS OF GALLIFREY

Once, there was a planet called Gallifrey, orbiting twin suns at the centre of the universe and home to the oldest and most powerful race in the cosmos. Sometimes known as the Shining World of the Seven Systems, its endless mountain ranges were slopes of silver-leaved trees and deep red grass, capped with snow that shone in the dual sunlight under burnt-orange skies. In the mountains of Solace and Solitude on the continent of Wild Endeavour, there was a vast glass dome, surrounding and protecting the Citadel of the Time Lords.

This great civilisation had perfected the science of time travel when the universe was young. Every Time Lord had two hearts and the ability to regenerate – to completely transform his physical appearance. At the age of eight, Gallifreyan children left their families and entered the Academy, and were taken as novices to the Untempered Schism to look into the whole of the Vortex and the raw power of Time and Space. Some saw and fled; a few would witness this eternity and be driven insane. But others were inspired to devote their lives to observe the galaxies below them, and swore never to interfere. On occasion, however, the Time Lords saw fit to intervene in the affairs of others...

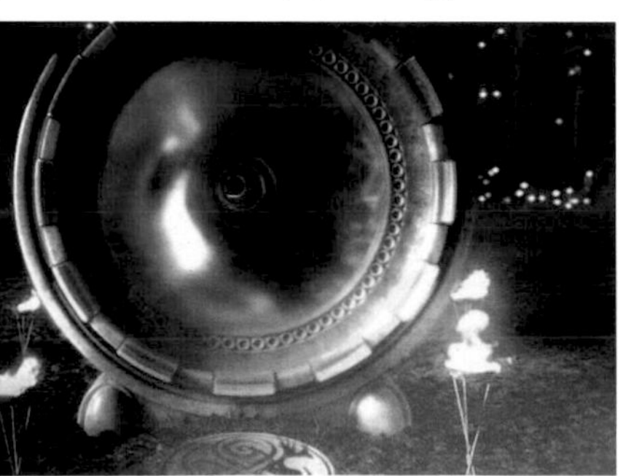

THE GENESIS OF THE DALEKS

> **Van Statten:** Genetically engineered by whom?
> **The Doctor:** By a genius ... By a man who was king of his own little world. *(Utah, 2012)*

On the planet Skaro, after a thousand-year war, the Kaled scientist Davros devised a life-support and travel machine for the mutation that he realised his people would ultimately evolve into. At the same time, he experimented with the mutated Kaled form, removing emotions that he regarded as weaknesses and instilling an overriding desire for supremacy. The result he named Daleks.

The Time Lords realised that the Daleks would one day destroy all life in the universe, so they despatched the Fourth Doctor to Skaro with instructions to avert or alter their development. This he failed to do, deciding that he could not wipe out an entire species. Instead he delayed their progress by a mere thousand years.

This was the first of a series of clashes between the Daleks and the Time Lords over the course of the millennia that followed, and ultimately led to a far bigger and much more devastating conflict.

THE LAST GREAT TIME WAR

The Time War raged through every time and no time and left the universe in an infinite state of temporal flux, yet no one knows how it started, few know what happened, and only one man truly knows how it ended.

Soon after the Tenth Dalek Occupation, the Daleks vanished from time and space as the Dalek Emperor led his entire race into the Vortex and let loose the Deathsmiths of Goth. At the same time, the Time Lords were deploying a fleet of Bowships, Black Hole Carriers and N-Forms gathered from their own history. In the first year of the War, Davros was killed when his command ship flew into the jaws of the Nightmare Child at the Gates of Elysium. The Time Lords resurrected the Master, an insane Time Lord whose criminal schemes had eventually cost him his life, to fight on their behalf – the perfect warrior in a Time War. But when he witnessed the Emperor Dalek take control of the Cruciform, the Master ran away and disguised himself as a human child in the Silver Devastation 100 trillion years into the future, hoping never to be found.

Both Daleks and Time Lords rejected Sontaran requests to join the greatest war in history. Most other Lesser Species were entirely unaware of the way that the histories of their worlds were being changed and unchanged. Higher Species like the Forest of Cheem, though, watched and despaired, and some were directly affected. The Nestenes lost not only their foodstocks, but also their protein planets. The Gelth were reduced to a gaseous state in search of physical form. The Greater Animus and its Carsenome were destroyed. The Eternals left this reality entirely. So did a small group of Daleks – the Cult of Skaro. They took with them a Time Lord prison ship that contained millions of Daleks, and travelled into the Void between realities, fleeing the Time War and waiting for an opportunity to re-emerge into this universe.

For a time, the Doctor led the Time Lords in battle, and fought on the front line. He witnessed the devastating fate of Arcadia, and tried but failed to save the Nestene home world and many others. He tried everything to end the conflict but, eventually, he had the chance to end the Time War completely and he chose to take it. Both great battle fleets of tens of millions of ships and both home worlds were obliterated, and both races died burning and screaming in an inferno that lasted just a single second. The Doctor saw Gallifrey and Skaro reduced to rocks and dust, and walked away from the ruins entirely alone – the only survivor, as far as he knew, of the Last Great Time War.

THE DARK TIMES

There was life in the universe from its earliest, darkest and most chaotic times, when the cosmos was many times smaller than it is now. The scriptures of the Veltino told of the imprisonment of a mighty Beast. The Lonely Assassins were almost as old as the universe itself – they spread through time and space and became known as the Weeping Angels. The Eternals, before they abandoned this reality, banished the Carrionites to the Deep Darkness, and both races became legends. The Nestenes and the Great Vampires stormed through space, feeding on life wherever they found it. Stories are still told of the Great Old Ones, beings with godlike powers that roamed the universe affecting the development of Lesser Species. One of these is known to have perished in the Hesperus galaxy, lost and alone and sheltering in the wreckage of the *Infinite*. And a race of omnivorous giant arachnids called the Racnoss multiplied across the galaxies and devoured whole planets. In one of their earliest acts of intervention, long before the Time War, the Time Lords joined an alliance of Fledgling Empires and went to war against the Racnoss, all but wiping them out.

THE CREATION OF THE EARTH

When the Fledgling Empires routed the forces of the Racnoss, just two Webstars survived. One carried the Empress of the Racnoss, who hibernated at the edge of the universe for 4.6 billion years until she was finally awoken by the cry of newborn Racnoss. The other, the *Secret Heart*, bore the eggs for a new hatching of Racnoss, and it drifted through space until it was caught in the gravity of a young star, just beginning to burn, and began to orbit it. The solar system had yet to form; this new sun was surrounded by rocks, dust and gas, swirling through space. When the *Secret Heart* arrived, its mass was greater than that of the elements around it, and it attracted them. Watched by the Doctor and Donna Noble, the Racnoss ship's gravity pulled the gas and dust towards it, and a new world gradually formed with the Webstar at its core – the planet Earth.

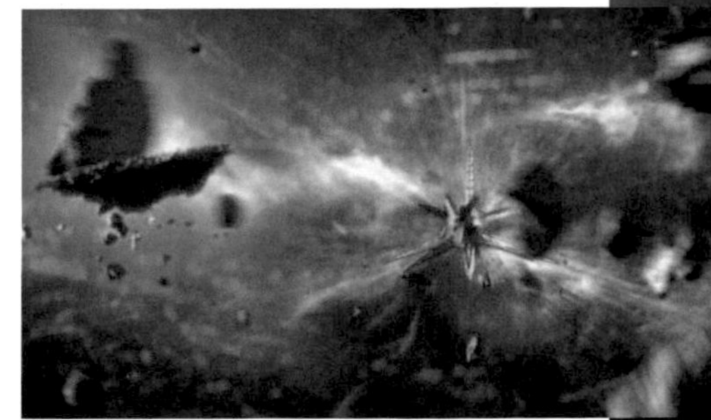

BRAVE NEW WORLD

THE FALL OF TROY

1184 BC

"I saw the fall of Troy.
– The Doctor to Rose Tyler (Cardiff, 1869)

By 1184 BC, the armies of Greece had been besieging the city of Troy for ten years. On the plains outside the city, the Greek leaders Agamemnon and Odysseus encountered an old man that they took to be the mighty god Zeus, arrived to win the war for them. When they realised that the old man was simply a traveller, the First Doctor, they gave him two days to devise a plan to capture Troy. Reluctantly, the Doctor provided plans for the construction of a wooden horse, inside which the Greeks could conceal their forces – an idea he had initially dismissed as an invention of the poet Homer. The finished horse was about 40 feet (12 metres) high, and its hollow belly was filled with 40 of the Greeks' best soldiers. The Trojans believed that it was the Great Horse of Asia, which they worshipped, and dragged the wooden imitation inside their city walls. The Greeks emerged in triumph and destroyed the city.

THE CENSUS OF QUIRINIUS

AD 6

"**Astrid Peth:** This Christmas thing, what's it all about?
The Doctor: Long story. I should know I was there. I got the last room.
(The Titanic, *2008)*

Caesar Augustus decreed that the governors of Syria and Judaea should conduct a tax census, requiring all citizens to travel to their ancestral homes. A carpenter named Joseph, a descendant of King David, journeyed to Bethlehem with his pregnant wife, Mary. When they reached the town, they found that all the rooms at the inn had been taken, and Mary was forced to give birth in a stable. The child was named Jesus, and these events, when recounted in the Gospel of Saint Luke, formed the basis of the Christian celebration of Christmas.

THE GREAT FIRE OF ROME

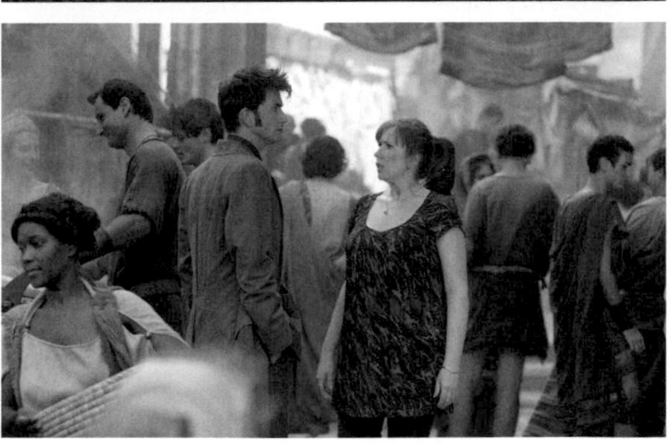

"And before you ask, that fire had nothing to do with me. Well, a little bit.
– The Doctor to Donna Noble (Pompeii, AD 79)

One night in the summer of the year 64, a great fire began in Rome. It lasted a week, and it destroyed or damaged as much as three-quarters of the city. Earlier that evening, the Emperor Nero had seen his plans for a New Rome destroyed by a small fire inadvertently caused by a visiting musician, Maximus Pettulian (actually the First Doctor). At first furious, Nero realised that the Senate's rejection of his plans to rebuild the city would be overturned if Rome itself were destroyed. He sent his guards into the city to round up torch-bearers, who were then paid to start the fires that would allow the construction of a new city – 'Neropolis', 'Nerossysum', or simply 'Nero'. As Rome burnt, Nero sat in his palace, playing his lyre.

FIRST-CENTURY POMPEII

The Roman town of Pompeii stood in the shadow of Vesuvius, near the Southern Italian city of Naples. By the time of its destruction, the town had a population of at least 20,000, who had no idea that the mountain was a volcano. Traders filled the streets, selling food, livestock and ceramics. At the centre of the town was the public Forum, with an amphitheatre nearby, and three sets of public baths, a food market and an aqueduct. Then there was the thermopolium, a bar that served as a gathering place for rebellious subcultures like the Etruscans and the Christians. Buildings in Pompeii used an under-floor heating system – a hypocaust – with heat carried in trenches from the hot springs around Vesuvius. Pompeii was unusual in relying on hot springs in this way – in Rome, for example, household heating was still provided by wood-burning furnaces.

BRAVE NEW WORLD

AD 79

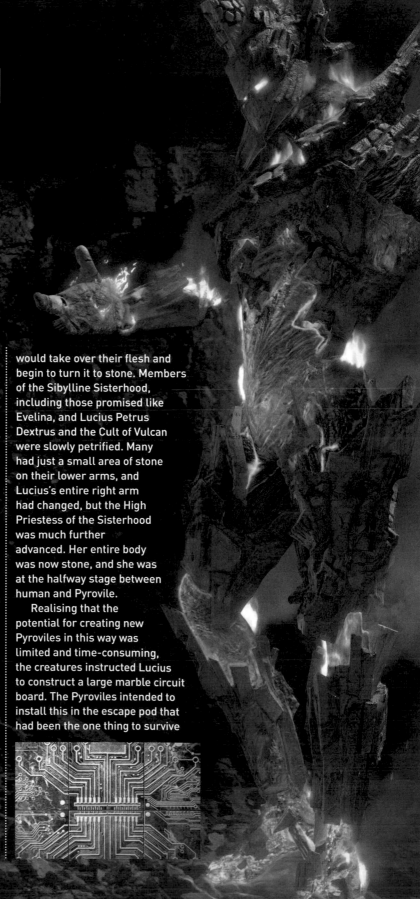

THE PYROVILES

Fleeing the loss of their home world, the Pyroviles crashed on Earth in southern Europe, disintegrating on impact. Fragmented and dormant, their essence spread through the underground heart of a mountain. Thousands of years later, the ancient Roman city of Pompeii had been established in the shadow of that mountain – Vesuvius. The earth tremors from the first stirrings of the mountain reawakened the Pyroviles in AD 62, and the creatures began to plan their escape. Drawing power from the volcanic potential of Vesuvius, they forced their way into the minds of nearby Pompeian people with latent psychic abilities.

The Pyroviles were able to make use of the local religious and spiritual customs of the people of Pompeii. Those deemed to have the gift of prophecy would inhale vapours from their hypocausts, breathing in the dust of Mount Vesuvius. They were in fact consuming tiny particles of rock containing the essence of the aliens, which seeded their bodies and began a physical transformation from human being into fully formed Pyrovile. The dust in their lungs would take over their flesh and begin to turn it to stone. Members of the Sibylline Sisterhood, including those promised like Evelina, and Lucius Petrus Dextrus and the Cult of Vulcan were slowly petrified. Many had just a small area of stone on their lower arms, and Lucius's entire right arm had changed, but the High Priestess of the Sisterhood was much further advanced. Her entire body was now stone, and she was at the halfway stage between human and Pyrovile.

Realising that the potential for creating new Pyroviles in this way was limited and time-consuming, the creatures instructed Lucius to construct a large marble circuit board. The Pyroviles intended to install this in the escape pod that had been the one thing to survive

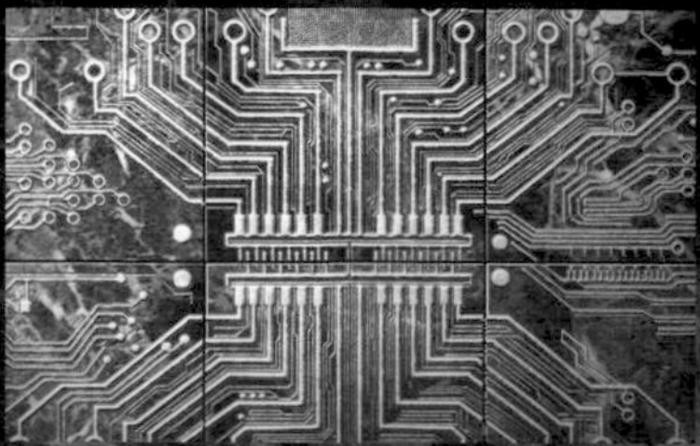

PLANET OF ORIGIN
Pyrovillia

APPEARANCE
8 metres tall; rock shell, held together by magma

ABILITIES
Psychic contact and manipulation

WEAPONS
Exhaled flame

WEAKNESS
Water

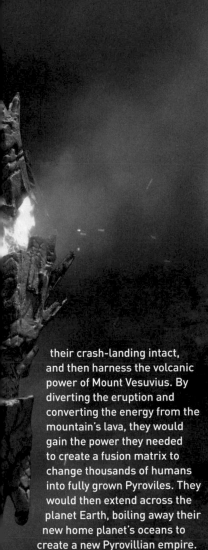

their crash-landing intact, and then harness the volcanic power of Mount Vesuvius. By diverting the eruption and converting the energy from the mountain's lava, they would gain the power they needed to create a fusion matrix to change thousands of humans into fully grown Pyroviles. They would then extend across the planet Earth, boiling away their new home planet's oceans to create a new Pyrovillian empire.

When the Doctor and Donna inverted the Pyrovillian systems, causing the eruption of Vesuvius, the power of the volcano was turned back on the Pyroviles, and the creatures were destroyed.

PYROVILLIA

The lost home planet of the Pyroviles, Pyrovillia had been transported across time and space by the Daleks and linked into web of 27 planets to form an enormous energy converter to produce the vast amounts of power needed to operate their ultimate weapon – the Reality Bomb.

VOLCANO DAY

VESUVIUS

On the morning of 24 August, a volcanic eruption from Mount Vesuvius began, which was to last more than 24 hours and had a destructive force equivalent to the impact of 24 nuclear bombs. For as much as 20 hours, flaming pumice rained down on the town, before the pyroclastic flow of hot gas and rock came streaming down from the mountain to engulf Pompeii. Those still trapped in the area had already suffocated or been burnt to death by the time the lava flow reached the town. Some had fled to the beach, but failed to escape the devastation.

THE PYROVILLIAN ALTERNATIVE

Had the Pyroviles' plan succeeded, there would have been no eruption, and Pompeii would not have been destroyed. Instead, the town would have been at the heart of a new, global empire. When the Doctor caused the eruption, a rift in time was briefly opened over Pompeii. Echoing back through the previous 17 years, this time rift caused the gift of accurate prophecy that all the soothsayers and fortune-tellers in Pompeii had enjoyed.

GREAT LIVES

THE FAMILY CAECILIUS

Lobus Caecilius was a Pompeian marble merchant who lived in Foss Street with his wife Metella, son Quintus and daughter Evelina. He was commissioned by Lucius to carve one of a series of marble circuit boards to Pyrovillian design.

Evelina could see the future, and she had been promised to the Sibylline Sisterhood. Her consumption of the vapours from the hypocaust that led to Vesuvius had already begun her mutation into a Pyrovile by the time the Doctor and Donna reached Pompeii.

After the family was saved by the Doctor, they moved to Rome, where Quintus studied to become a doctor, and Caecilius invested in the marble granaries of Alexandria.

AN AGE OF OFFICIAL SUPERSTITION

The Roman Empire of the first century had a civic and political culture that deferred to the wisdom of seers and soothsayers. Decisions, from warfare to trade, would be taken on the advice of the Chief Augur of the City Government, an elected position. Augurs like Pompeii's Lucius Petrus Dextrus deciphered the will of the gods by studying the weather, the flight patterns of birds or entrails. His gift of prophecy was greatly enhanced after the earthquake of AD 62. Lucius also led the local Cult of Vulcan, and he and its members were being transformed into new Pyrovile creatures.

The Sibylline Sisterhood were distinguished by their scarlet robes and the distinctive eye designs on the backs of their hands. They gathered in the Temple of Sibyl, under the leadership of their High Priestess and Sister Spurrina. To aid their gift of prophecy, the Sisterhood inhaled sulphurous fumes derived from the hot springs of Vesuvius, and those, like Caecilius's daughter, promised to the Sisterhood would also have to consume these vapours.

The Sisters guarded the Books of the Sibylline Oracle, the 13th of which predicted the arrival in Pompeii of a blue box at a time of storm, fires and betrayal. Through the High Priestess, the Pyroviles foretold an empire of Pompeii that would reach out to topple Rome and encompass the entire world. After the earthquake of AD 62, the Sibylline Sisters, like Lucius, were transformed from somewhat vague oracles into unfailing seers, able to foretell the weather and the success or failure of local farmers' crops. According to Lucius, this was the gift of Pompeii – that every oracle in the town told the truth. He and Caecilius's daughter Evelina could both see the Doctor and Donna's real names and identify their places of origin, even describing the fate of Gallifrey.

Ordinary Roman families worshipped household gods, and the Caecilius family adopted new ones when they moved from Pompeii to Rome: a new shrine displayed a marble depiction of the Doctor, Donna and their 'temple', the TARDIS.

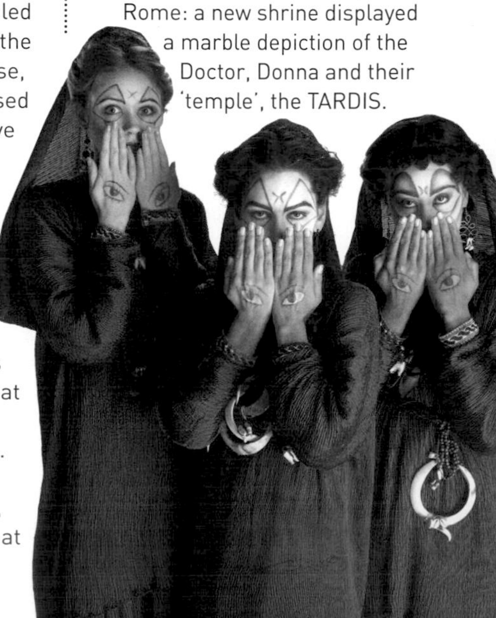

742–1540

GREAT LIVES

CHARLEMAGNE

742–814

Agatha Christie: Charlemagne lived centuries ago.
The Doctor: I've got a very good memory.
(Eddison Hall, 1926)

Charlemagne, or Charles I of France, ruled the Frankish Empire for 46 years until his death, uniting Western and Central Europe for the first time since the Roman Empire. His reign saw a renaissance in European culture: architecture, art, literature and music all flourished, while Medieval Latin developed as Europe's first common language. When Charlemagne was kidnapped by an insane computer, the Doctor journeyed into the forests of the Ardennes to rescue him, armed only with bow and arrows and a machete.

GENGHIS KHAN

1162–1227

The assembled hordes of Genghis Khan couldn't get through that door, and believe me, they've tried.
– The Doctor to Rose Tyler (London, 2005)

Born near Burkhan Kaldun mountain in Mongolia, Temüjin was the founder of the Mongol Empire, which he ruled as Genghis Khan from 1206. The Empire was formed by uniting the confederations of the Keraits, Merkits, Mongols, Naimans, Tatars and Uyghurs, and Genghis Khan's forces went on to conquer the Western Xian Dynasty, the Jin Dynasty, the Kara-Khitan Khanate, the Khwarezmid Empire, Georgia and Volga Bulgaria. His armies were notoriously brutal, and his was widely regarded as a genocidal and destructive regime.

14TH-CENTURY JAPAN

Then we went to... Kyoto, that's right, Japan, in 1336, and we only just escaped.
– The Doctor to Lynda Moss (Game Station, 200,100)

Japan's imperial court was established in 794 at the city of Heian-kyō, which was renamed Kyoto ('capital city') three centuries later. During the 14th century, the rule of the Kamakura shogunate was ended with the restoration of the Emperor Go-Daigo, but this was short-lived: civil war eventually forced the Emperor to flee to Yoshino in 1336, and Kyoto was captured by the Ashikaga shogunate, beginning the Muromachi period in Japanese history.

CAPTAIN JACK HARKNESS

REPORTED SIGHTING #8

ESTIMATED AGE: 35

LOCATION: Kyoto, 1336

AVAILABLE INFORMATION: Captain Jack was with the Doctor and Rose Tyler, shortly after their trip to Raxacoricofallapatorius.

THE HOWLING BEGINS

In the year of our Lord 1540 under the reign of King James the Fifth, an almighty fire did burn in the pit.

On 6 October 1540, a shooting star fell to Earth at the Glen of Saint Catherine in Scotland. It burned with an unearthly glow and left the ground scorched. Local monks were reported to have taken the object to their nearby monastery. Soon the area became prey to an unseen creature which would attack and devour livestock and, occasionally, people. These attacks were accompanied by the strange cry that gave the threat its name – the Howling. The meteorite's crash had in fact brought to Earth a single cell from a lupine-wavelength haemovariform, a light-modulating species whose transformations were triggered by specific wavelengths. Periodically, it would take a fresh human host but, when there was a full moon, it would transform into the wolf creature that carried out the attacks. Stories of the wolf persisted for over 300 years, until the visit of Queen Victoria to the nearby Torchwood Estate in 1879.

1599

ELIZABETHAN LONDON

ALL HALLOWS STREET

The architect and builder Peter Streete met witches in this street in London's Southwark area. The witches were actually three Carrionites, who had taken a house in All Hallows Street. A local boy, Wiggins, was lured here by one of the Carrionites, Lilith, and murdered by her and her mothers, Bloodtide and Doomfinger. The Doctor and Martha later found the house, where they too were attacked by Lilith.

NORTH JETTY, SALINGER WAY

A Bankside jetty on the River Thames between London Bridge and Southwark Bridge. Vessels would harbour here. The SS *Rose*, under the command of a Captain Beardsworthy, departed from North Jetty on 10 May 1599, having advertised around Southwark for crew.

MARKET WAY

Every Thursday, Southwark's Market Way would hold its market at which local householders could stock up on cheese, eggs, beef, pork, herbs and spices.

THE GLOBE

Situated in Southwark, just south of the River Thames, the Globe was a theatre constructed in 1599 by the Lord Chamberlain's Men to plans by architect Peter Streete. Streete was manipulated by the Carrionites to build the theatre as a tetradecagon; he told Shakespeare that 14 walls would best carry sound in the theatre. Here the Lord Chamberlain's Men presented *Love's Labour's Lost* and gave the first and last performance of its sequel, *Love's Labour's Won*. That play's final lines allowed thousands of banished Carrionites to escape the Deep Darkness into the Globe. The audience assumed that these events were a particularly spectacular climax to Shakespeare's new play, and word spread through London, finally drawing a royal visit by Queen Elizabeth I.

THE ELEPHANT

An inn in London's Southwark area, playwright William Shakespeare was living here in 1599, writing plays in his rooms. The inn's landlady, Dolly Bailey, had outlasted three local bouts of the plague, but died of fright when she encountered an undisguised Carrionite and her heart gave out. The Carrionite, Lilith, had been working as a serving wench in the inn in order to keep an eye on Shakespeare. The Doctor and Martha stayed at the Elephant during their visit, though their rest was interrupted by Dolly's death.

CARRIONITES

The Carrionites vanished when the universe was still young – banished to the Deep Darkness by the Eternals. In 1596, William Shakespeare's grief at the death of his son allowed three Carrionites to escape to Earth. Lilith and her mothers, Doomfinger and Bloodtide, assumed humanoid female guise and lived largely unnoticed in London for the next three years. Occasionally, Lilith would lure victims to their house in All Hallows Street. Some, like Wiggins, were lured to their deaths. Others, like the architect Peter Streete, would be manipulated to advance the Carrionites' plans: Streete constructed the Globe under Carrionite influence. Using the power of Shakespeare's words, they opened a portal through which the rest of their race could return to this universe. The Doctor, Martha and Shakespeare managed to thwart their plan and close the portal again, returning the Carrionites to the Deep Darkness. Lilith, Doomfinger and Bloodtide were trapped in a crystal ball, which the Doctor put in a trunk in the TARDIS.

PLANET OF ORIGIN
Rexel 4 in the Rexel Planetary Configuration

APPEARANCE (1)
Wraithlike, skeletal ravens

APPEARANCE (2)
Female crones

ABILITIES
Physical transformation; flight; teleportation; psychic powers

WEAPONS
Words; puppets; witchcraft

LONDON SOCIETY

Urban houses in Elizabethan England had no indoor toilets – instead, people would fill buckets and then hurl the waste out of the window, contributing to the awful smell in the streets. When emptying the bucket, people would shout 'Gardez l'eau!' – watch out for the water! Although animal waste was recycled, the dirtiness of London's streets helped to spread disease, and plague remained a problem in the country's towns and cities: it had been more than 30 years since the last great outbreak in England, but the residents of Southwark had still undergone three bouts of plague in recent memory. With little medical knowledge, the population would readily ascribe unnatural deaths to plague or witchcraft, but would equally readily accept 'a sudden imbalance of the humours' if the explanation was offered authoritatively.

Mental illness was also rife and was catered for by London's Bethlem Hospital, widely known as Bedlam. Those thought to be mad were locked in filthy cells, often with their heads shaved, sometimes being brought out to be whipped for the entertainment of visiting gentry.

CARRIONITE SCIENCE

Carrionite science was based on deriving power from sequences of words – much as mathematics uses sequences of numbers. The right words said with the right emphasis at the right time could change everything. While it seems to have inspired accounts of witchcraft, particularly Shakespeare's in *Macbeth*, this science actually made use of psychic energy, channelled and converted through the manipulation of shapes. The construction of the Globe theatre as a 14-sided building, for example, reflected the shape of the Rexel

Planetary Configuration. This tetradecagon could act as an energy converter for the Carrionites' words, activated by a co-radiating crystal.

A cauldron was used in a similar way to allow the Carrionites to watch events elsewhere, and they were well versed in chemical mixtures and potions that could give them power over other beings. They were able to kill or incapacitate victims by invoking 'the power of the name'. The Carrionites also made

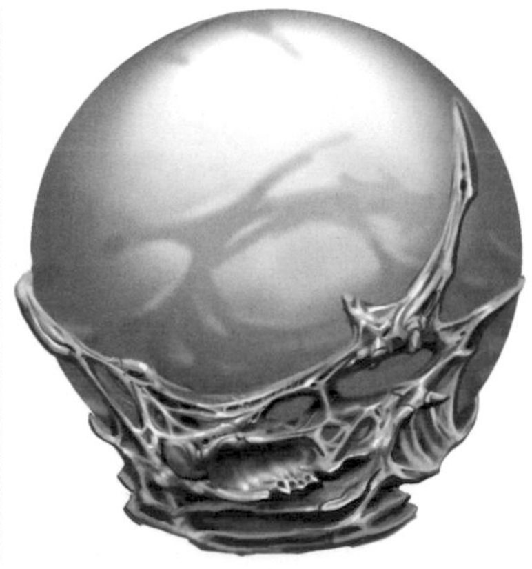

use of replication devices – puppets and dolls to which were added samples of a potential prey's DNA. The Carrionites generally stole hair for this purpose, linking the dolls to their victims and manipulating them to act on their behalf, or to suffer a seemingly magical death. In one case, a man appeared to drown on dry land when the device containing his DNA was submerged in water and the correct sequence of words was spoken by Lilith.

THE REXEL PLANETARY CONFIGURATION

The 14 points of the Rexel Planetary Configuration include Rexel 4, Dravidia and the hollow moon of Shadmoch.

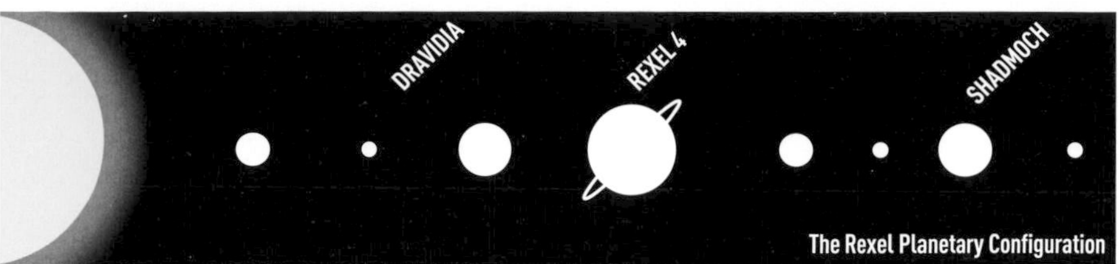

GREAT LIVES

QUEEN ELIZABETH I

1533–1603

The daughter of King Henry VIII and his second wife, Anne Boleyn, Elizabeth succeeded her elder sister Mary to the throne of England on 17 November 1558 and was crowned on 15 January 1559. By the time of her death in 1603, her country was one of the most powerful and prosperous in the world. Like all monarchs at the time, she had many sworn enemies, and she counted the Doctor as one of them. During a visit to the Globe theatre in 1599, she recognised him from an earlier encounter. She ordered the Doctor's execution; her guards pursued him, but were not quick enough to catch him.

WILLIAM SHAKESPEARE

1564–1616

William Shakespeare was described by the Doctor as '*the* genius – the most human human there's ever been'. Born in Stratford in 1564, Shakespeare married Anne Hathaway in 1582. The couple had three children, and the family remained in Stratford when Shakespeare moved to London. He was in London when his son, Hamnet, died at the age of 11 in 1596, and his guilt drove him mad; he told the Doctor that only his fear of Bedlam restored his sanity. In fact, it was this madness that allowed three Carrionites to escape the Deep Darkness and gain a foothold in Elizabethan England.

By 1599, Shakespeare was a member of the Lord Chamberlain's Men, London's playing company, who built the Globe theatre in Southwark. Here the Doctor and Martha Jones watched a performance of *Love's Labour's Lost* and saw Shakespeare – under Carrionite influence – announce the premiere of its sequel, *Love's Labour's Won*. This is among the 'lost plays' of William Shakespeare – there are occasional contemporary or near-contemporary references to it, but there has never been any trace of the play itself.

Shakespeare was induced to complete the new play with a sequence of words that would free the rest of the Carrionites from the Deep Darkness. Encouraged by the Doctor and helped by Martha, Shakespeare improvised a counter-spell that banished the Carrionites again.

THEATRE AND THE ARTS

LOVE'S LABOUR'S LOST AND LOVE'S LABOUR'S WON AT THE GLOBE THEATRE, LONDON

When the Lord Chamberlain's Men first performed *Love's Labour's Lost* at the Globe, William Shakespeare announced that the next night would see the premiere of its sequel, *Love's Labour's Won*. This came as a surprise to William Kempe and other actors in the playing company, and was almost prevented by Lynley, the Master of the Revels. Lynley's responsibilities included the censorship and license of every new play in Elizabethan London, and he threatened a banning order when Shakespeare was unable to show him a completed script. Lynley's death allowed the performance to go ahead, however. *Love's Labour's Won* revisited several of the characters of *Love's Labour's Lost*, including the clown Costard and Maria, a lady-in-waiting, and was acted, as always at the time, by an all-male cast. The performance was disrupted by the appearance on stage of its author, who attempted to stop the play. Every copy of *Love's Labour's Won* was lost when the Carrionites' portal from the Deep Darkness was closed.

THE BEST WORDS: NEW, BEAUTIFUL, BRILLIANT WORDS

The strange events at and around the Globe prompted Shakespeare to write several of his more famous works, including *Hamlet* and *Macbeth*. He also included several words and phrases that he had heard the Doctor use. The Doctor had been quoting Shakespeare quoting the Doctor quoting Shakespeare...

The Doctor: Good luck, Shakespeare. Once more unto the breach...
Shakespeare: I like that! Wait a minute... That's one of mine!

Once more unto the breach,
dear friends, once more,
Or close the wall up with our
English dead.
The Life of Henry the Fifth (1599)

Shakespeare: I must to work – I have a play to complete. But I'll get my answers tomorrow, Doctor, and I'll discover more about you and why this constant performance of yours.
The Doctor: All the world's a stage.
Shakespeare: Mm. I might use that.

All the world's a stage,
And all the men and women
merely players.
As You Like It (1600)

THEATRE AND THE ARTS

The Doctor: That's it! They used you. They gave you the final words, like a spell, like a code. *Love's Labour's Won*, it's a weapon – the right combination of words, spoken in the right place, with the shape of the Globe as an energy converter. The play's the thing! And yes, you can have that.

The play's the thing
Wherein I'll catch the
conscience of the King.
The Tragedy of Hamlet, Prince of Denmark (1602)

The Doctor: You lost your son.
Shakespeare: My only boy. The Black Death took him. I wasn't even there.
Martha Jones: I didn't know. I'm sorry.
Shakespeare: It made me question everything – the futility of this fleeting existence. To be or not to be— Ooh... that's quite good.
The Doctor: You should write that down.
Shakespeare: Maybe not. Bit pretentious...?

To be, or not to be; that is the
question...
The Tragedy of Hamlet, Prince of Denmark (1602)

The lodging house, the Elephant Inn, sign swinging in the breeze...

In the south suburbs
at the Elephant
Is best to lodge.
Twelfth Night, or What You Will (1602)

Martha Jones: I saw a witch, big as you like, flying, cackling away. And you've written about witches.
Shakespeare: I have? When was that?
The Doctor: Not... not quite yet.

Thunder and lightning.
Enter three witches.
The Tragedy of Macbeth (1606)

Lilith: Then watch this world become a blasted heath.

Say from whence
You owe this strange intelligence,
or why
Upon this blasted heath you stop
our way
With such prophetic greeting.
The Tragedy of Macbeth (1606)

Shakespeare: Martha, let me say goodbye to you with a new verse. A sonnet for my Dark Lady...
Shall I compare thee to a summer's day? Thou art more lovely, more temperate—

Shall I compare thee to a
summer's day?
Thou art more lovely and more
temperate.
Sonnet 18 (first published in 1609)

The Doctor: Peter, I'm the Doctor. Go into the past. One year ago. Let your mind go back, back to when everything was fine and shining. Everything that happened in this year since happened to somebody else. It was just a story. A winter's tale.

A sad tale's best for winter.
I have one
Of sprites and goblins.
The Winter's Tale (1611)

The Doctor: Good props store back there! Not sure about this, though. Reminds me of a Sycorax.
Shakespeare: Sycorax. Nice word. I'll have that off you as well.
The Doctor: I should be on ten per cent.

Hast thou forgot
The foul witch, Sycorax, who with
age and envy
Was grown into a hoop?
The Tempest (1611)

The Doctor: Outside this door – brave new world.

How beauteous mankind is! O
brave new world
That has such people in't!
The Tempest (1611)

Jailer: Does my Lord Doctor wish some entertainment while he waits? I could whip these madmen. They'll put on a good show for you – bandog and Bedlam.

Oh, master, is't you that speak
bandog and Bedlam this morning?
The Shoemaker's Holiday by Thomas Dekker (1599)

1727–1773

GREAT LIVES

BENJAMIN FRANKLIN

1706–1790

"**Mr Stoker:** ... lightning being a form of static electricity, as first proven by, anyone?
The Doctor: Benjamin Franklin ... My mate Ben! That was a day and a half, I got rope burns off that kite. And then I got soaked.

(Royal Hope Hospital, London, 2008)

One of the Founding Fathers of the United States of America, Benjamin Franklin was also a pioneering scientist and inventor. He theorised that lightning was a form of electricity in 1750, and proposed to prove this by flying a kite in a storm. He conducted this experiment two years later, on 15 June 1752, during which he managed to extract sparks from a cloud. The theory led him to invent the lightning rod, a conductor placed on the roofs of tall buildings to attract lightning and divert it from striking other targets.

KING LOUIS XV

1710–1774

Born on 15 February 1710, Louis became King of France and Navarre at the age of five, following the deaths of his great-grandfather, Louis XIV, and much of his immediate family. France was ruled in his name by a succession of regents until he was officially crowned in 1722. He moved to the Royal Court at Versailles in 1723, and married in 1725, before taking a series of mistresses, among them Madame de Châteauroux and Madame de Pompadour. He first encountered the Doctor in 1758 during the attack on the Palace of Versailles by clockwork robots. They met again in April 1764, when the King gave the Doctor a letter from Madame de Pompadour, shortly after her death. Louis XV died on 10 May 1774.

GREAT LIVES

JEANNE-ANTOINETTE ('REINETTE') POISSON, MADAME DE POMPADOUR

1721–1764

Often hailed as one of the most accomplished women of her age, Jeanne-Antoinette Poisson gained longer-term renown as the mistress of King Louis XV of France from 1745 to 1764. Her skills and interests included acting, art, music, dance and horticulture, and her political influence was such that she was considered the uncrowned Queen of France.

The life of Madame de Pompadour

1721 *29 December*. Birth of Jeanne-Antoinette Poisson in Paris, France, known to her family as Reinette.

1727 Reinette encounters a man in the fireplace in her bedroom. He claims to be conducting a routine fire check. Later the same year, the fireplace man appears in her bedroom, discovering a clockwork robot under her bed. The clockwork robot had been scanning her brain and stated that Reinette was 'incomplete'. Identifying himself as the Doctor, the man lures the robot away through the fireplace. Reinette comes to think of the Doctor as an imaginary friend.

c.1740 The Doctor reappears in Reinette's Paris bedroom.

1741 Reinette marries Charles-Guillaume Le Normant d'Étoiles and becomes Madame d'Étoiles.

1744 *8 December.* The mistress of King Louis XV, Madame de Châteauroux, becomes ill and dies. Reinette and her friend Katherine are observed by the Doctor as they discuss Reinette's ambition to become the King's new mistress.

1745 *25 February.* On the day of the Yew Tree Ball at the Palace of Versailles, Reinette discovers another of the clockwork robots. The Doctor emerges from a mirror to protect her, and she takes him to the masked ball. She dances with King Louis at the Ball, and soon becomes his mistress. Louis subsequently purchases the marquisate of Pompadour for her. She takes up residence at Versailles, and has the fireplace from her Paris bedroom transported brick by brick to her new home. She also befriends the King's wife.

1753 Rose Tyler visits her at the Palace to warn her that the clockwork robots will attack again five years later.

1758 On the night of another masked ball, the robots attack again, announcing that Reinette is now 'complete'. They are about to remove her head when the Doctor arrives on horseback through a plate-glass mirror on the ballroom wall. The mirror is the latest in a series of time portals, which is deactivated when the horse smashes through it. The clockwork robots cease to function. The Doctor leaves through the last working time portal – the fireplace in Reinette's bedroom.

1764 Reinette becomes ill and writes a letter to the Doctor, entrusting it to Louis to deliver. *15 April.* The death of Madame de Pompadour. Her body is taken in a horse-drawn hearse from the Palace of Versailles back to Paris, watched by the Doctor and the King.

1727–1773

18TH-CENTURY FRANCE

PARIS

Although Paris was not the political capital of France at this time, the city remained the social hub of the country. Fashionable society centred on salons, including one founded by Madame de Pompadour, which attracted many of France's leading philosophers and writers.

PALACE OF VERSAILLES

King Louis XIV established Versailles as the seat of French power in 1682, and his great-grandson continued to use the Palace as both home and Royal Court during his own reign. During Louis XV's reign, Versailles was home not only to his mistresses but also to as many as 20,000 courtiers, and the costs of maintaining the Royal Court were estimated at 25 per cent of the French government's expenditure. Louis often held masked balls here – at one he first danced with Madame d'Étoiles, who was to become Madame de Pompadour and his mistress; another was attacked by clockwork robots in 1758.

18TH-CENTURY LONDON

10 DOWNING STREET

> Fascinating history, Downing Street ... 1730, it was occupied by a Mr Chicken. Nice man.
>
> – *The Doctor to the Slitheen (London, 2006)*

In the early 1730s, King George II offered the house to the then First Lord of the Treasury (in effect the Prime Minister, although that term was not yet in use), Sir Robert Walpole. Walpole suggested that the property be made available to all future Prime Ministers, and the King agreed. The last private tenant of the property, Mr Chicken, moved to another house in the street, and the property was refurbished and extended, incorporating stables and another house to produce one official residence. Walpole moved into 10 Downing Street in 1735.

THE BOSTON TEA PARTY

1773

> I pushed boxes at the Boston Tea Party.
>
> – *The Doctor to Rose Tyler (Cardiff, 1869)*

The chain of events leading to the American Revolution effectively began on 16 December 1773, when colonists protested against both British rule and British taxation policies. As many as 8,000 campaigners took over a ship, the *Dartmouth*, which had brought a consignment of East India Company tea to Boston, and emptied its cargo into the harbour: 342 casks containing over 90,000 lbs of tea, worth an estimated £10,000, were chucked into the water, with no other damage to people or property. These events inspired many other peaceful protests around the world.

CAPTAIN JACK HARKNESS

REPORTED SIGHTING #10

ESTIMATED AGE: 35

LOCATION: Cardiff, 1869

AVAILABLE INFORMATION: Captain Jack used his Vortex Manipulator to travel from the Game Station in the year 200,100 to Earth. The Manipulator burnt out, leaving him stranded.

GREAT LIVES

CHARLES DICKENS

1812–1870

Dickens: My books, Doctor. Do they last?
The Doctor: Oh yes.
Dickens: For how long?
The Doctor: For ever.

(Cardiff, 1869)

Charles John Huffham Dickens was Victorian England's most successful writer, the author of numerous novels, short stories, essays, poetry and plays. He used many of his novels to examine great social causes, initially inspired by his own childhood experiences: from the age of 12, Charles worked ten hours a day in a boot-blacking factory after his father was imprisoned for debt.

As a young man, he became a journalist and then began to establish himself as an author with *The Pickwick Papers*. He became a great campaigner against poverty and social injustice, championing children, the poor and the oppressed.

Dickens married Catherine Thompson Hogarth in 1836, and they had ten children. The couple separated in 1858, however, by which time Dickens was involved with an actress, Ellen Ternan. He once commented that he had 'been rather... well, let us say, clumsy, with family matters'.

With the end of his marriage, Dickens embarked on a long series of tours of Britain and America, on which he would read from his most popular works to packed houses. Despite serious ill health, he continued with these tours almost to the end of his life, and he read from *A Christmas Carol* at Cardiff's Taliesin Lodge on Christmas Eve 1869. Events that night seemed to have revitalised him, and he returned to London intending to incorporate mysterious blue elementals into the plot of his latest novel.

Charles Dickens died on 9 June 1870, leaving his final work, *The Mystery of Edwin Drood,* unfinished.

Notable works by Charles Dickens

Oliver Twist *(1837–1839)*
The Old Curiosity Shop *(1840–1841)*
A Christmas Carol *(1843)*
Martin Chuzzlewit *(1843–1844)*
Bleak House *(1852–1853)*
Great Expectations *(1860–1861)*
The Signal-Man *(1866)*
The Mystery of Edwin Drood *(1870, unfinished)*

VICTORIAN CARDIFF

TEMPERANCE COURT

Situated in the north-western Cardiff suburb of Llandaff, 7 Temperance Court was the home of undertakers Sneed and Company. The undertakers' premises comprised four floors of rooms including a chapel of rest, a parlour and a kitchen, and a basement, housing the morgue. The building was constructed on a rift in space and time, which led to suggestions that the house was haunted. On Christmas Eve 1869, an explosion in the morgue destroyed the building, killing the owner, Gabriel Sneed, and his maid, Gwyneth.

1869

THE GELTH

Once they had solid form, but the Gelth were among the higher life forms affected by the Time War – they lost their physical bodies and became intelligent gaseous creatures able to exist within other gases. While their physical state had been compromised, the Time War did not reduce their numbers – there were billions of them – and the Gelth remained a belligerent force. They reasoned that, since recently deceased corpses break down and produce gases, they could inhabit and animate human cadavers. These possessed bodies would be used to murder the rest of the Earth's population, so creating still more vessels for them. Travelling to Earth via the Rift that runs through Cardiff, the Gelth began to take over the bodies of the dead that they had located at the local undertakers, Sneed and Company. They had made contact with Sneed's housemaid, Gwyneth, who had psychic abilities and could establish a bridge through the Rift. Their gaseous state, however, left them both susceptible to attraction by other gases and flammable. Their attacking force was destroyed by fire when Gwyneth struck a match in the gas-filled morgue as the Gelth were pouring through the Rift.

PLANET OF ORIGIN
Unknown

APPEARANCE
Non-corporeal; blue; gaseous; humanoid

ABILITIES
Possession and animation of fresh corpses; psychic powers

VICTORIAN SOCIETY

> **Rose:** So did you even go to school, or what...?
> **Gwyneth:** Course I did, what d'you think I am, an urchin? I went every Sunday, nice and proper ... We had to do sums and everything.

Before the 1870 Education Act, there was no single or compulsory form of education in Britain, and a child's access to schooling was entirely dependent on class, wealth and gender. About two-thirds of Britain's working-class children between the ages of 5 and 15 attended Sunday school each week. These were generally operated on a voluntary basis, and they instructed the children in religious morals and the basics of reading, writing and arithmetic.

There were about 1.2 million domestic servants in Britain in the 1860s, about 4 per cent of the population. Domestic service was the second-largest source of employment, after agricultural labour, in Victorian Britain. The average wage for a live-in maid was £6 per year – Gabriel Sneed was comparatively generous paying Gwyneth £8. Approximately 25 per cent of the people of Britain were living in poverty at this time, with 40 per cent of the country's wealth held by 5 per cent of the population. Between the two extremes was the growing middle class – those, like Sneed, who had at least one servant.

Sneed was likely to be charging at least £4 for a funeral, an impossible sum for most people. Llandaff's Bishop would have had little trouble finding the money needed to bury his nephew, whose body had been in a local weir for a fortnight. The average annual episcopal income was in excess of £6,000, although Llandaff was a poorer diocese.

SPIRITUALISM

Seances were at the heart of much Victorian spiritualism. Its advocates claimed contact with the spirit world and the recently deceased; its detractors unveiled a series of parlour tricks – 'luminous tambourines and a squeeze-box concealed between the knees'. The European origins of the seance go back to Anton Mesmer (1734–1815), and several notable mid-Victorian figures were intrigued enough to investigate the phenomenon. Dickens, like Browning and Darwin, dismissed it all as a hoax and a travesty, until he encountered the Gelth.

MUSIC

'Nadolig Llawen!'

POPULAR CHRISTMAS CAROLS

Hark! The Herald Angels Sing

First published in 1739 in *Hymns and Sacred Poems*, this carol was written by Charles Wesley and subsequently altered and rewritten by many composers, including Felix Mendelssohn.

God Rest Ye Merry Gentlemen

This is a traditional English Christmas carol, first published in 1833 in *Christmas Carols Ancient and Modern*, although it had been sung for several centuries by that time.

SCIENCE AND TECHNOLOGY

THE RIFT

A weak point or rip in time and space that runs across Cardiff. The Rift connects various times and places to Earth and allows other life forms through. The Gelth's use of the Rift to reach Victorian Cardiff gave rise to a number of ghost stories, centred on the local undertakers' house. The psychically sensitive maid Gwyneth had her abilities heightened by living in proximity to the Rift. The Gelth therefore selected Gwyneth to act as their bridge from the Rift to fully emerge into Cardiff.

The explosion that Gwyneth caused in Temperance Court closed the gateway she had opened and ended the Gelth attack, but the Rift itself remained active in Cardiff. It is not always active, and can open at any location in the city at any time.

Other recorded instances of Rift activity in Cardiff: 2006; 2008

GASLIGHT

Gas was the most widespread means of illumination until the development of electric lighting. The gas required to fuel lamps was produced through burning coal at very high temperatures in the presence of controlled quantities of oxygcn (gasification).

1879

GREAT LIVES

QUEEN VICTORIA

1819–1901

The longest-reigning monarch of Great Britain, Victoria came to the throne at the age of 18 following the death of her uncle, William IV, on 20 June 1837. She was crowned Queen of the United Kingdom of Great Britain and Ireland, Defender of the Faith on 28 June 1838 and became Empress of India on 1 May 1876. During her reign, Britain expanded its industry and its empire, extending the country's power and influence across the globe.

Victoria married her cousin, Prince Albert of Saxe-Coburg, in 1840, and the couple had four sons and five daughters over the next 18 years.

The Prince had a great interest in a range of subjects, including science and technology, and in 1842 he accompanied Victoria on the first train journey by a reigning monarch. His death from typhoid fever in 1861 affected the Queen profoundly and she withdrew from public life for much of the 1860s, rarely visiting London, although she continued to perform her constitutional duties in private.

For the rest of her life, she wore black as a sign of mourning and divided her time between Windsor Castle, the Isle of Wight and Balmoral Castle in Scotland.

An attempted assassination in 1840 proved to be the first of several, and further attempts were made in May and July 1842, 1849, 1850 and 1872.

Victoria was the first carrier of haemophilia in Britain's royal family, passing the disease on through the royal houses of Europe, including those of Germany, Russia and Spain. Neither her parents nor her ancestors were carriers, and not all of her children inherited the mutation, but it was passed on to Victoria's daughters Alice and Beatrice, and her son Leopold eventually died from it.

The last British monarch of the House of Hanover, Victoria died on 22 January 1901.

'We are not amused...'

Queen Victoria's most famous saying was not actually attributed to her until 1919, when Caroline Holland mentioned it in her *Notebooks of a Spinster Lady*. According to Holland, an equerry had tried to entertain dinner guests at Windsor Castle with a mildly scandalous tale. When he'd finished his story, Her Majesty spoke on behalf of the room: 'We are not amused.'

LUPINE-WAVELENGTH-HAEMOVARIFORM

Having arrived on Earth in 1540, this light-modulating creature was protected and worshipped for 339 years by the Brethren of St Catherine. Once a generation, the Brethren would procure a Host for the haemovariform – a young boy would be snatched from the local area, and the haemovariform would inhabit his body, heart and soul. Each full moon, the Host would transform into a wolf and scavenge the surrounding countryside, savaging and devouring the local farmers' livestock. In the 19th century, the haemovariform planned to transfer its essence to Queen Victoria and advance humanity's technological progress to create the Empire of the Wolf. The Doctor was able to destroy the creature with focused and intensified moonlight, effectively drowning it in the energy that usually strengthened it.

APPEARANCE
2.7-metre wolf

ABILITIES
Physical transformation; bodily possession; transfer of DNA via bite

OTHER SIGHTINGS
Glen of St Catherine, Scotland, 1540

1879

SOCIETY AND RELIGION

THE BRETHREN OF THE MONASTERY OF ST CATHERINE

The monks of the Glen of St Catherine in Scotland, having retrieved a falling star from the Glen in 1540, became ever more reclusive – legends said that they turned their backs on God and started to worship a wolf, and the Brethren became unpopular with the local populace. Over the next three centuries, the monks protected the light-modulating life form that they had rescued, periodically snatching local boys to become hosts for the 'werewolf'. For their own protection, the Brethren trained the wolf to avoid the scent of mistletoe. Under the leadership of Father Angelo, the Brethren waited many years for one of Queen Victoria's annual visits to Scotland to coincide with a full moon. In 1879, this finally occurred, and the monks sabotaged the train line, forcing the Queen to travel by horse-drawn coach. Knowing that the royal party would therefore need to stop overnight, the Brethren attacked and occupied the nearby Torchwood Estate, imprisoning the household staff and Lady Isobel, wife of the landowner, Sir Robert MacLeish. Garlanding themselves in mistletoe to prevent themselves becoming victims of the wolf, the Brethren drugged the Queen's guards and unleashed the wolf. When Father Angelo was shot by Queen Victoria and the wolf was destroyed, the Brethren surrendered.

SCIENCE AND TECHNOLOGY

VISCUS ALBUM

A species of mistletoe native to Europe. Mistletoe features in many legends and customs, from Greek and Norse mythology to a Christian tradition that the Cross was constructed from the wood of the mistletoe tree. It bears fruit around the time of the winter solstice and is a common Christmas decoration. Perhaps because of its mythological significance, it was used by the Brethren of St Catherine to subdue the wolf and, aware of this, Sir George MacLeish protected much of Torchwood House by varnishing interior doors with oil from the plant.

KOH-I-NOOR

In the 19th century, this was the largest diamond in the world, found in India perhaps as early as 3,200 BC. It was held by a series of Indian rulers until the British conquest of the subcontinent in 1849, when the diamond was presented to Queen Victoria. It was displayed at London's Great Exhibition of 1851, but poor lighting made it a disappointing attraction: the shine was not quite right. Prince Albert subsequently supervised the cutting of the stone – at a cost of at least £8,000, the Koh-i-Noor's weight was reduced by more than 40 per cent.

TORCHWOOD HOUSE

Built in the 15th century and extended and renovated during the next 200 years, this Highland estate was the home of the MacLeish family for over three centuries. When ownership passed to Sir George MacLeish in the 1800s, the House began to fall into disrepair, as Sir George focused his attention and funds on the construction of an observatory at the top of the building. He also had the House's interior doors varnished with oil of mistletoe and reconstructed the central Great Staircase with timber from the North American torchwood tree. Sir George's son, Robert, was the last of the MacLeish line – he died during the wolf attack of 1879, and his widow Isobel left the Estate. On her death in 1893, the Torchwood Estate was purchased by the Crown.

TORCHWOOD

After the death of Sir Robert MacLeish, Queen Victoria vowed never to forget the events at Torchwood House or the Doctor's part in them. Horrified by the implications of the Doctor's presence and actions, she decided to found an institute to battle against alien incursions, with the Doctor listed among the foremost enemies of the British Empire. She purchased the House and Estate from Lady Isobel MacLeish, and established the new Torchwood Institute.

THE TORCHWOOD OBSERVATORY

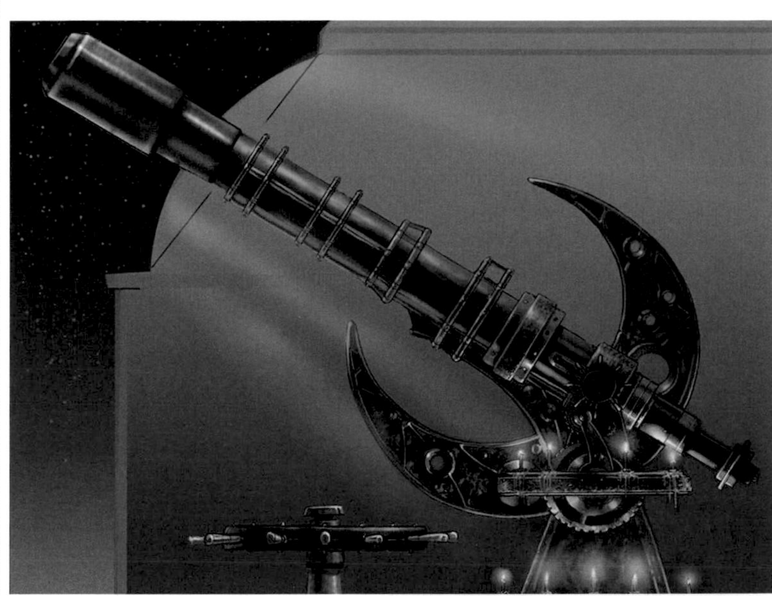

The 'famous endeavour' of Sir George MacLeish, the construction of the observatory and telescope at Torchwood House almost bankrupted the Estate. Sir George's enthusiasm for the project was supported by Prince Albert, and the pair devised a plan to trap and destroy the local werewolf. The telescope was deliberately constructed with too many prisms, which made it useless as an astronomical tool but perfect for focusing and concentrating incoming light...

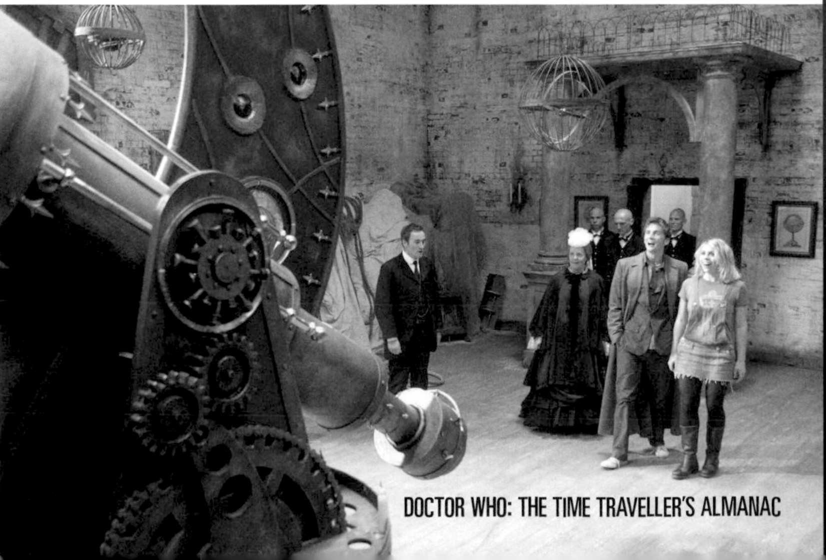

1883–1892

THE ERUPTION OF KRAKATOA

1883

The volcano on Krakatoa, an Indonesian island, has erupted many times, but the most devastating eruption began on 20 July 1883, intensifying over the next few weeks to reach a peak at the end of August and destroying two-thirds of the island, which all but disappeared. Four huge explosions on 27 August were heard up to 3,000 miles away, as 25 cubic kilometres of rock and volcanic ash obliterated 300 towns and villages, killing more than 36,000 people. The eruption caused a series of tsunamis, bringing more devastation to the region. Among the few survivors washed up on the shores of Sumatra on the night of the first main explosion was the Doctor.

THE GRASKE

A Graske was observed on Earth in London in December 1883, when it kidnapped a street urchin. The Graske are a race with a penchant for abducting and imprisoning other species. They replace their victims with changeling replicas, allowing them to take over other planets by stealth. They use transmat technology with time-travel capability to materialise in different periods and places, removing their prey via a quick blast from a hand-held weapon. The kidnapped specimens are then held in stasis capsules on the Graske home world, Griffoth. There is evidence that the Graske have sometimes abducted victims to order on behalf of employers.

PLANET OF ORIGIN
Griffoth

APPEARANCE
Short; brown skin; three tentacles on their heads

ABILITIES
Time-travel; transmat

WEAPONS
Hand-held blaster

OTHER SIGHTINGS
Cardiff, 2006; London, 2008

SCIENCE AND TECHNOLOGY

THE FIRESTONE

One night in 1885, at the height of the British Raj in India, 19-year-old Lady Clemency Eddison saw a dazzling purple light in the sky above the city of Delhi – a falling star. The following day, she met an attractive young man calling himself Christopher, and she fell in love with him. Christopher then revealed his true form to her: a giant wasp. He was a Vespiform from the Silfrax galaxy, who had come to Earth and adopted human form, he said, to learn about mankind. The couple were soon parted, when a great monsoon began and the River Jumna broke its banks, and Christopher was among those lost in the floods. Before he died, however, he gave Clemency a jewel – the Firestone. Clemency returned to her Surrey home, pregnant by Christopher and compelled to give up her son at birth. She wore the Firestone for the next forty years, until it was identified as a Vespiform Telepathic Recorder by the Doctor in a Surrey house in 1926...

CAPTAIN JACK HARKNESS

REPORTED SIGHTING #11

ESTIMATED AGE: 58

LOCATION: Ellis Island, New York Harbor, 1892

AVAILABLE INFORMATION: Captain Jack got into a fight with a man who shot him through the heart. With his subsequent resurrection came the realisation that he could no longer die.

GREAT LIVES

EMMELINE PANKHURST

1858–1928

Martha Jones: What else have you got? Laser spanner?
The Doctor: I did, but it was stolen by Emily Pankhurst, that cheeky woman

(London, 2008)

A leading British women's rights activist, who founded the movement to win the right for women to vote.

SERVICE ROBOTS

Sarah Jane Smith: I saw things you wouldn't believe.
Rose Tyler: Try me.
Sarah: Mummies.

(London, 2007)

When a 7,000-year-old pyramid was opened by archaeologists in Egypt in 1911, the ancient and powerful alien being trapped within began to engineer his escape. Sutekh the Destroyer had been imprisoned there by his fellow Osirans, the force field that held him being controlled from a second pyramid on the planet Mars. Sutekh's awakening reanimated the ancient mummies that accompanied him in his tomb. But these were not the embalmed, eviscerated corpses usually found inside the pyramids. They were disguised service robots controlled by Sutekh's mental energy via a ring that sent signals to a small triangular device on their backs. The metal frames and circuitry of the robots were protected from corrosion by their chemically impregnated bindings, and the Fourth Doctor made use of this when he disguised himself as one of the robots during his and Sarah's successful bid to prevent Sutekh's return.

MAFEKING

Reading some military memoirs, fascinating stuff ... Took me right back to my days in the army. Started reminiscing about Mafeking, you know.

– Colonel Hugh Curbishley (Eddison Hall, 1920)

From 14 October 1899 to 16 May 1900, British forces laid siege to the South African town of Mafeking, in one of the earliest and most significant actions of the Second Boer War. Colonel Curbishley, however, had fonder memories of Parisian cabaret...

THE RMS TITANIC

I was on this other ship once, they said that was unsinkable. I ended up clinging to an iceberg, wasn't half cold.

– The Doctor to Jabe (Platform One, 5.5/apple/26)

On 10 April 1912, the RMS *Titanic* left Southampton in the UK and headed for America. Four days later, the ship struck an iceberg and sank. The British-registered, four-funnelled ocean liner was at the time the largest passenger steamship ever constructed, and had taken three years to build at Belfast's Harland and Wolff shipyard. The death toll of 1,495 made this one of the world's greatest maritime disasters in peacetime, although one family had a lucky escape. Mr and Mrs Daniels of Southampton had planned to take their four children on the voyage. They were dissuaded by the Doctor, who then took their place on board.

THE SHIP

✦ **LENGTH:** 264.9 metres
✦ **DECKS:** Nine
✦ **PROPULSION:** Three propellers
✦ **ENGINES:** Two reciprocating steam engines and one Parsons turbine
29 boilers
159 coal-burning furnaces

1913

SOCIETY AND EDUCATION

FARRINGHAM SCHOOL FOR BOYS

In the early years of the 20th century, England had a thriving private education system. Farringham School for Boys was a typical fee-paying 'public' school, which accepted boys from the wealthier sections of English society and prepared them for their future roles as aristocrats, diplomats, lawyers and officers in the military. The intention was to produce the next generation of English gentlemen: boys of 'sound' character, ready to assume responsibilities in the wider world – religious and moral instruction took priority over intellectual development, with emphasis placed on teamwork and team-leading skills and sporting and military prowess. The boys, who entered the school at the age of 13 after five years of preparatory school, would leave at 18 ready to lead and govern the rest of the country.

They would have spent much of that five years living in the school as boarding pupils. The school staff therefore included resident nurses, cooks and cleaning staff, who were regarded as socially inferior to the boys they served, and were generally employed from among the local populace. This class hierarchy was reflected among the pupils themselves, with younger pupils acting as servants ('fags') to the older boys: their 'duties' included shoe-polishing and completing homework. The senior pupils were also entitled, with permission, to punish the younger boys.

The teaching staff, too, lived in the school. Each master was given his own set of rooms, with a bedroom and a book-lined study. A member of the school's domestic staff would be assigned to him, delivering breakfast and afternoon tea to his rooms, cleaning and tidying, perhaps even drawing the curtains at the start and end of each day.

Academic instruction was essentially limited to rote-learning of an established core curriculum of Classics, Religious Instruction, Geography, History and Physical Education, with cursory attention

paid to Science and Mathematics. Farringham's pupils left the school well versed in the defeat of Napoleon at the Battle of Waterloo in June 1815 or Britain's decisive and crushing Boer War victory at the siege of Mafeking in 1899–1900, for example. They were also familiar with the great works of the Classics, having been instructed in the translation of Latin poets like Catullus, Horace, Ovid and Virgil.

Farringham School was not one of England's foremost public schools, and some of its pupils hoped that promotion and advancement for their fathers might mean a better school for themselves.

School Hymn

To Be A Pilgrim – words by John Bunyan; music by Ralph Vaughan Williams

Cadets

Just as important to a country preparing for war was the readiness of its army leaders. All schoolboys at Farringham were members of the School's cadet corps. Schoolmasters supervised regular training, during which the pupils practised loading, aiming and firing machine guns at dummy targets. Classes were drilled in marching, maintenance of weapons, and other military duties.

ROLL OF HONOUR

Farringham School for Boys and the local village came under attack on the night of 11 November 1913. The staff and pupils fought bravely. Among the casualties were:

Mr Rocastle
Headmaster, Farringham School)

Mr Phillips
(Bursar, Farringham School)

Mr Smith
(History master, Farringham School)
– missing in action

Mr Clark
(landowner, Oakham Farm)

Jeremy Baines
(pupil, Farringham School)

Mr Chambers
(Farringham Village)

Mr & Mrs Cartwright, and their daughter Lucy
(Farringham Village)

Jenny
(housemaid, Farringham School)

Martha
(housemaid, Farringham School)
– missing in action

The school later recognised and honoured the bravery of those who had assisted in the defence of Farringham:

Staff

Mr Snell *(master)*
Mr Pool *(master)*
Nurse Joan Redfern *(matron)*

Pupils

Hutchinson *(House Captain)*
Armitage
Ashington
Baxter
Jackson
Jenkins
Latimer
Lockley
Morris
Pemberton
Peterson
Redford
Smythe
Thwaites
Wicks
Williams

THE FAMILY OF BLOOD

A species with a very limited life span, the Family were parasites that prolonged their lives by inhabiting the bodies of other species. They had strong familial ties, addressing each other in terms of their relationships: Father of Mine, Mother of Mine, Son of Mine, Daughter of Mine.

When a member of the Family took over a new form, they gained the memories of their victim, who instantly perished. They also retained the physical weaknesses of the forms they possessed, including mortality. When the Family first scented the Doctor's Time Lord essence, they recognised that his Gallifreyan anatomy offered the perfect vehicle for a near-eternal existence. Using a stolen Vortex Manipulator to travel through time, they followed him to Earth in their spaceship, which could be rendered invisible on landing. They tracked him to Farringham School for Boys in Herefordshire, England, only to find that he had physically changed himself into a human being and was now a schoolmaster named John Smith.

With no moral inhibitions, the Family was quite prepared to sacrifice hundreds of innocent lives in pursuit of the Doctor's essence, and they attacked both the school and the local village without mercy. The Doctor, once restored to his Time Lord self, was similarly ruthless: the Father was bound in unbreakable chains forged from a dwarf star and imprisoned underground; the Mother was cast into the event horizon of a collapsing galaxy; the Son was immobilised inside a Scarecrow in an English field; and the Daughter was hidden inside every mirror for eternity.

PLANET OF ORIGIN
Unknown

APPEARANCE
Unknown

ABILITIES
Telepathy; strong sense of smell; bodily possession

WEAPONS
Scarecrows; energy blasters

SCIENCE AND TECHNOLOGY

MOLECULAR FRINGE ANIMATION

The Family of Blood had an extensive arsenal of stolen technology and usurped powers – including an invisible spaceship, a Time Agent's Vortex Manipulator and telepathic powers. They also used the technique of molecular fringe animation to fashion and control an expendable army of foot-soldiers, which, when they arrived in England, they drew from the Scarecrows found on the local agricultural land. Molecular fringe animation used a mental source – in this case Son of Mine – to pinpoint the subject (the Scarecrow). A cerebral impulse, through which background radiation was reflected from the source, was transmitted to the Scarecrow, forming an alternating energy pattern. This energy pattern stimulated the subject at a molecular level, and activated it. The resultant physical movement was largely autonomous, but took its cue from the source, so that the Scarecrows' movements effectively mimicked those of their controllers, within the constraints of their physical composition. An obvious sign of their connection to the Family was their shared trait of tilting their heads to one side. The animated Scarecrows were used to abduct the individuals whose forms the Family then took. The Scarecrow soldiers were subsequently used both as sentinels and as an attack force when the Family besieged Farringham School. When the staff and pupils of the School defended themselves with rifles and machine guns, the Scarecrows seemed at first to be susceptible to bullets. They collapsed to the ground, apparently dead, but were quickly reanimated by a simple spoken command from Son of Mine.

1914–1922

THE FIRST WORLD WAR

"In June 1914, an Archduke of Austria was shot by a Serbian. And this then led, through nations having treaties with nations, like a line of dominoes falling, to some boys from England walking together in France.

– *The Doctor (1913)*

On 28 June 1914, a Serbian assassin named Gavrilo Princip shot and killed Archduke Franz Ferdinand of Austria. The Archduke was heir to the throne of Austria-Hungary, which then attacked Serbia. Russia was bound by treaty to Serbia, and began to mobilise troops against Austria-Hungary. Germany was allied to Austria-Hungary, so declared war against Russia. France had a treaty with Russia, so entered the war against Germany, which invaded Belgium (allied with France). Britain, at the time also allied with France, therefore declared war against Germany. This brought in Britain's colonies – including Australia, New Zealand, Canada, South Africa and India – as well as Japan, which had an agreement with Britain. Italy, although bound by treaty to Germany, held back from the war for a year, before siding with the Anglo-French alliance against Germany in 1915. The USA joined the fight against Germany in April 1917, hastening the end of the conflict the following year.

GREAT LIVES

DAVID LLOYD GEORGE

1863–1945

The only Welsh Prime Minister of Great Britain, Lloyd George took office on 7 December 1916. The Liberal MP for Caernarvon served as President of the Board of Trade, Chancellor of the Exchequer, Minister of Munitions and Secretary of State for War before heading the coalition government that led the country through the second half of the First World War. Lloyd George was an aggressive campaigner against alcohol, famously declaring that Britain had three enemies: 'Germany, Austria and Drink; as far as I can see, the greatest of these three deadly foes is Drink.' His attempt, as Chancellor, to ban alcohol entirely led to the introduction of licensing laws to increase taxes on alcohol and to restrict its sale and the opening hours of public houses. In private, however...

"Telling you, Lloyd George, he could drink me under the table.

– *The Doctor to Rose Tyler (London, 2006)*

MISSING PERSON

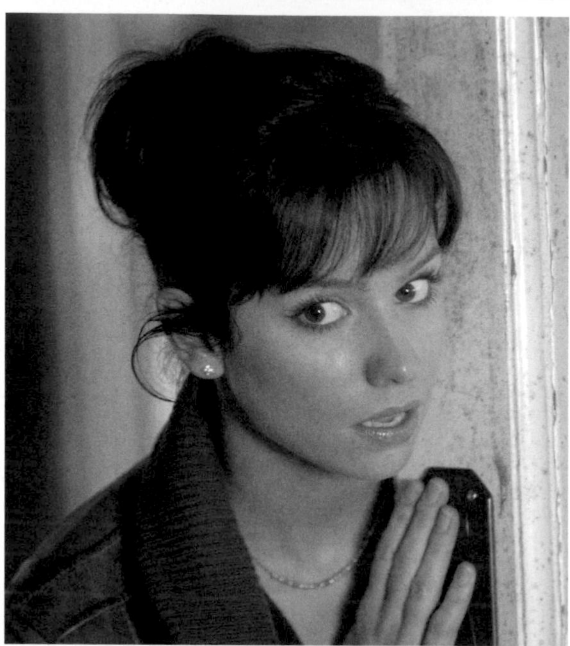

1920 – KATHY NIGHTINGALE

Kathy Nightingale was born in Lancashire in the late 1980s. In 2007, she was attacked in London by a Weeping Angel, which despatched her to Hull 87 years earlier. She arrived in a cow field outside the city in early December where she met a local farmer, Ben Wainwright. Kathy, who lied about her age, claiming to be just 18, married Ben and settled down to her new life. The couple had three children: Matthew, Joseph, and Sally, who was named after Kathy's friend Sally Sparrow. In 1962, Ben died of influenza, and Kathy grew old among her children and grandchildren. In 1987, Kathy realised that she did not have long left to live and wrote a letter to Sally Sparrow, entrusting it to her grandson Malcolm to deliver in 2007.

(See also: 1969; 2007; 2008)

VESPIFORM

The Vespiform are an amorphic race from the hives of the Silfrax galaxy. Although they can adapt and alter their appearance to mimic other species, the natural appearance of a Vespiform is that of a giant wasp. After a physical transformation, Vespiform leave traces of a morphic residue – a honey-like goo deposited when they genetically re-encode. They feed on insects, which they kill with their giant stings. They can grow replacement stings.

The first Vespiform known to have reached Earth landed in Delhi in 1885 and adopted human form. There it met and fell in love with Lady Clemency Eddison, who became pregnant and returned to England after her lover's death in a monsoon flood. At birth, the child was taken to an orphanage and, forty years on, he had become a church minister, Reverend Golightly, in the vicinity of his mother's home in Surrey. Neither he nor Lady Eddison had any idea of their relationship to one another. Her only reminder of events in India was the Firestone jewel that her lover had given her before he died.

Eight days before the arrival at Eddison Hall of Agatha Christie, the Reverend Golightly began a series of transformations into a Vespiform, the first of which activated the Firestone – a Vespiform Telepathic Recorder, which transmitted details of his identity and heritage into Golightly's mind. The Recorder also absorbed Lady Eddison's knowledge of the crime novels of Agatha Christie, and it transmitted this information too. The new Vespiform was effectively modelled on the early mysteries of the Queen of Crime. It began to kill the house guests at Eddison Hall in revenge for the denial of its human and Vespiform birthrights.

PLANET OF ORIGIN
Unknown

APPEARANCE
2.4-metre wasp

ABILITIES
Flight; physical transformation; telepathy; space travel

WEAPON
Giant sting

GREAT LIVES

AGATHA CHRISTIE

1890–1976

On 15 September 1890, Agatha Mary Clarissa Miller was born in Torquay, Devon. She was the second of three children. She was taught at home by her mother before attending a Parisian finishing school in 1906. She married Colonel Archibald Christie as the First World War was beginning, and they had a daughter. In 1920, her first novel, *The Mysterious Affair at Styles*, was published, in which she introduced the Belgian detective Hercule Poirot.

Over the next six years and for many years after, the Queen of Crime's bestselling detective novels and short stories made her a household name in Britain, a notable addition being *The Murder of Roger Ackroyd* in 1926. Behind the popular and financial success, however, her personal life was unhappy – her mother died, and, in August, her husband confessed to having an affair. Agatha was opposed to divorce, and refused to annul her marriage. One Friday, Colonel Christie left their Berkshire home to spend the weekend with his mistress.

That weekend, Agatha went to stay at Eddison Hall in Surrey as a guest of Lady Clemency Eddison and her husband, Colonel Hugh Curbishley. That afternoon, as cocktails were served on the lawn, one of Lady Eddison's other house guests – Professor Peach – was murdered in the library with a piece of lead piping. Soon afterwards, Lady Eddison's companion and housekeeper, Miss Chandrakala, was killed by a falling stone gargoyle. Later the same evening, Roger Curbishley, son and heir of Lady Eddison and the Colonel, was stabbed with a breadknife in the dining room.

The Doctor and Donna Noble posed as investigators from Scotland

Yard and began to investigate the murders, soon discovering that they were the work of a Vespiform from the Silfrax galaxy. The infant Vespiform mind had taken Agatha's first six novels as the template for its actions. Its mind was linked to hers, so she was able to lure the creature to its death in a nearby lake, the Silent Pool. The danger over, Agatha collapsed, losing her memory of the night's events. Her car was discovered abandoned by the lakeside the next morning, sparking a police search and fevered press speculation. The Doctor and Donna took her in the TARDIS to a hotel in Harrogate, Yorkshire, where she was discovered ten days after the events at Eddison Hall.

Agatha swiftly resumed her writing career, producing more than eighty novels and short-story collections and twenty plays for theatre, radio and television, as well as several works of non-fiction. She never mentioned her disappearance or the events surrounding it. In 1971, she was made a Dame Commander of the Order of the British Empire. On 12 January 1976, Agatha died of natural causes at her home in Oxfordshire.

ARTS AND MEDIA

PLAYING ON THE GRAMOPHONE...

Girls And Their Swinging Pearls
– Perry Anderson and The Anderson Ragtime Band
Jazz Makes The Flowers Bloom
– Ragtime Orchestra
My Heart Is Like A Cuckoo Clock
– Harry Jarmin and The Morris Hess Jazz Orchestra
Walk, Walk, The Blue Walk
– Russy Sherman and The Sherman Players

CHRISTIE IN THE PRESS

MYSTERY WRITER DISAPPEARS
– The Daily Courier
CHRISTIE MYSTERY DEEPENS
– The National Herald
MANHUNT FOR MISSING CHRISTIE – The Enquirer

LITERATURE

SUGGESTED READING

"Thing is, I don't think she ever quite forgot ... Some of the details kept bleeding through, all the stuff her imagination could use. Like Miss Marple! ... Somewhere in the back of her mind, it all lingered.
– The Doctor to Donna Noble (Surrey, 1926)

The Secret Adversary
Murder at the Vicarage
Murder on the Orient Express
Death in the Clouds
Why Didn't They Ask Evans?
Cards on the Table
Appointment with Death
Murder Is Easy
N or M?
The Body in the Library
The Moving Finger
Sparkling Cyanide
Death Comes as the End
Taken at the Flood
Crooked House
They Do It with Mirrors
Dead Man's Folly
Cat among the Pigeons
Endless Night
Nemesis

Facsimile of the 1957 Earth edition (Sol 3)
Published in the year 5,000,000,000
'Death in the Clouds' first published in Great Britain in 1935

HIGH SOCIETY

Lady Clemency Eddison

Clemency Eddison spent her youth in India in the days of the British Raj. She returned to England aged 19 in 1885 and locked herself in a bedroom in Eddison Hall for six months, claiming that she'd contracted malaria in Delhi. She was in fact pregnant, something which her maid, Miss Chandrakala, helped her to conceal. Society would not have accepted her as an unmarried mother, and the scandal would have destroyed the Eddison family name, so she gave the newborn child to Miss Chandrakala, who took him to an orphanage. Some years later, Lady Eddison married Colonel Hugh Curbishley.

Colonel Hugh Curbishley

Curbishley was a British army officer during the Boer War, given to reminiscing about the siege of Mafeking. In service, he'd devoted himself as much to the Can-Can girls of Les Folies Bergère as to combating the enemy; in later life, he would claim to be reading military memoirs in his study, but was usually perusing scandal rags. Having married Lady Clemency Eddison, a woman fifteen years his junior, Curbishley worried that she would leave him for a younger man. After the 1918 flu epidemic, Curbishley confined himself to a wheelchair, believing that his faked disability would stop his wife from straying.

Roger Curbishley

The Honourable Roger Curbishley was the son of Lady Clemency Eddison and Colonel Hugh Curbishley. He had a relationship with one of the household's footmen, Davenport. The Eddison title and estate was passed down through the female line, so Roger stood to inherit the Hall from his mother and become Lord Eddison. But, when he was still in his early 30s, he was killed in the dining room, with the breadknife.

Reverend Golightly

The Reverend was raised in an orphanage by the Christian Fathers, and by the age of 40 was the vicar in the parish local to Eddison Hall. Unknown to anyone, he was the illegitimate son of Lady Eddison and Christopher, the first Vespiform to reach Earth. When his church was broken into, his anger broke the genetic lock that held him stable in his human form, and the two thieves became the first victims of the Vespiform – killed in the church, with the giant sting. Having absorbed both his full identity and the works of Agatha Christie, the Golightly-Vespiform set out to take his revenge at Eddison Hall.

Professor Peach

A university professor in his 60s, Peach was researching the family history at Eddison Hall when he discovered evidence of Lady Eddison's first child. He was promptly killed in the library, with the lead piping.

Robina Redmond

The absolute hit of the social scene in 1926, Miss Redmond, 28, was in fact Ms Ada Mullins, otherwise known as the Unicorn, a famous jewel thief. Her most recent victim, Lady Barrington, lost her pearls, and Lady Eddison's Firestone was next on the Unicorn's list. When Roger Curbishley was murdered, she managed to purloin the Firestone, but was forced to return it when she was unmasked by Agatha Christie. Agatha theorised that the real Robina Redmond was at home in London, and that Ada Mullins had taken her place at Eddison Hall.

1930s NEW YORK

Established by Dutch colonists in the 1620s, who named the town New Amsterdam, it became a city in 1653. Eleven years later, New Amsterdam was attacked and taken by the English, who renamed it New York. Over the next century the population of New York grew, and it had become the largest city in the newly independent United States of America by 1790. The city is made up of five boroughs, including Manhattan, and is famous for its culture and many architectural landmarks.

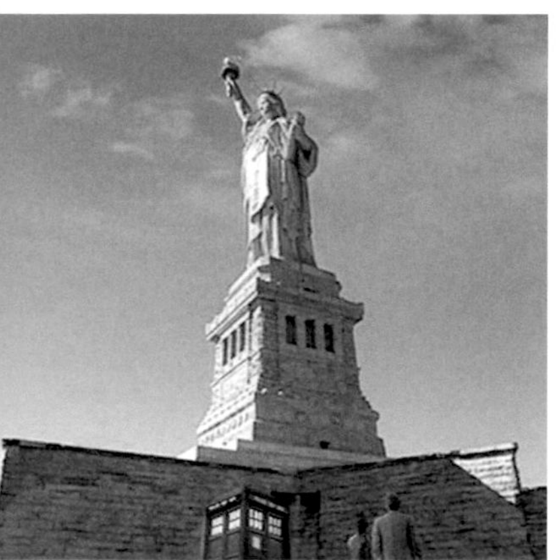

THE STATUE OF LIBERTY

Travellers entering New York State by New York Harbor are greeted by the large statue of Liberty Enlightening the World on Liberty Island. Commonly referred to as the Statue of Liberty, it was donated to the USA by the people of France in 1886. The statue welcomes visitors, immigrants and returning Americans to the USA, and stands at 46.5 metres from its base to its highest point – the tip of the torch it holds in its right hand. A sonnet by poet Elizabeth Lazarus appears on a plaque inside the statue's pedestal, and includes the renowned lines:
Give me your tired, your poor,
Your huddled masses yearning to breathe free

THE EMPIRE STATE

In 1929, a new corporation – Empire State, Inc. – was formed by a consortium of leading New York businessmen. Their aim was to construct the tallest building in the world, the first to have more than 100 floors, situated in the heart of New York City and named the Empire State, a popular nickname for the state of New York. The architect was Gregory Johnson of Shreve, Lamb and Harmon, and he designed an art-deco skyscraper in less than a fortnight. Excavation of the site began on 22 January 1930, and construction work was started on St Patrick's Day (17 March). A 3,000-strong workforce erected the building's 103 storeys at a rate of 4.5 storeys per week between June and November. The construction work cost $40,948,900 and claimed the lives of six workers.

A few weeks before work was finished, new masters took over the project: the Cult of Skaro directed the completion of the skyscraper through Mr Diagoras, who hired and fired the workforce and supervised the final stages. Working to plans supplied by the Daleks, Diagoras had three panels of Dalekenium fixed to the base of the antenna that topped the building. He also advanced the schedule, insisting that work be completed by the night of 1 November. Shortly after this had been done, lightning struck the mast for the first time – something that happens about a hundred times every year. The Daleks also established an underground base beneath the foundations, 17 metres below the tower, with a lift shaft running through the foundations of the building and all the way up to the 102nd floor.

LOCATION
Fifth Avenue, New York

HEIGHT
443.2 metres to top of antenna; 337 metres to 102nd floor

AREA
7,240 square metres

FLOORS
103

CONSTRUCTION TIME
410 days (7 million man hours)

ARTS AND MEDIA

ON BROADWAY

The Laurenzi theatre, Broadway, Manhattan
Doors open: 7pm, Monday to Friday;
12pm and 8pm, Saturday
Tickets: available from the front desk in advance
or on the night
Presented throughout October and November 1930:
New York Revue
written and directed by Mr Franz Wheeler
starring Barker's Belles:
Ella Lane, Frankie Manelli, Lois Shaw, Loretta Forbs,
Mitzy Segal, Susi Blanco, Tabitha Lee,
and Tallulah Francis (replacing Heidi Chicane)
singing 'Heaven & Hell (My Angel Put the Devil in Me)'

Earlier smash hits at The Laurenzi
Barker's Big Band Bonanza by Mr Franz Wheeler, starring Barker's Belles
Songs of Home by Mr Jackson Pope,
starring Barker's Belles
Manhattan in the Fall by Mr Dean Knight,
starring Barker's Belles
Remembering You, starring Barker's Belles
Forget Your Troubles by Mr Rob Dicks, music by Mr RS Williams, starring Barker's Belles
Summer in the Windy City by Mr Rob Dicks,
music by Mr RS Williams, starring Barker's Belles
Manhattan in the Fall by Mr Dean Knight,
starring Jackson Pope and Nadia Dand
Stars and Songbirds by Mr Franz Wheeler,
starring Lilly Malone

THE NEW YORK RECORD

New York's daily newspaper, published on
1 November 1930:

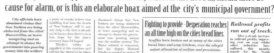

New York Record

Saturday, November 1st 1930

HOOVERVILLE MYSTERY DEEPENS

-As reports of disappearances from the city's Hooverville flood in, should there be cause for alarm, or is this an elaborate hoax aimed at the city's municipal government?

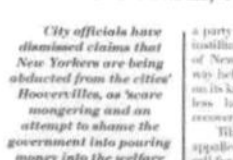

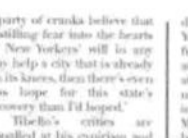

City officials have dismissed claims that New Yorkers are being abducted from the cities' Hoovervilles, as 'scare mongering and an attempt to shame the government into pouring money into the welfare

Fighting to provide - Desperation reaches an all time high on the cities bread lines.

Scuffles have broken out at many of the cities bread lines and soup kitchens, over the alleged unfair allocation of welfare and provisions.

Railroad profits run out of track.

THE GREAT DEPRESSION

The Republican Herbert Clark Hoover was inaugurated as President of the United States of America on 4 March 1929. He took office during what seemed to be a time of wellbeing and prosperity but, within seven months, a stock market crash sent the USA and the world into a sharp economic downturn. The Great Depression that followed caused mass unemployment and homelessness throughout America's cities, with much of the country's industry suffering. Many saw shanty towns develop in their public spaces, like New York's Central Park, as people lost their livelihoods and with them their homes. These shanty towns were named Hoovervilles, since the President's administration was blamed for non-interventionist and protectionist economic policies that were only worsening the situation. Hoover encouraged voluntary solutions to the economic crisis rather than government help, and each Hooverville took him at his word. Desolate areas were colonised by penniless construction workers, lawyers and stockbrokers – people from all walks of life settled in makeshift tents and crates, building temporary 'homes' out of cardboard and scrap metal. Their only hope lay in temporary construction work, with atrocious working conditions for pitiful rewards: Mr Diagoras offered wages of just a dollar a day for clearing sewer tunnels. Even with those conditions, unemployment proved a great incentive to take such work, since there was always someone else just as desperate who would take over an abandoned job. Labour was cheap, yet the abandoned poor of New York's Hooverville lived in the shadow of the construction of a national monument that would cost $40 million.

THE FINAL EXPERIMENT

Fleeing the Battle of Canary Wharf in 2007, the Cult of Skaro found themselves stranded in 1930s New York, their power cells drained by the emergency temporal shift they had used in their escape. The Dalek race had been brought to the brink of extinction, with apparently just the four-strong Cult left, hidden on a planet inhabited by millions of humans. Their leader Dalek Sec – who had been instructed by the Emperor of the Daleks to imagine new ways for the Dalek race to survive – formulated a plan for the Daleks to become supreme again.

Having established an underground base under the Empire State Building, the Cult constructed a vast genetics laboratory, with storage bays extending beneath Manhattan. At first they attempted to breed new Dalek mutants, with genetic material extracted from the members of the Cult. Their experiments were unsuccessful, lack of power preventing them from creating sustainable life. The resulting lifeless genetic matter was discarded in the nearby sewers.

Sec then made telepathic contact with a suitable human mind – Mr Diagoras, a man whose experiences in the First World War had left him determined to survive and prosper at any cost. Diagoras was instructed to procure humans, and he arranged for the abduction of scores of men

from the nearby Hooverville in Central Park. The Daleks divided their captives into two groups according to intelligence. Those of lower intellect were used as test subjects for experimental fusion of genetic elements, creating hybrids of pigs and human beings. These hybrids walked upright, but their facial features were porcine, they had lost the power of speech and they had a very limited life span. The Daleks referred to them as Pig Slaves and used them to collect further human specimens from around Manhattan. Those of greater intellect were held in suspended animation – more than a thousand of them.

Having mastered the genetic splicing of two different races to create the Pig Slaves, the Cult of Skaro moved on to their Final Experiment. This comprised two phases. In the first, Dalek Sec himself would absorb and merge with a human subject to create the first Human-Dalek hybrid. Walking upright, the Dalek Sec Hybrid's single-eyed head resembled the mutant found within each Dalek's casing.

The second phase involved the 1,000-plus captured humans the Cult held in storage. These men were kept near death, their minds already prepared to be receptive to new input. The Daleks planned to infuse these empty human shells with Dalek DNA to create a new race, a mobile army of Dalek-Human hybrids, freed

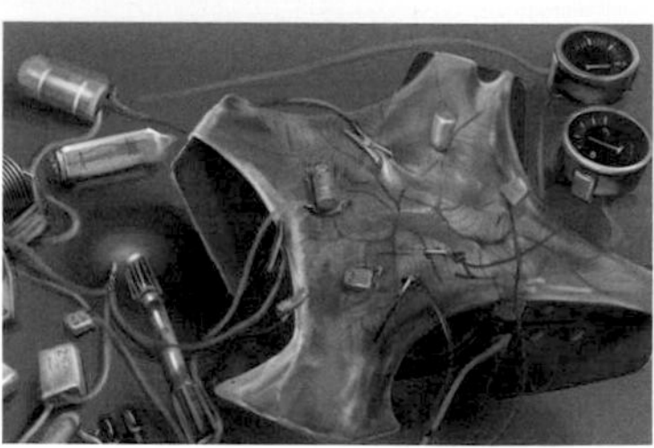

from protective casings yet loyal to the Daleks. The children of Skaro would walk again. This plan required enormous reserves of power, which the Daleks planned to obtain by harnessing the energy from a blast of gamma radiation from an eruption of solar flares. Having calculated the date and time when the gamma radiation would strike the Earth, they had instructed Diagoras to complete the construction of the antenna atop the Empire State Building by the night of 1 November. The final stage of construction work was to fix plates of Dalekenium to the base of the antenna. The skyscraper

was to act as an energy conductor for gamma radiation-carrying lightning, transmitting the power down through the building to the Dalek systems below, activating the Final Experiment and splicing Dalek DNA with the stored humans.

With the work on the antenna mast complete, the Cult of Skaro were able to set their plans in motion. Diagoras himself was absorbed by Dalek Sec to create the Human-Dalek Hybrid. The Dalek Sec Hybrid, however, absorbed more than he had expected, gaining aspects of humanity that the Daleks had discounted as irrelevant. As he began to experience emotions and feel compassion, Sec concluded that the Dalek plan was flawed: the Daleks could benefit more from regaining the emotions that their creator had considered a weakness. He and the Doctor attempted to revise the Final Experiment so that the new race of Daleks could start again. The rest of the Cult rejected Sec's analysis and turned on their leader, removing the hybridised DNA from the chromatin solution destined for the stored humans and replacing it with pure Dalek DNA to create the intended Dalek-Human army, which they would arm with Dalek weapons.

When the lightning struck the skyscraper, the Doctor interposed his own body between the gamma radiation and the Dalekenium, so that Time Lord DNA was added to the mix. This gave the activated Dalek-Humans a measure of independence and free will, quickly leading them to question the Daleks' orders. The Cult promptly declared the experiment a failure and exterminated the race that they had just created.

These events cost the lives of Sec and two of the Dalek members of the Cult of Skaro, Jast and Thay. Only Dalek Caan remained. Using what remained of the energy from the gamma strike, Caan activated another emergency temporal shift and escaped New York, travelling across his own timeline and back into the Time War itself.

DALEKS (4)

The arrival of the Cult of Skaro in New York was not the Daleks' first visit to the Empire State Building. Centuries earlier (in their own timeline), a squad of Daleks pursued the Doctor through time and space, and the chase led them to the Empire State in 1966. They were too late to capture the TARDIS, and only stayed long enough to conduct the unproductive interrogation of a bemused tourist from Alabama named Morton Dill.

Other sightings: 2007; 2009; 2012; 200,100

1941

BRAVE NEW WORLD

THE LONDON BLITZ

The London Blitz began on 7 September 1940. The city was attacked by 348 German bombers escorted by 617 fighters, and 448 people were killed. There were similar attacks on each of the next 56 days or nights, with bombardments continuing until 10 May 1941. The Blitz claimed at least 20,000 lives and made 1.4 million people homeless. The ARP ('Air Raid Precautions') organisation was formed to coordinate protection and defence, and nearly one in six Londoners was involved in civil defence. The ARP issued gas masks to citizens and publicised the constant need for vigilance and caution. To avoid attracting or guiding enemy aircraft, there were strict

'blackout' rules: all windows were covered, rooms were left in darkness, and no car headlights were to be used, or torches or cigarettes lit in the open air, although these restrictions were relaxed a little a few months into the war. The illumination of the famous Clock Tower of the Palace of Westminster was also switched off. Procedures were well established for what people should do when the sirens signalled an approaching raid. The Civil Defence Ministry distributed 2.25 million free air-raid shelters for people to erect in their back gardens, with London tube stations also used for protection. The ARP put up around fifty huge barrage balloons, secured with strong cables which would destroy any low-flying aircraft that collided with them. Occasionally, one of these balloons would come loose, and the RAF were rumoured to use them for target practice.

SOCIETY AND WAR

THE SPIRIT OF THE BLITZ

'The walls of London may be battered, but the spirit of the Londoner stands resolute and undismayed,' said King George VI. In many ways, Britain remained undaunted during the serial bombardment of its cities, with many of the people of London adapting their lives to the constant bombing and attempting to carry on as normal. Some would spend evenings in dimly lit nightclubs and drinking dens, watching singers and entertainers, dancing and mixing with locally stationed troops. When the sirens sounded, lights were extinguished and everyone moved to the nearest shelters.

A major part of the war effort was a constant stream of propaganda, the most visible signs of which were the many public-information posters seen all over the city. Some reminded people of the precautions needed in blackout – always carry your gas mask, Hitler will send no warning. Others emphasised how important it was that nothing was wasted – Your Empties Wanted. Next to the loss of life and destruction of property, the biggest problem for the country's morale came from the shortages of food, clothing and other necessities. For some, the Black Market offered a means to buck the rationing system, with expensive prices illicitly paid for stolen goods or for supplies of food beyond the official entitlement.

MARXISM IN ACTION

Although the government arranged the evacuation of almost 3 million children and teachers from Britain's towns and cities when war broke out in September 1939, many were unhappy among strangers in unfamiliar countryside villages and farms. Some, like Algy, Jim, Ernie and Alf, experienced ill treatment and abuse and eventually made their way back to their home towns. These children lived as homeless scavengers, sleeping rough and emerging from their hiding places during air raids to steal food from still-occupied houses, while the owners were in the shelters.

A teenage mother called Nancy, who had raised her son Jamie as her brother, was out looking for food one night during an air raid. Jamie followed her out and was caught in the blast from a German bomb near Limehouse Green Station. Still wearing his gas mask, Jamie suffered massive trauma to the left side of his head and a partial collapse of his chest cavity on the right-hand side. He later died in the nearby Albion Hospital.

CAPTAIN JACK HARKNESS

REPORTED SIGHTING #5 CONFIRMED

ESTIMATED AGE: 35

LOCATION: London, 1941

AVAILABLE INFORMATION:
Captain Jack arrived on Earth at the height of the London Blitz, planning to execute a 'self-cleaning con'. He posed as an American volunteer in the Royal Air Force's 133 Squadron, and lured the Doctor and Rose Tyler to London, believing that they were 51st-century Time Agents. He then attempted to sell them a burnt-out Chula medical transporter, which he claimed was a fully equipped warship and which he knew would soon be destroyed by a German shell falling on the cylinder's Limehouse Green Station location. Jack was devastated to discover that he was ultimately responsible for the chaos that ensued, and helped the Doctor to put things right by capturing the incoming German bomb in his own ship's tractor beam and taking it onboard. This almost cost him his life, but he was rescued by the TARDIS and joined the Doctor and Rose on their travels.

1940s LONDON

BIG BEN

The popular name for the Clock Tower at the north-eastern end of the Palace of Westminster. 'Big Ben' is actually the nickname of the tower's Great Bell. The tower was designed by the English architect Augustus Pugin when the Palace was rebuilt following a fire in 1834, and the clock was started in September 1859. Although the Palace was hit fourteen times during the Blitz, the clock remained operational and accurate throughout the Second World War, although it was not illuminated.

Jack Harkness chose Big Ben as a memorable parking place for his spaceship, which he rendered invisible and tethered to the tower. For the only time between September 1939 and April 1945, Big Ben's lights were switched back on as Jack danced with Rose on top of his craft alongside the tower. It is not recorded whether this itself led to one of the successful German strikes on the Palace of Westminster.

LIMEHOUSE GREEN STATION

The Limehouse area of East London was the city's original Chinatown. Large numbers of Chinese immigrants settled there during the 1880s, establishing restaurants and shops, and opening laundry houses where lime was used to clean clothes, giving the area its popular name. This area of London was particularly badly hit during the Blitz, forcing much of the population to relocate to Soho. Limehouse Green Station was abandoned and, when the Chula medical transporter landed and buried itself in the ground there, the army sealed off the station with barbed-wire fences, covered the cylinder with tarpaulin, and posted troops to guard what they believed might be Hitler's latest secret weapon.

SCIENCE AND TECHNOLOGY

CHULA SPACECRAFT

Some time before his arrival in wartime London, Captain Jack Harkness stole a spaceship from a female from an advanced race of warriors, the Chula.

The ship's onboard computer was capable of two-way voice communication, and responded to an extensive series of emergency protocols that Jack had installed, including #471 (which mixed him a large martini). The craft could be rendered invisible, and had tractor-beam and teleport technology, as well as Om-Com – the capacity to communicate through anything with a speaker grille, including telephones, radios and even a child's toy. Jack used the tractor beam to rescue Rose Tyler as she fell from a barrage balloon cable during an air raid, projecting a light field out from his ship into the London skyline, noting as he did so that signals from Rose's mobile phone interfered with his instruments. As Jack later discovered, the ship had no escape pods.

While Jack had reprogrammed the ship's computer to recognise him as its commander, he did not have total control over the ship's systems: having security-keyed the teleporter to his own molecular structure, he had

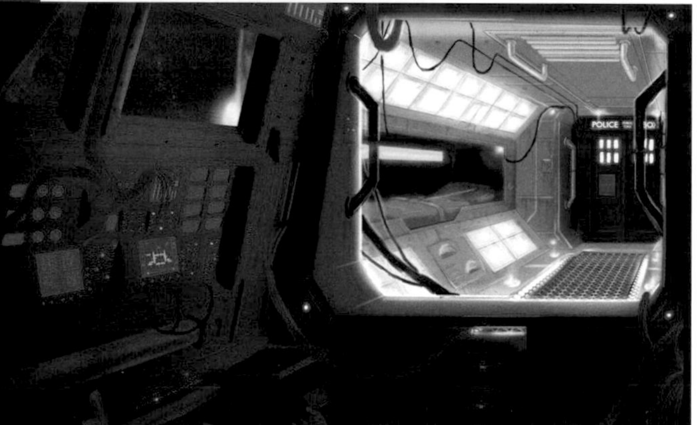

to disable the ship's navigation controls and override the security protocols in order to teleport anyone else. The ship was also equipped with nanogenes – airborne sub-atomic robots that repaired any ailments or injuries sustained by the crew.

Jack had brought a second Chula ship to London, a medical transporter. Like the main Chula craft, this mauve-coloured cylinder was full of nanogenes. Jack programmed the transporter's flight computer to crash in East London, taking care to avoid hitting any living creatures. On impact, however, the cylinder leaked its nanogenes, which began to spread through the local area.

NANOGENES

Every Chula ship contained billions of nanogenes, sub-atomic robots that activated when the craft's bulkhead was sealed. On activation, they located nearby life forms, assessed them for physical damage, and fixed the flaws – the Chula war effort required that their injured warriors were restored to peak condition as rapidly as possible. When Jack crashed the stolen Chula ambulance into Limehouse Green Station, nanogenes escaped from the damaged cylinder and set about fulfilling their programming. The first life form they encountered was the recently killed child, Jamie, just after he had fallen victim to a bomb blast in an air raid. With their Chula programming, the nanogenes were unfamiliar with the human form and registered Jamie's physical state as the human norm: the child's head had been partially crushed; the gas mask he was wearing had melded with the remains of his skull; his chest cavity had collapsed; and his hand was scarred. Having reanimated the child and absorbed his condition as their human template, the nanogenes proceeded to apply it to every human that they subsequently encountered. As the Doctor suggested, human DNA was being rewritten... by idiots.

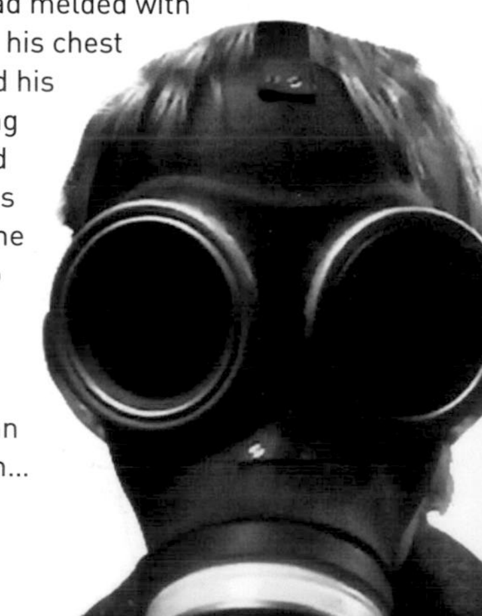

ALBION HOSPITAL

In the aftermath of the air raid, the injured Jamie was taken to the nearest hospital. He was treated in room 802 on the top floor, where it was discovered that he had survived his injuries, yet seemingly had no real consciousness or physical life signs. Before breaking out of the hospital, the child drew dozens of pictures of his mummy, which were stuck on the walls of the room. Within hours of beginning to treat the boy, the staff were in the grip of a plague, which soon spread to the other patients. The last to succumb was Dr Constantine, who had recorded his attempt to communicate with the child on state-of-the-art equipment. The hospital was closed and quarantined; the authorities seem to have devised a plan to destroy it during an air raid, hoping to contain the plague and blame the loss on a German air attack.

The Doctor's intervention eventually undid the damage done by the nanogenes, and he reprogrammed the robots to heal all the affected people in the vicinity. Soon, Dr Constantine was being hailed as a miracle healer, with reports of patients recovering so completely that years of physical problems had been reversed – one, Mrs Harcourt, discovered that she'd had an amputated leg restored to her.

GAS-MASKED ZOMBIES

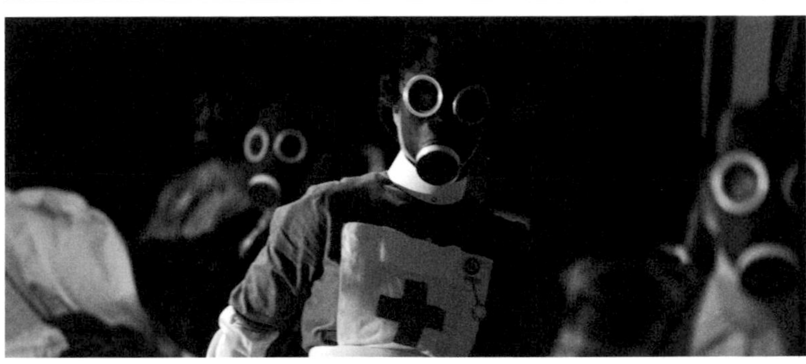

The victims of Albion Hospital's 'plague' were suffering from an exact replication of the boy's injuries: head and chest trauma and scarring to the back of the hand. Worst of all, they, like Jamie, developed gas masks which fused to the flesh of their faces, composed of their own flesh and blood. Soon the apparent infection had affected hundreds of doctors, nurses and patients, and the hospital was full of zombies. They did not die, but they had no heartbeat or other signs of life.

Like the Chula spacecraft, the gas-masked boy could communicate via Om-Com, contacting people through anything with a speaker grille. All the gas-masked people retained the ability to speak but generally repeated a simple phrase: 'Are you my mummy?' When the nanogenes had restored Jamie, they had also revived his overriding need to find his mother, and this instinct was shared with the other gas-masked people. As a fully equipped Chula warrior, the child was capable of tearing the world apart in his search for his mother. This provided the key to ending the crisis: when the Doctor realised that Nancy was Jamie's mother not his sister, he persuaded her to admit the fact to her son. The nanogenes then recognised the parental DNA as superior to the infant DNA, and corrected their previous error by following the new template. Jamie was properly restored to life, and the Doctor reprogrammed the nanogenes to do the same for the rest of the gas-masked people.

ALIEN ACTIVITY

1947 – ROSWELL INCIDENT

> "That's the milometer from the Roswell spaceship...
>
> *– The Doctor to Rose Tyler (Van Statten's museum, Utah, 2012)*

In July 1947, the US military recovered what it claimed was a research balloon from a ranch near Roswell, New Mexico. There was, however, much speculation that what had actually been captured – and concealed – was the debris from an alien spacecraft that had crash-landed on Earth.

XIV OLYMPIAD

> "Last one they had in London was dynamite. Wembley, 1948. I loved it so much, I went back and watched it all over again.
>
> *– The Doctor to Rose Tyler (Stratford, London, 2012)*

The 1948 Summer Olympics opened in London on 29 July. The torchbearer's name was John Mark.

1953

1950s BRITAIN

Britain was finally starting to recover from the effects of its massive war effort. The rationing of food, clothing and non-essential items, imposed in 1940, was lifted in stages from 1948. By June 1953, most restrictions had been lifted, and even confectionary was no longer rationed, although it would be another year until the final controls were abolished.

Meanwhile, Everest – the world's highest mountain – was conquered by the ninth British expedition to make the attempt. The Communist Party leader of the USSR, Josef Stalin, died in March, and Winston Churchill, the UK Prime Minister, was awarded the Nobel Prize for Literature in recognition of his six-volume history of the Second World War. And, as the first colour television broadcasts were permitted in the USA, and Technicolor announced improvements to its colour and 3-D film processes, the British Broadcasting Corporation began to plan the most ambitious and successful television outside broadcast yet seen.

THE CORONATION

Upon the death of her father King George VI on 6 February 1952, Princess Elizabeth succeeded to the British throne. Her Coronation was then scheduled to take place the following year, on Tuesday 2 June, after a sufficient period of mourning for the deceased monarch. The Queen gave permission for the event to be televised, against the advice of the Prime Minister, Winston Churchill, and about 56 per cent of the country's population of 36.5 million were estimated to have watched the live broadcast by the BBC, which ran from 10.15am to 5.20pm.

The broadcast began with cameras following the Queen and her husband as they left Buckingham Palace in the Golden State Coach. The Coach made its way along the processional route to Westminster Abbey, arriving a little over an hour later. The Queen was crowned at 12.34pm. The live coverage, presented by commentator Richard Dimbleby, continued into the afternoon, as the Queen left the Abbey shortly before 3pm, and the State Coach made its way through London's streets back to Buckingham Palace. As the official event concluded, the population began to celebrate with street parties and fireworks.

HERMETHICANS

Not naturally a formless species, one small group of criminals on the planet Hermethica discovered a means to convert themselves into beings of plasmic energy. In this state, they had the capacity to direct electrical signals, enabling them to take over Hermethica's major cities.

Their leader was the Wire, and her capture brought an end to their short reign of terror. Before her execution could take place, however, the Wire converted herself once more, transmitting herself through a communications device and travelling across the stars until she reached the Earth.

PLANET OF ORIGIN
Hermethica

APPEARANCE
Bolts of plasmic energy

ABILITIES
Extraction of life force; mental control

MAGPIE ELECTRICALS

Mr Magpie owned a small shop on Mafeking Terrace in North London's Muswell Hill district, selling and repairing radio and television sets. It was not a successful business – Magpie's bank account was £200 overdrawn. That changed with the arrival of the Wire. The Wire travelled via a lightning storm and transmitted herself through the aerial on the roof of Magpie's shop and into one of his television sets. Once there, the Wire took on the appearance of a television presenter, and spoke to Magpie. At first, the Wire fed off the electrical energy in his brain and began to remove the man's face, then relented and decided that Magpie would be more useful as a servant. The Wire gave Magpie instructions on how to modify televisions that would allow her to absorb the life forces of viewers, and a smaller device, resembling a portable television made from Bakelite, that would turn a transmitter into a receiver. To ensure the best possible take-up, Magpie was now selling his Wire-infested television sets locally for just £5. As more and more people bought telly-boxes, more and more of the screens in Magpie's shop began to show silent and disembodied faces...

TELEVISION

By March 1953, there were 2.14 million licensed television sets in Great Britain, representing about 14 per cent of households and up from 1.45 million twelve months earlier. The number continued to grow throughout the year, and an estimated audience of 20.4 million people crowded around their friends' and neighbours' small screens to watch June's live broadcast of the Coronation. For the first time television overtook radio as the nation's medium of choice for a major event. As Rose observed to the Doctor, most people did not have a television, so TV aerials were a rare sight. Except in Muswell Hill, where Mr Magpie's bargain-priced sets were soon to be found in many more homes...

Top Telly

✦ *Muffin the Mule*, presented by Annette Mills, ran on weekday afternoons from 1946 until 1955, as part of BBC Television's *For the Children* and *Watch With Mother* strands. ✦ *What's My Line?* was hosted by Eamonn Andrews from 1951 to 1963, each Sunday at 8.30pm. ✦ *Animal, Vegetable, Mineral?* was a successful panel game for archaeology experts that ran from 1952 to 1959. ✦ Hours of broadcast were strictly limited by the government, and each evening's broadcasts from Alexandra Palace ended between 10.30 and 11pm with the National Anthem.

TORCHWOOD

Seventy-four years after the Institute was founded by Queen Victoria, its shadowy influence was keenly felt by the more senior officers of the Metropolitan Police Force. To add to Detective Inspector Bishop's worries over the phenomenon of the faceless people was the fear that such unusual events in the run-up to the Coronation would soon attract the attention of Torchwood.

FACELESS PEOPLE

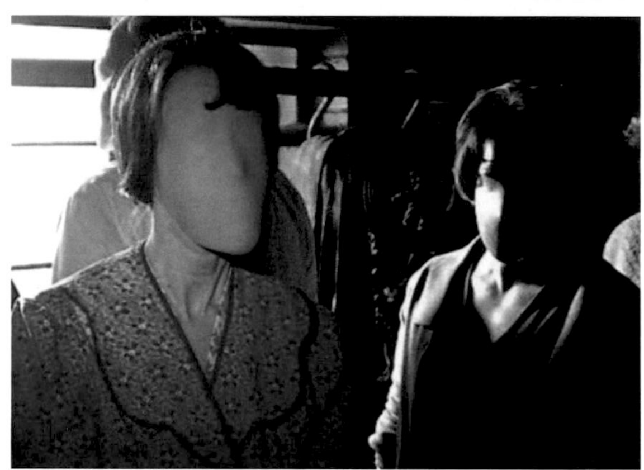

Rumours and scare-stories abounded of the disturbing powers of television – some, like Tommy Connolly's grandmother, believed that it rotted the mind, or made your brain come out of your ears. She was closer to the truth than she knew: she became one of the Wire's earliest victims, straight after a man from Magpie's Electricals had delivered and installed the Connolly family's new television set. Plasmic energy streamed from the TV, attached itself to her head and began to extract her life force, as the Wire gorged on her brain. Gran was left mute and faceless, unable to communicate or even feed, with the only real indication that she remained alive being the constant clenching and unclenching of her fists.

Several other residents of Florizel Street had already experienced the same fate. As rumours of monsters began to circulate in the area, Eddie Connolly decided to inform on his friends and neighbours. He reported their whereabouts to the authorities, and the police, scared of any disruption to the upcoming royal event, swiftly removed the faceless victims. They were kept locked up and hidden away from public view.

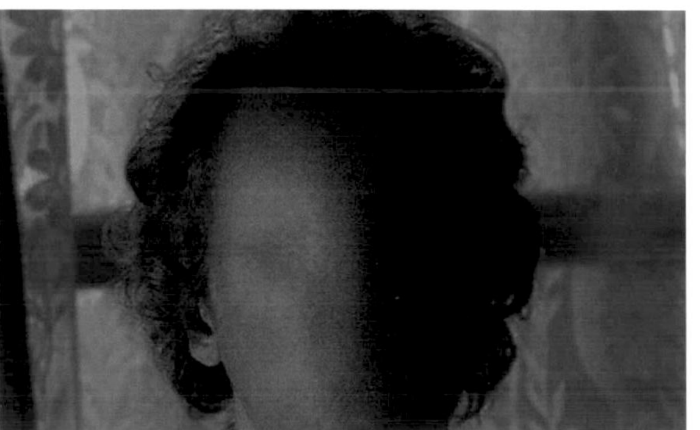

ALEXANDRA PALACE

The BBC began to lease the eastern part of the building in 1935, and it was the main production and transmitter centre for the Corporation's television service for more than twenty years. Two television studios were installed, and a steel lattice radio tower was added to the top of the building.

This antenna was vital to the Wire's plans. As the Coronation broadcast began, and the largest single viewing audience up to that time gathered around their television screens, the Wire ordered Magpie to climb the radio tower and attach the portable television device. With the device plugged in, the radio tower stopped transmitting and started receiving – bolts of plasmic energy linked the antenna to every television aerial, and the Wire began to feast on the life essences of more than 20 million people. All over Britain, viewers' faces were slowly sucked into their TV screens. She intended to fully restore her energies and then transmit herself back to Hermethica.

The Doctor followed Magpie to the top of the radio tower and attached a link to his own invention: a prototype home video recorder, some thirty years ahead of its time. There was a brief setback when a component in the Doctor's machine failed, but Tommy Connolly, helping from inside one of the Alexandra Palace TV studios, replaced the part. As the Wire killed Magpie, who had now served his purpose, the Doctor restored the transmitter function of the radio tower and recorded the Wire onto videotape, where she would remain trapped until he taped over her.

THE KENNEDY ASSASSINATION

On Friday 22 November 1963, John F Kennedy, the President of the United States of America, was assassinated during a public appearance in Dallas, Texas. Among the onlookers lining the streets was the Doctor...

APOLLO MOON LANDING

The spacecraft *Apollo 11* achieved the first manned landing on the Earth's moon on Sunday 20 July 1969. Approximately one-fifth of the world's population watched on television as the astronauts, Neil Armstrong and Buzz Aldrin, made their 'giant leap for mankind'. Also watching – though not on TV – were the Doctor and Martha Jones, who enjoyed it so much they used the TARDIS to go back and watch it all another three times.

MISSING PERSONS

THE DOCTOR AND MARTHA JONES

Martha Jones's fifth visit to 1969 was not by TARDIS. She and the Doctor were attacked by a Weeping Angel in 2007 and sent thirty-eight years back in time. Stranded, Martha was forced to get a job in a shop to earn enough to support the two of them. Meanwhile, the Doctor – armed with Sally Sparrow's 2008 notes on what had happened – ensured that all the pieces were in place for Sally to return the TARDIS to them from 2007. He wrote messages to Sally on the walls inside Wester Drumlins house; he constructed his timey-wimey detector so they could make contact with Billy Shipton; he filmed his half of a conversation with Sally, reading his part of Laurence Nightingale's 2007 transcript from an autocue; and he gave the film to Billy to hide on DVDs that Sally would own in the future; and then the Doctor and Martha waited for the TARDIS to arrive and rescue them.

BILLY SHIPTON

Detective Inspector Billy Shipton, a Metropolitan Police officer, was in charge of investigations into disappearances at Wester Drumlins house in the early twenty-first century. In 2007, soon after meeting Sally Sparrow, he was attacked by a Weeping Angel, which despatched him to 1969. When he arrived, he was met by the Doctor and Martha Jones, who had tracked him down using a timey-wimey detector. The Doctor explained to Billy that he could not be returned to 2007, and that he should not try to contact Sally Sparrow over the thirty-eight years that would pass before they would meet again – if he did, he would tear a hole in the fabric of space and time and destroy two-thirds of the universe. Instead, Billy would have to settle in 1969 and live out the rest of his life: he would marry a girl named Sally, and begin a career in book publishing, before moving on to making videotapes and then DVDs. The Doctor asked Billy to take a filmed message to Sally Sparrow, and to hide it as an Easter Egg on 17 specific DVDs. He also said that Billy would meet Sally Sparrow just once more, and it would be on the night of his death.

(See also: 1920; 2007; 2008)

1979: HELL OF A YEAR

✦ **17 February** The Sino-Vietnamese war begins as China invades Vietnam

✦ **4 May** Margaret Thatcher leads the Conservative Party to victory in the UK's General Election

✦ **22 June** The Jim Henson Company releases *The Muppet Movie*

✦ **11 July** The US space station *Skylab* begins its return to Earth, several years ahead of schedule, and with a little help from the Doctor

✦ **5–10 November** ABBA perform at Wembley Arena in London, as seen by Rose Tyler

✦ **21 November** Ian Dury and the Blockheads perform at the Top Rank in Sheffield, as missed by the Doctor and Rose Tyler

1970s–1980s

UNIT

UNIT, under the command of Brigadier Alistair Gordon Lethbridge-Stewart, and the Third Doctor

File QQ

File CCC

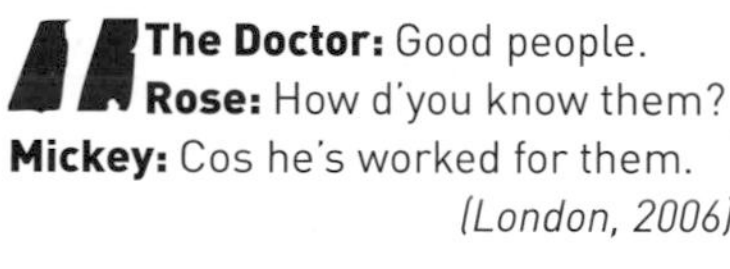
The Doctor: Good people.
Rose: How d'you know them?
Mickey: Cos he's worked for them.
(London, 2006)

File TTT

File 4A

UNIT records contain files on countless alien incursions and other strange phenomena encountered by its operatives and its one-time scientific adviser the Doctor. Among the most notable are:

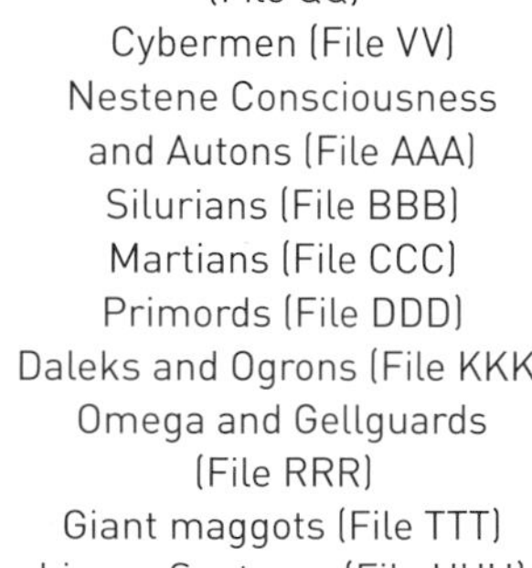

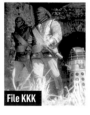

Great Intelligence and robot Yeti (File QQ)
Cybermen (File VV)
Nestene Consciousness and Autons (File AAA)
Silurians (File BBB)
Martians (File CCC)
Primords (File DDD)
Daleks and Ogrons (File KKK)
Omega and Gellguards (File RRR)
Giant maggots (File TTT)
Linx, a Sontaran (File UUU)
Dinosaurs (File WWW)
Giant spiders (File ZZZ)
K-1 robot (File 4A)
Zygons and Skarasen (File 4F)
Kraals and androids (File 4J)
Krynoid (File 4L)

File VV

File DDD

File AAA

File UUU

File BBB

File RRR

File ZZZ

File 4L

UNIT

Additional files relate to the Master, a renegade from the same race as the Doctor. He made a series of attacks on Earth, often with alien support. Among those covered in the UNIT files are:

✦ A second incursion by the Nestene Consciousness, again using Autons (File EEE)
✦ A plot to provoke a world war using a stolen missile and an alien brain parasite (File FFF)

File GGG

✦ An attempt to hand the Earth to the parasitic Axons (File GGG)
✦ An unfortunate case of mistaken identity – UNIT arrested the Spanish ambassador in London, briefly believing him to be the Master (File HHH)

File LLL

✦ The reawakening of the Dæmon Azal (File JJJ)
✦ The revival of an ancient colony of undersea reptiles – 'Sea Devils' – that planned to retake the Earth (File LLL)
✦ The development of a matter-transmission device to unleash a Chronovore (File OOO)

The Master

DINOSAURS

Sarah Jane Smith: I saw things you wouldn't believe.
Rose Tyler: Try me.
... Sarah: Real living dinosaurs!
(London, 2007)

Prehistoric creatures were transported through time to appear in 20th-century London, provoking the evacuation of the city. The conspirators intended to return Earth to a Golden Age before the planet had been ruined by humans. The Doctor altered the programming of the time machine they were using, and the plotters themselves were returned to the age of the dinosaurs.

File WWW

ZYGONS AND SKARASEN

... Sarah: The Loch Ness Monster. *(London, 2007)*

Buried in their crashed spaceship for centuries, a band of Zygons awoke in Scotland and planned to conquer and restructure the Earth to make it fit for their race to inhabit. They controlled a gigantic cyborg sea creature, the Skarasen, on which they were dependent for food, and used it in a series of attacks on oil rigs and, finally, central London. The Zygons were all destroyed and the creature returned to its adopted home: Loch Ness.

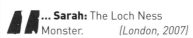

File 4F

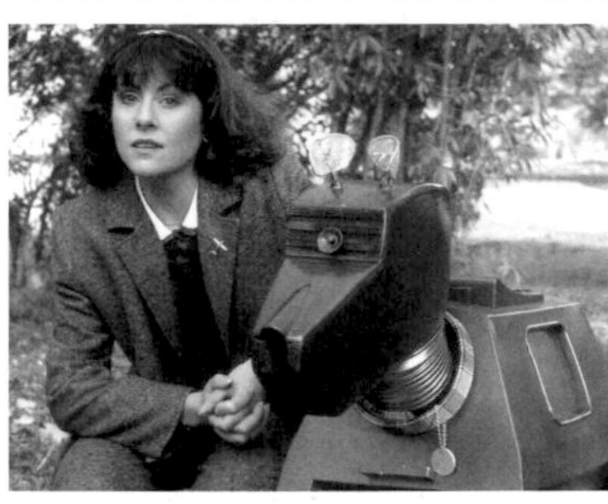

ROBOTS

... Sarah: Robots ... Lots of robots. *(London, 2007)*

Developed at the Thinktank research centre, the K-1 robot was used by corrupt scientists to hold the world to ransom. It briefly grew to enormous size after absorbing energy from a disintegrator gun, but was destroyed with a metal-eating virus.

The Kraals of the planet Oseidon planned an invasion using android doubles. When the invasion began, the Doctor jammed the androids' control signals.

Sarah Jane Smith's travels with the Doctor ended when he took her back to Earth, accidentally leaving her in Aberdeen rather than Croydon. He later sent her a gift – K-9 Mark III.

LIVING SHADOWS

LIVING SHADOWS

An elemental shade had escaped from the Howling Halls, and the Doctor tracked it to a terraced house in London. He stopped it, but was too late to save the life of the young mother of four-year-old Elton Pope. This was Elton's first encounter with the Doctor.

(See also: 2007)

1987

REAPERS

Reapers are parasitic extra-dimensional beings that exist outside time. The creatures are attracted by the creation of a wound in time – they seal off the affected area then sterilise it by slaughtering all living beings inside it. When they feed off their victims, their heads and necks give off an amber glow.

They were brought to 1980s Earth by a combination of factors: time was already weakened by the simultaneous presence of two versions of the Doctor and Rose; and when Rose averted her father's death, the weakness became a wound or breach. As the Reapers spread across the planet devouring all life they encountered, several concentrated on the church where Pete Tyler and the rest of the wedding party were sheltering. The only defence against the Reapers being physical obstructions – the older the better – the Doctor led everyone inside the church, hoping that its centuries-old walls would delay them long enough for him to find a way to end the menace.

When 19-year-old Rose had physical contact with her infant counterpart, however, a paradox was added to the time wound, and this allowed a Reaper to breach the church walls. The Doctor's last hope was that he might himself prove old enough, at 900 years, to hold back the Reapers and protect the humans. It was a vain hope – the Reaper devoured him.

The only means of ridding the Earth of the Reapers was to heal the wound in time caused by Pete Tyler's survival. The Doctor had quickly realised this but hoped to avoid it. Once he had died, Pete himself realised that the car that should have killed him offered the only chance for everyone else.

With his sacrifice, the Reapers instantly disappeared from this dimension.

PLANET OF ORIGIN
Not applicable

APPEARANCE
Dragon-like; four-armed; winged; red eyes; scythe-like tail; sharp-toothed mouth in abdominal area

ABILITIES
Flight; extra-dimensional travel

HIT AND RUN

VISITORS RECORD B

ate	Name	Company	Car
	Peter Alan Tyler		
	Jacqueline Andrea Suzette Prentice		

Pete Tyler

Peter Alan Tyler (born 15 September 1954) married Jacqueline Andrea Suzette Prentice (born 1 February 1967) in a South London registry office. Pete got Jackie's name wrong as the couple took their vows: 'I, Peter Alan Tyler, take you Jacqueline Susan... Suzette... Anita?' Hidden among the guests were the Doctor and 19-year-old Rose Tyler, who had travelled back in time to see the wedding.

Pete was a wannabe entrepreneur, pinning his hopes on the potential success of a range of ventures – health drinks called Vitex, solar power, cut-price detergents, Betamax videotapes – none of which had paid off for him. In fact, his proudest achievement to date was probably winning third prize in a bowling competition.

Pete and Jackie had one child – Rose Tyler, who was still a baby at the time of her father's death.

On 7 November, Pete Tyler was hit by a speeding car as he crossed the road to his flat in South London on the day of the wedding of his friends Stuart Hoskins and Sarah Clark. The driver didn't stop, and Pete was dead by the time an ambulance reached him. The only witnesses were the Doctor and 19-year-old Rose Tyler, who had travelled back in time and watched the accident.

Wedding Day

As the family and friends of Stuart Hoskins and Sarah Clark gathered at a South London church for their wedding, the Maid of Honour, Jackie Tyler, realised that her husband had not turned up. She didn't find out until after the wedding that he had died. Jackie brought Rose Tyler up single-handed for the next 18 years.

ON THE AIRWAVES

Eighties Hits

✦ *Never Can Say Goodbye* – The Communards

✦ *Never Gonna Give You Up* – Rick Astley

BAD WOLF

That's been there for years, it's just a phrase, it's just words...

– Mickey Smith to Rose Tyler (South London, 2006)

The first recorded outbreak of 'Bad Wolf' graffiti in the Powell Estate area of South London was on flyposters advertising 20 November's Energize event. Over the next 19 years, 'Bad Wolf' was scrawled on the walls and ground of the local play area and could often be seen on posters in the windows of shops and cafés.

A WOUND IN TIME

On 7 November, Pete Tyler was almost hit by a speeding car on the day of the wedding of his friends Stuart Hoskins and Sarah Clark. As he crossed the road to his flat in South London, a stranger managed to knock him out of the path of the vehicle, which didn't stop. Pete's rescuer was called Rose, and the only other witness was a man called the Doctor. They had crossed their own timeline to watch the accident a second time, which caused a weak point in time. As a result, the car that should have killed Pete became trapped in a short time loop, appearing and disappearing again and again. When Rose saved her father, the weak point in time had become a wound through which streamed extra-dimensional creatures.

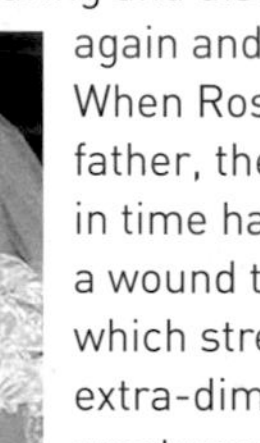

As the family and friends of Stuart and Sarah gathered at a South London church for their wedding, it soon became apparent that many of the expected guests were missing. Then the Reapers attacked, forcing the Doctor, Rose Tyler, Pete Tyler and the rest of the wedding party to lock themselves in the sanctuary of the church building.

ON THE AIRWAVES

Not out yet...

✦ *Don't Mug Yourself* – The Streets

Mobile telephones

In the late 1980s, the portable, wireless telephone was just beginning to break out from its niche market as an expensive toy for businessmen. Large and unwieldy, these mobile phones required sizeable batteries. The Doctor cannibalised one of these to provide power to retrieve his lost TARDIS. The phone had belonged to the father of the groom, Sonny Hoskins, a victim of the Reapers. It had provided some of the first evidence that something was wrong with time, receiving nothing but a very strange, repeated message.

The first telephone call

" Watson, come here, I need you.

– *Alexander Graham Bell, 1876*

THE MAN WHO SAVED THE WORLD

On 7 November, the wedding day of his friends Stuart Hoskins and Sarah Clark, Pete Tyler ran in front of a speeding car in the street outside a South London church and was killed. The driver stopped and waited for the police, and the only other witness was 19-year-old Rose Tyler, who stayed with him as he lay dying. Hearing the noise, the wedding guests emerged from the church to find that Pete Tyler had died.

Rose Tyler

As Rose grew up, her mother Jackie would sometimes show her photographs of her father, and tell her the story of the car accident that took his life in 1987.

CAPTAIN JACK HARKNESS

REPORTED SIGHTING #12

ESTIMATED AGE: 157–166

LOCATION: Powell Estate, London, 1990s

AVAILABLE INFORMATION: Captain Jack, still stranded on Earth and working for Torchwood, occasionally visited South London's Powell Estate and watched Rose Tyler growing up.

EVERYTHING CHANGES

21ST-CENTURY LONDON

HENRIK'S DEPARTMENT STORE

One of Central London's largest and best-known department stores, Henrik & Son was located within walking distance of Trafalgar Square. The Central London branch was opened in 1928, and expanded over the next eight decades to occupy a ground floor, three upper floors and a basement, having combined five adjacent premises. It boasted a food hall and several restaurants and cafés, and sold a wide range of consumer goods, including electrical goods, books and clothing.

On the evening of Wednesday 3 March, as the store was closing, one of the shop's employees – Rose Tyler from the women's clothing department – took a store lift to the basement. She needed to give the week's staff lottery money to the shop's chief electrical officer, H.P. Wilson, but there was no sign of him. Instead, Rose was attacked by seven walking shop-window dummies, then rescued by a stranger called the Doctor.
As the pair fled, and as many as sixty of the moving mannequins joined their pursuit, the Doctor explained that Wilson had been killed by the dummies. They were Autons, creatures made of living plastic and controlled via a relay device in the roof of the shop – which he was going to blow up. Sending Rose home, the Doctor headed to the top of the empty building and set off a bomb that ripped Henrik's apart in a huge fireball. The whole of Central London was swiftly closed off as the police investigated the fire. According to news reports, there was just one fatality – the shop's electrician, Wilson.

AUTONS

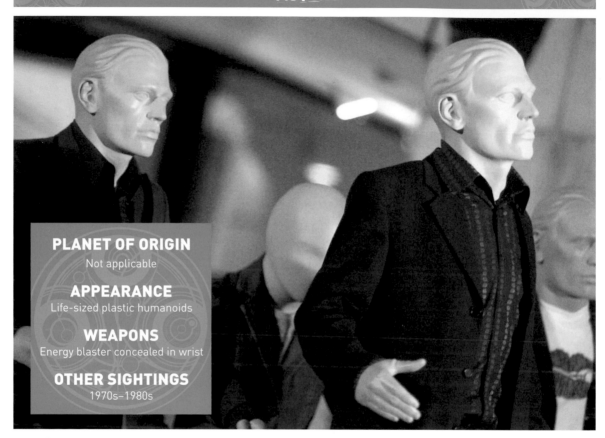

PLANET OF ORIGIN
Not applicable

APPEARANCE
Life-sized plastic humanoids

WEAPONS
Energy blaster concealed in wrist

OTHER SIGHTINGS
1970s–1980s

Artificial life forms created, animated and controlled by the Nestene Consciousness. There were two basic types of Auton. The most common was the basic humanoid, with undeveloped features and stiff, awkward movement. This form resembled display mannequins found in shop windows across planet Earth. The Nestene Consciousness animated these via radio-transmitted signals, and used them as shock troops when it was ready to begin an invasion.

The second type was the much more sophisticated replica. These were exactly modelled on individuals, both physically and vocally, although they were not perfect – their 'skin' could appear rather shiny, and their grasp of vocal mannerisms could be erratic. These superior Autons were also able to manipulate parts of their plastic bodies to form new shapes, and each element of them (head, torso, limbs) could be operated independently of the others, even when detached from the main creature.

When the controlling signal from the Nestene Consciousness was interrupted or halted, the Autons ceased functioning.

21ST-CENTURY LONDON

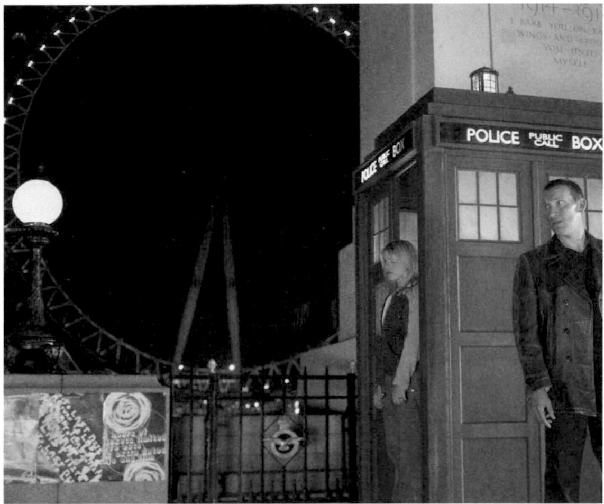

LONDON EYE

Constructed to mark the end of the second millennium, the London Eye was a huge Ferris wheel – at the time, the largest in the world. Construction work was completed by the end of 1999, although the wheel itself was not ready for public use until some months later. It quickly became a familiar and immediately recognisable part of the London skyline, alongside St Paul's Cathedral, Big Ben and the Houses of Parliament, its night-time illuminations ensuring it was always visible. It stood on the South Bank of the River Thames, within easy reach of London's West End via Westminster Bridge.

LOCATION
Westminster Bridge Road, London
HEIGHT
135 metres

As the Nestene Consciousness embarked on the infiltration and conquest of Earth, it established a lair beneath the London Eye, and used the Ferris wheel itself as the transmitter for the activation signal for its Autons.

PICCADILLY CIRCUS

This landmark is the junction between the busy London streets of Regent Street, Shaftesbury Avenue and Piccadilly. Famous for its statue of Anteros, this is where Rose Tyler had her final glimpse of London in the year 2005. Here, the Doctor told her of the Time War that had destroyed his planet and his people, and Rose decided to stay with the Doctor on his travels, once they'd had some chips. The next time they saw London, twelve months would have passed...

NESTENE CONSCIOUSNESS

The Nestene Consciousness was a collective intelligence, which manifested as a form of liquid plastic, although it was once a disembodied intelligence able to shape itself at will to suit different environments. The Consciousness used warp shunt technology, which enabled the super-lucent movement needed for interplanetary travel, and had been invading and colonising industrialised worlds throughout history, creating a chain of 'protein planets', from which it fed on smoke, oil, and the toxins, dioxins and other chemicals polluting the air. These planets had, however, been lost or destroyed during the Time War, making the heavily polluted Earth a highly attractive target.

PLANET OF ORIGIN
Unknown

APPEARANCE
A vat of orange molten plastic

WEAPONS
Autons; all plastic

OTHER SIGHTINGS
1970s–1980s

The Nestenes had made at least two earlier attempts to infiltrate and conquer the Earth, each of which was prevented by the Doctor. On this latest occasion, the Nestene Consciousness followed its familiar pattern of animating and controlling anything made of plastic – wheelie bins, phones, cables – and operating Auton troops to slaughter the local populace. As soon as it sent out an activation signal, the living plastic it commanded began to attack. The signal was deactivated only when the Nestene Consciousness was destroyed by a vial of antiplastic, a blue liquid that caused the vat of molten plastic to boil and dissolve, turning a fierce white before it exploded.

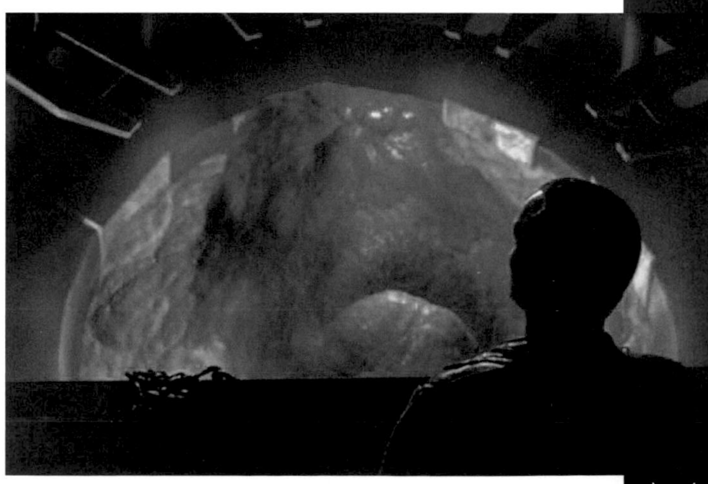

LATE-NIGHT SHOPPING

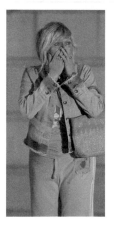

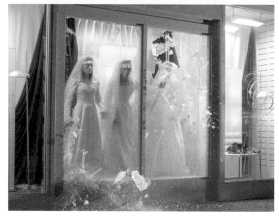

The first public sign of the Nestene invasion attempt came as hundreds of shop-window dummies came to life in the Queen's Arcade shopping mall at 7.40pm on Thursday 4 March. As the nearest to the source of the activation signal, these were the first Autons to receive it and come to life. They smashed through shop windows and attacked shoppers indiscriminately. The first to die was Clive Finch, who had been running a website devoted to sightings of the Doctor throughout history. His wife and son managed to get away. Rose's mother, Jackie, also had a lucky escape – three Autons dressed in bridal gowns had just surrounded her and levelled their weapons when the Nestene was destroyed and its signal stopped.

Elton Pope, who was passing the Arcade when the first Autons crashed through the shop windows, also survived the experience, and counted it as the first of the series of alien encounters that led him to join L.I.N.D.A. in 2007.

SUPERPHONE

The longest-distance telephone call in history was received by Jackie Tyler in her kitchen in South London, at 11am on Wednesday 3 March 2005. The call lasted forty seconds, and the caller was her daughter, Rose, speaking from a space station named Platform One, orbiting the Earth five billion years, one day,

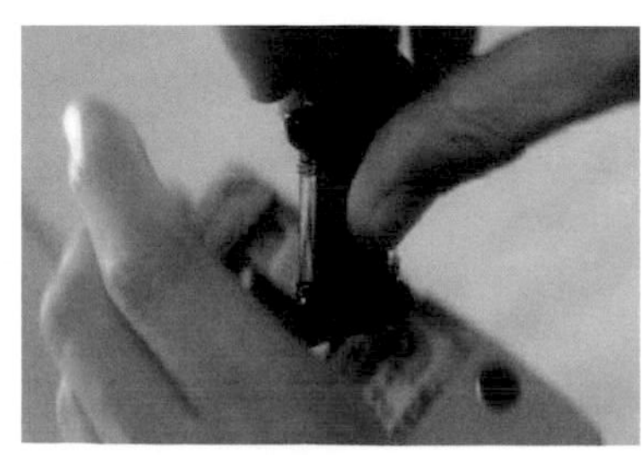

nine hours and two minutes into her future. The Doctor had replaced the battery in her ordinary mobile phone with a jet-black device that enabled her to call home from almost anywhere in the universe in any time period. Jackie, oblivious to all this, discussed the washing and asked Rose to put a quid in the lottery.

SONIC SCREWDRIVER

The Doctor's sonic screwdriver has at least two and a half thousand settings.

Amongst many other functions, the device can:

✦ short out electronic controls ✦ track transmitter signals ✦ disconnect relay signals ✦ lock and unlock doors ✦ connect items to the TARDIS console ✦ access computer systems ✦ open and close viewing panels ✦ deactivate robots ✦ make repairs to the TARDIS ✦ scan objects ✦ pilfer from cash machines ✦ release manacles and handcuffs ✦ blow up simple machines ✦ recharge batteries ✦ perform medical examinations ✦ resonate concrete ✦ reattach barbed wire ✦ override personal teleporters ✦ remotely activate the TARDIS ✦ disassemble machinery ✦ repair machinery ✦ disable machinery ✦ amplify remote-control devices ✦ light candles ✦ distract Cyberforms ✦ deactivate Cyberforms ✦ cut rope ✦ detect power sources ✦ disrupt an absorption matrix ✦ (partially) reverse an absorption matrix ✦ shrink graphite ✦ make precise technical adjustments ✦ crack glass ✦ remotely set off explosions ✦ adjust holograms ✦ destroy robots with (externally amplified) sonic vibrations ✦ increase the radiation output of an X-ray machine ✦ break into cars ✦ loosen screws ✦ bypass security systems ✦ deactivate security systems ✦ disable teleport devices

NB The sonic screwdriver cannot penetrate a deadlock seal and has no effect on wood.

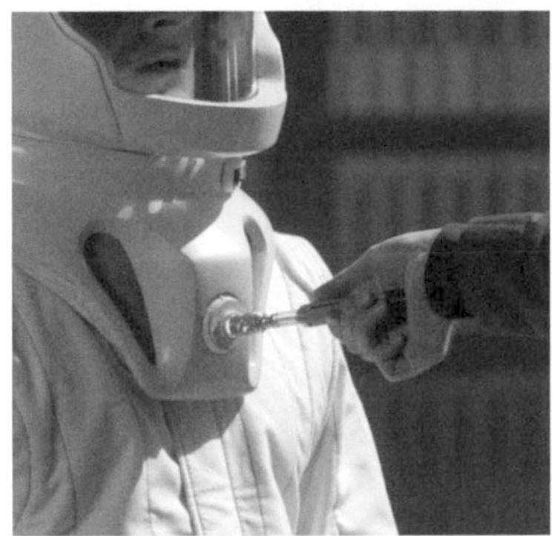

2006

RAXACORICOFALLAPATORIANS

Huge creatures, native to the planet Raxacoricofallapatorius. They are hatched from large, tendrilled eggs in the family hatcheries, and their skins are entirely composed of living calcium, which makes them vulnerable to acetic acid. Adult Raxacoricofallapatorians sleep in nests.

There is a strict political and legal system, led by a Grand Council and an Assembly, with harsh penalties for offenders – dangerous criminals are subject to the death penalty. The implementation of a death sentence is highly ritualised: it takes place in the planet's largest temple, the Palace of Enforced Atonement, in which the convicted criminal is lowered into a cauldron of acetic acid. As the liquid is boiled, the victim's skin is eaten away. A soup is formed as the remaining internal organs dissolve into the boiling liquid, which is then drunk by the presiding officials and priests.

Raxacoricofallapatorians begin to educate their young in poetry, mathematics and democracy as soon as they are hatched. Their main form of contact with other worlds comes through trade in the planet's valuable spice, Offich.

The Raxacoricofallapatorians are divided into a number of clans, or families, notably the Family Blathereen, the Family Rackateen, the Family Hostrozeen, the Family Jingatheen and the Family Slitheen.

RAXACORICOFALLAPATORIUS

Part of a star system that includes its twin planet Clom. The beautiful planet's four poles are marked by spectacular ice-caves, and sapphire and chalk cliffs meet huge, burgundy oceans.

There is one major continental landmass – Raxas Prime – with many other island groups found across the planet, such as the Islands of Hisp. The planet is noted for its white poppito trees and the scent of cinnamon that pervades the air, as well as the huge, white marble cliff-top temples that the Raxacoricofallapatorians have built across their world.

Among the species populating the planet are Venom Grubs, found on several planets in the Isop galaxy.

RAXACORICOFALLAPATORIANS

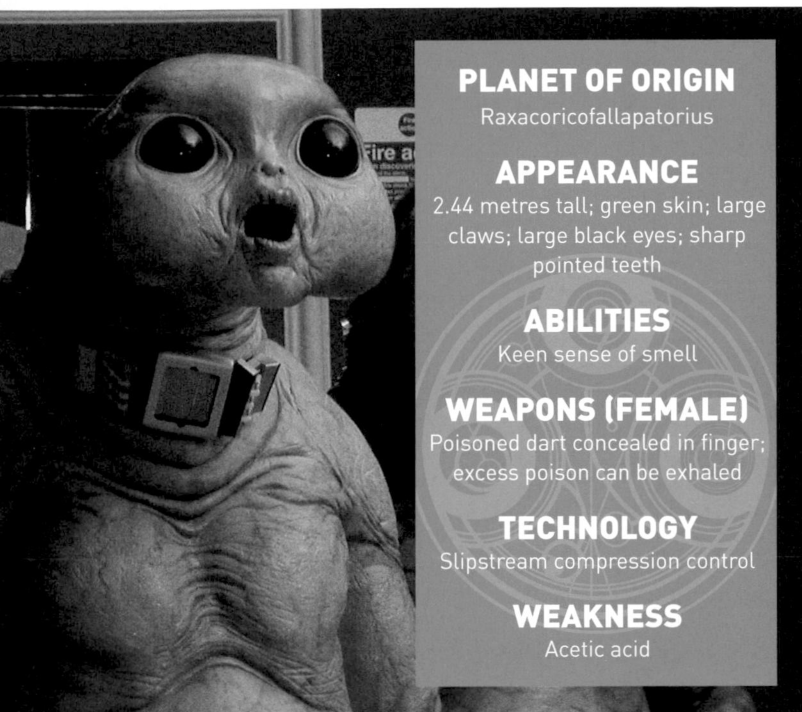

PLANET OF ORIGIN
Raxacoricofallapatorius

APPEARANCE
2.44 metres tall; green skin; large claws; large black eyes; sharp pointed teeth

ABILITIES
Keen sense of smell

WEAPONS (FEMALE)
Poisoned dart concealed in finger; excess poison can be exhaled

TECHNOLOGY
Slipstream compression control

WEAKNESS
Acetic acid

THE FAMILY SLITHEEN

A criminal family, descended from the Huspick Degenerate and cousins of the Blathereen and the Rackateen. The children of the Slitheen were trained to hunt, and would be fed to the Venom Grubs if they failed or refused. The family infiltrated every level of government on Raxacoricofallapatorius, until a purge saw them all removed from office. Those that escaped arrest fled the planet and spread across the galaxy, but the family was tried in its absence. An unending death sentence hangs over the head of every Slitheen, with no appeal permitted.

Having left their homeworld, the Slitheen turned their criminal attentions elsewhere, operating drug-running, arms-dealing and chizzle-waxing operations across the cosmos.

In 2006, part of the family devised a plan to make a profit out of the Earth by provoking a nuclear war that would destroy the planet, then selling off the resultant radioactive chunks as cheap fuel.

The Slitheen used slipstream compression technology to compress their large bodies inside skinsuits made from the remains of their fatter murder victims. This process was controlled by a limitation device worn around their necks. The shrinking of their physical forms caused a frequent, malodorous and audible release of gas – when they were disguised in their skinsuits, this flatulence was the biggest clue to their true identities.

Slitheen family members

Blon Fel Fotch Pasameer-Day Slitheen: Disguised herself as Margaret Blaine of MI5 and murdered the British Prime Minister. After the Doctor's intervention to stop the Slitheen plot, she escaped the destruction of Downing Street and made her way to Cardiff, where she managed to become the Lord Mayor.

Jocrassa Fel Fotch Pasameer-Day Slitheen: Disguised himself as Joseph Green and became Acting Prime Minister after the Big Ben spaceship crash.

Sip Fel Fotch Pasameer-Day Slitheen: Disguised himself as Police Commissioner Strickland and attempted to kill Jackie Tyler. Mickey Smith prevented this and, under instruction from the Doctor, he and Jackie attacked Sip Fel Fotch with acetic acid – the vinegar from jars of gherkins, pickled onions and pickled eggs.

FIRST CONTACT

PHASE 1: ARRIVAL AND INFILTRATION

The Family Slitheen landed their spacecraft 500 fathoms beneath the surface of the North Sea, where it remained initially undetected while family members began to emerge and infiltrate the UK's political and administrative establishment. Having identified the people with the necessary political and physical weight, the Slitheen murdered these key figures and disguised themselves in their skins. At the same time, they began to broadcast an intergalactic signal, advertising their forthcoming sale of radioactive chunks of the planet Earth.

Victims of the Slitheen

✦ **General Asquith** (British Army)
✦ **Margaret Blaine** (MI5)
✦ **Oliver Charles** (Transport Liaison Officer)
✦ **Sylvia Dillane** (Director, North Sea Boating Club)
✦ **Joseph Green** (Member of Parliament for Hartley Dale and Chairman of the Parliamentary Commission for Monitoring of Sugar Levels in Exported Confectionery)
✦ **Group Captain Tennant James** (Royal Air Force)
✦ **Ewan McAllister** (Deputy Secretary for the Scottish Assembly)
✦ **Assistant Commissioner Strickland** (Metropolitan Police)

PHASE 2: SPACE PIG

As UK authorities moved to investigate a radiation blip from the alien vessel, the Slitheen moved to the next stage of their attack. They captured a farmyard pig and wired technology into its brain that allowed it upright movement and rudimentary piloting skills. Dressing the pig in a spacesuit, they placed it at the controls of their spaceship, which they sent on a slingshot orbit of the planet, pre-programmed to return to Earth in Central London.

FIRST CONTACT

PHASE 3: SPACESHIP RE-ENTRY

09.57.55 Enters London's airspace from the south east

09.57.57 Flies over North Peckham

09.58.17 Narrowly misses Tower Bridge

09.58.23 Flies between St Paul's Cathedral and the City of London
09.58.32 Approaches the Houses of Parliament

09.58.39 Strikes the Clock Tower of the Palace of Westminster

09.58.50 Crashes into the River Thames

PHASE 4: STATE OF NATIONAL EMERGENCY

Emergency situation

✦ City closed down ✦ Roads gridlocked
✦ Widespread civilian panic
✦ Looting and civil disturbance
✦ Assaults on suspected 'aliens' reported
✦ Disappearance of UK Prime Minister
✦ All Cabinet ministers stranded outside London

Emergency measures

✦ State of national emergency declared
✦ Army closes Central London
✦ Police reinforcements drafted in from across the country
✦ Telephone helpline opened: 08081 570980
✦ Army divers sent into Thames to investigate spaceship wreckage
✦ Appointment of Acting Prime Minister
✦ Release of Emergency Protocols to Acting Prime Minister
✦ Two flights allowed from Geneva and Washington to bring alien specialists to London
✦ Downing Street conference of alien specialists
✦ Acting PM holds press conference

International response

✦ Special session of the United Nations
✦ UN Secretary General asks people to watch the skies
✦ US military on lookout for more spaceships
✦ All flights in North American airspace grounded
✦ US President addresses nation live from White House

WORLD WAR THREE

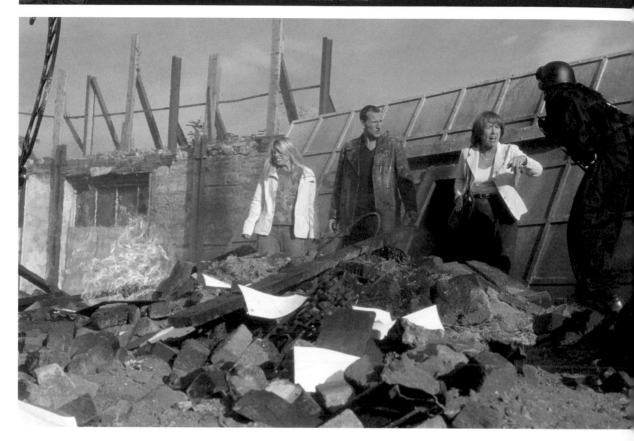

POLITICAL SITUATION

Two Slitheen, wearing Margaret Blaine and Oliver Charles skinsuits, had infiltrated 10 Downing Street before the destruction of Big Ben. They claimed to have escorted the Prime Minister to his official car but had in fact murdered him and hidden his body in a cupboard in the Cabinet Room. With the PM missing and the Cabinet stranded outside London, the most senior MP available in London was Joseph Green – by now another disguised Slitheen. Green was quickly installed as Acting Prime Minister and summoned the world's experts in extraterrestrial life to Downing Street, where he killed them all.

DODGY DOSSIER

Acting Prime Minister Joseph Green made a live televised address to Britain and the world, announcing that alien aggressors had murdered the world's experts on extraterrestrials and that massive weapons of destruction were in orbit around the planet. These weapons, he claimed, could be turned on the Earth within 45 seconds. He appealed for the release of defence codes that would allow a pre-emptive nuclear strike against the threat. Still in emergency session, the UN quickly decided to accede to Britain's request and released the codes.

DESTRUCTION OF DOWNING STREET

Shortly before the defence codes could reach Downing Street, a missile was launched from HMS *Taurean*, a Trafalgar Class submarine stationed ten miles off the coast of Plymouth. The Sub Harpoon UGM-84A missile hurtled across London and struck 10 Downing Street, destroying the building and killing all the Slitheen still gathered in the building. The missile had been launched by Mickey Smith, instructed by the Doctor.

Harriet Jones MP was one of the survivors and revealed what had truly happened, and that there was no alien threat from above the Earth.

HOAX!

The authorities swiftly decided to attempt to conceal the truth of what had happened, feeding a story to London's *Evening Standard* newspaper that the whole thing had been a gigantic hoax.

ALBION HOSPITAL

Central London's Albion Hospital was located on the Thames Embankment. Its imposing wrought-iron gates stood at the entrance to the grounds of a hospital building that had survived the London Blitz of the early 1940s.

The hospital was evacuated and commandeered by the army in the aftermath of the destruction of Big Ben. Since London's roads had been closed off, they needed to use a hospital that could be reached by boat, and Albion Hospital was quickly chosen – the slightly nearer Royal Hope Hospital would have presented greater operational difficulties, because it housed many more staff and patients.

The body recovered from the spaceship wreckage was taken there by troops, with press and camera crews kept outside the hospital grounds.

(See also: 1941)

ALIENS FAKING ALIENS

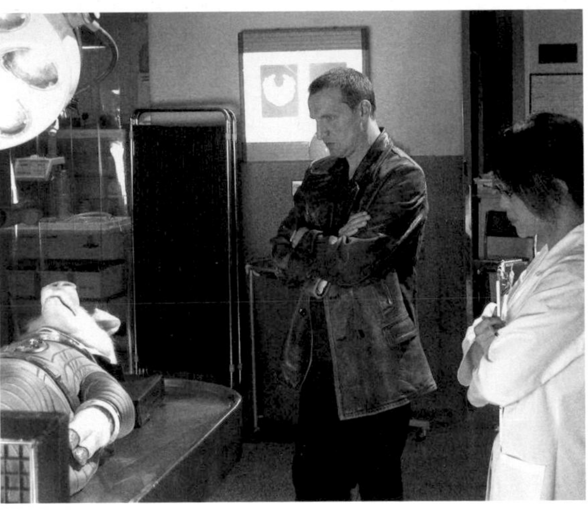

The alien body found in the crashed spaceship was examined by 'Dr' Toshiko Sato under the supervision of General Asquith. Toshiko (an undercover Torchwood agent) discovered that the alien invader resembled an ordinary pig dressed in a spacesuit, and that it was not, in fact, dead. Attempting to escape, the revived animal attacked her and fled but was shot by the army. By now, the Doctor had arrived at the hospital, and he established that the creature didn't just resemble an ordinary pig – it was an ordinary pig. But alien technology had been wired into its brain, allowing it to walk upright and pilot the crashed spaceship. Aliens had faked an alien.

CARDIFF EARTHQUAKE

September brought a seemingly natural disaster to the Welsh capital of Cardiff, as the city was apparently struck by an earthquake. This was centred on the Cardiff Bay area, with much of the damage affecting Roald Dahl Plass. Witnesses saw a bright column of light reaching from the square's water tower sculpture up into the sky throughout the duration of the tremor. The clean-up operation revealed that the new Mayor, Margaret Blaine, was among the missing, and her plans to build a nuclear power station in the heart of the city were soon abandoned.

THE BLAIDD DRWG PROJECT

Having escaped London, still disguised as Margaret Blaine, and taken up office as the Lord Mayor of Cardiff, Blon Fel Fotch Pasameer-Day Slitheen drew up plans for a new nuclear facility in the heart of the city. She ensured that the plans were fatally flawed: the design of the suppression pool would cause the hydrogen recombiners to fail as soon as the power station reached maximum capacity, causing the collapse of the containment isolation system. This would result in meltdown, opening Cardiff's space-time rift and destroying the Earth. The disappearance of the Mayor during September led to the abandonment of the plans.

THE CURSE OF BLAIDD DRWG

- ✦ A team of Safety Inspectors from the European Union died when explosives labelled only in Welsh went off during their visit
- ✦ The members of the Cardiff Heritage Committee were electrocuted in a swimming pool
- ✦ The Project's chief architect was hit by the Mayor's car during a storm
- ✦ The government's nuclear adviser, Mr Cleaver, was decapitated when he slipped on an icy patch

While local officials, construction workers and observant journalists attributed it to a curse, this series of accidents surrounding Blaidd Drwg was down to Blon Fel Fotch's efforts to prevent her plans being discovered. Cleaver was in fact attacked by Blon Fel Fotch in her own office, shortly after he'd informed her that he could not support the project because of its design flaws.

ALIEN TECHNOLOGY

TELEPORTS

Blon Fel Fotch's escape from Downing Street was by means of a teleport device whose components she had hidden in a brooch and earrings. This only transported one life form at a time, so she was unable to save any of her family. She was unable to program it with coordinates, and she found herself rematerialising in a rubbish skip in East London's Isle of Dogs. She attempted to use this teleport again to escape capture in Cardiff, but the Doctor easily overrode it with his sonic screwdriver.

The Sycorax also had teleport technology, using it to bring Harriet Jones and three associates onto their spaceship and then to bring the TARDIS on board, when their instruments identified it as superior technology. Having defeated the Sycorax leader, the Doctor used the alien's teleport to beam himself, Rose Tyler, Mickey Smith, Harriet Jones and the TARDIS back to South London. The Doctor was not the only one to make use of the Sycorax technology – the roboforms, too, had used it to travel to the Earth, unknown to the Sycorax.

The Graske used personal teleports to transmat themselves across space and time and to abduct their victims, including at least one Raxacoricofallapatorian, and send them to Griffoth.

TRIBOPHYSICAL WAVEFORM MACRO-KINETIC EXTRAPOLATOR

Brought to Cardiff by Blon Fel Fotch, the extrapolator was recognised by the Doctor and Captain Jack Harkness as an advanced means of transport. An extrapolator absorbs energy from nearby power sources, allowing its user to ride it like a pan-dimensional surfboard through space, protected by a force field. The Slitheen's initial plan was to power up her extrapolator from the Rift running through Cardiff, once Blaidd Drwg had gone into meltdown, and then escape the consequent destruction of Earth. The Doctor and Jack connected the device to the TARDIS, hoping to speed up the time machine's refuelling stop, but Blon Fel Fotch took advantage of this with pre-programmed instructions for the extrapolator to steal the TARDIS's own energy as well as that of the Rift, which would allow her to flee the planet. As the Rift opened, it caused huge earth tremors in the surrounding Cardiff Bay area. When she looked into the heart of the TARDIS, Blon Fel Fotch was reverted to an egg, which allowed the Doctor and Jack to shut down the TARDIS systems and end the extrapolator's power drain. They left the device attached to the time machine, thinking that it might be useful one day...

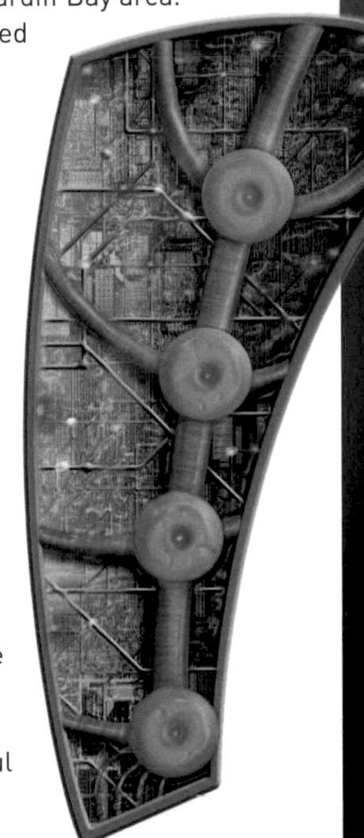

2006

REGENERATION

The only witness to the Doctor's regeneration from his ninth to his tenth body was Rose Tyler. Once he had convinced her that he was who he said he was, the Doctor programmed the TARDIS to take them to Bucknall House on the Powell Estate in South London on Christmas Eve. As the TARDIS began its journey, however, the new Doctor began to behave oddly – he told Rose he thought the regeneration was going wrong, and collapsed in front of Jackie Tyler and Mickey Smith as soon as the TARDIS reached Earth.

THE BRITISH ROCKET GROUP

Formed in the 1950s, the BRG's fortunes fluctuated for fifty years until the British government decided in the early years of the 21st century to revive the country's attempts at space exploration. The first public fruits of this renewed interest came with the launch in October 2006 of *Guinevere One*, an unmanned space probe headed for the planet Mars. Its mission was to land on the surface of the planet and beam live images back to Earth on Christmas Day. Aboard the probe were robot devices designed to conduct atmospheric and mineral analyses and send the results back to the BRG.

Following traditional practice for unmanned space probes, *Guinevere One* was also stocked with a number of items designed to help communication with alien species, should any be encountered:

- A data plaque, showing human male and female figures
- A diagram of the solar system
- Samples of natural sounds
- Spoken greetings in 120 languages
- Samples of international music
- A copy of the *Mappa Mundi*
- The London A-Z
- Chemical samples of life's building blocks

The chemical samples included a phial of human blood, type A+. Approximately one-third of the Earth's human population shares this blood group, and it was this that enabled the Sycorax to exert blood control over two billion people, once they had taken *Guinevere One* into their craft.

FIRST CONTACT (2)

In the early hours of the morning on Christmas Day, the *Guinevere One* space probe was expected to make its first live transmission from the surface of the planet Mars. Instead of pictures of the red planet, however, the British Rocket Group received images of an alien race – the Sycorax. The British Prime Minister, Harriet Jones, immediately sent a message of goodwill.

As governments and armed forces moved to an emergency footing for the second time in a year, a second broadcast was received from the Sycorax. Instantly, one-third of the Earth's population entered a trance-like state and proceeded to the tops of the world's tallest buildings.

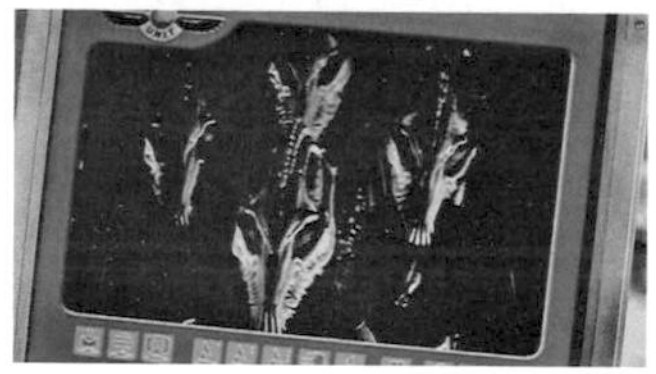

Before long, everyone with the A+ blood type – approximately two billion people – could be seen standing on the rooftops of tower blocks and landmarks across the planet, seemingly poised to jump. At 7.45am, the Sycorax spaceship entered the Earth's atmosphere and descended to hover over London. Harriet Jones made a live television broadcast appealing for help from the Doctor, before she led a small deputation to the Sycorax spaceship. Some time later, she returned to London and ordered the destruction of the departing vessel.

One undistinguished witness to the spaceship's arrival was Elton Pope, who was in bed when the sonic wave blew out the windows of his room. Unable to reach his shoes, he was forced to spend Christmas morning devising a rudimentary pulley system before he could get to the window and take a look at the spaceship. Elton tried to discover more about events surrounding the alien craft, but huge traffic sent the internet into meltdown.

GREAT LIVES

HARRIET JONES

As an undistinguished backbench MP, the Member of Parliament for Flydale North was notable only for voting against US-UK military action in the Middle East and her persistent efforts to have the British government adopt her Cottage Hospitals Initiative to improve the health service. But when she emerged from the ruins of 10 Downing Street after the Slitheen attack, she soon provided broadcasters with an image that would be constantly replayed – the heroic survivor, striding towards the cameras with words of reassurance and pride. In the General Election that followed, she was swept to government with a landslide majority. This was the start of Britain's Golden Age and what should have been a three-term administration for Harriet Jones.

As Prime Minister during the Sycorax invasion attempt, Harriet Jones refused to bow to American demands that the US President should take charge of the situation. Representing the Earth, she was taken aboard the Sycorax ship to act as her world's champion – a role that first Rose Tyler and then the Doctor quickly took over. Once the Doctor had defeated the Sycorax leader and ordered the spaceship to leave the Earth, Harriet decided that the risk of allowing the craft to depart was too great. She ordered its destruction by the Torchwood Institute, an action that the Doctor saw as murder.

Vowing to bring down her government, the Doctor commented to Alex Klein, the UNIT operative assigned to assist the PM, that Harriet was 'looking tired'. After Klein's UNIT debrief, word quickly spread that the Prime Minister's health might be in question and, before long, a media and political storm had forced her from office. She retired from politics and public life, but remained watchful for extraterrestrial incursion, and her intervention would prove vital during the Dalek attack in 2009.

SYCORAX

The inhospitable rock world of Sycorax lay many light years from Earth, in the wastelands of the galaxy. Its inhabitants were split into many small warring tribes but, when a crashed spaceship brought them the secrets of interstellar craft, these Sycorax tribes united to explore and exploit the rest of the cosmos. They split their planet into an armada of many smaller asteroids, which they piloted through the stars, taking over worlds by stealth or conquest.

One such asteroid starship – the *Fire Trap* – made its way to Earth's solar system and was just reaching Mars when it encountered the man-made probe *Guinevere One*. The British Rocket Group had planned that the probe would broadcast live images of Mars back to Earth on Christmas Day – instead, the first transmission was of the snarling face of the Sycorax Leader. Having examined the contents of the probe and discovered a human blood sample, the Sycorax were able to exert blood control on the population of the Earth. With two billion people apparently hypnotised and poised to kill themselves, the Sycorax demanded the surrender of the planet.

They brought human representatives aboard their craft, prepared to deal only with Earth's leaders. They dealt ruthlessly with two of these representatives, Major Blake and Professor Llewellyn, but were prepared to accept Harriet Jones as Earth's 'champion', until Rose Tyler arrived and briefly attempted to take on the role. The warlike Sycorax have their own code of honour, and the freshly regenerated and newly revived Doctor was able to exploit this. He challenged the Sycorax Leader, under the sanctified laws of single combat, with the planet as the victor's prize. The Doctor prevailed and, their leader dead, the Sycorax began their retreat from Earth.

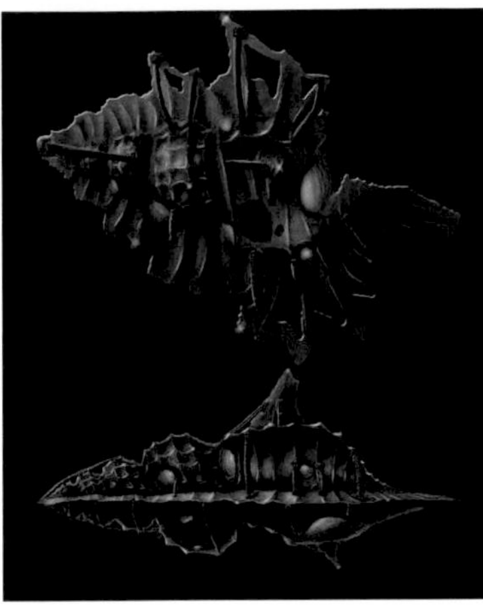

PLANET OF ORIGIN
Sycorax

APPEARANCE
1.90 metres tall; skinless, with exposed muscle and bone; red eyes; robed in blood-red velvet, adorned with trophies of their conquests, and with skull helmets

LANGUAGE
Sycoraxic

WEAPONS
Broadsword; staff; electrified whip

TECHNOLOGY
Blood control; interstellar flight by piloted asteroid remnants; teleportation; translation

MEDIA COVERAGE

TELEVISION

BBC News 24 (UK): Tom Hitchinson reported on the Big Ben spaceship crash and its aftermath.
Andrew Marr reported from Downing Street on the disappearance of the Prime Minister.
Jason Mohammad presented coverage of the *Guinevere* expedition.
Harriet Jones replaced the Queen's Christmas Day message with a televised appeal to the Doctor.

AMNN (USA): Trinity Wells reported from New York, and broke the news that the UN would release nuclear defence codes to the British government. She also anchored AMNN's coverage of the Sycorax attack.
BBC One: *Blue Peter*'s Matt Baker showed children how to bake an alien spaceship cake.

NEWSPAPERS

The Evening Standard: The first newspaper to report that the Slitheen attack was a hoax.
The Cardiff Gazette: Cathy Salt reported from Margaret Blaine's Blaidd Drwg press launch.
The Western Mail: Published the first photograph of Cardiff's new mayor, Margaret Blaine, taken at the Blaidd Drwg launch.

ROOFTOP DESTINATIONS

Sycorax blood control affected one-third of the world's population, with two billion people scaling tall buildings and standing on the edges of the rooftops. Many international locations and landmarks are known to have been affected, among them:

- **Paris, France** – various buildings around the Eiffel Tower and the Arc de Triomphe
- **Rome, Italy** – the Colosseum
- **Cairo, Egypt** – the Cairo Hotel
- **Giza, Egypt** – the Great Pyramid
- **Sydney, Australia** – the Sydney Harbour Bridge

BAD WOLF

The phrase 'Bad Wolf' continued to appear in graffiti across South London. Among the locations defaced were:

- The side of a police box in a courtyard area near Bucknall House on the Powell Estate
- An 'Extreme Species Club' poster, in the window of a fast-food restaurant in North Peckham
- A children's playground near the Powell Estate

The phrase also cropped up in Wales during 2006, when incoming Mayor Margaret Blaine announced plans for an urban nuclear power station, which she named 'Blaidd Drwg'. She thought it sounded good and had no idea that it translated from Welsh into English as 'Bad Wolf'.

ROBOFORMS ('PILOT FISH')

Robot scavengers that first appeared on Earth in advance of the Sycorax attack – they had covertly travelled through space alongside the Sycorax, and even made use of the Sycorax technology to teleport to the planet. They were attracted by a power source which proved to be the regenerative energy of the Doctor himself. In their efforts to track down and capture the Doctor, the Roboforms disguised themselves in Father Christmas outfits and masks, playing Christmas carols on brass instruments in the vicinity of a branch of Henrik's department stores in London. The musical instruments concealed weaponry, which they turned on Rose Tyler and Mickey Smith, hoping to weaken the Doctor by isolating him from his friends. When this attack failed, they utilised a remote-controlled Christmas tree, causing it to rotate at such speed that it could carve its way through doors and walls. The Doctor destroyed the tree with his sonic screwdriver, which he then used to ward off the Roboforms. The Roboforms beamed out using their stolen teleport technology, but seem to have escaped the destruction of the Sycorax vessel.

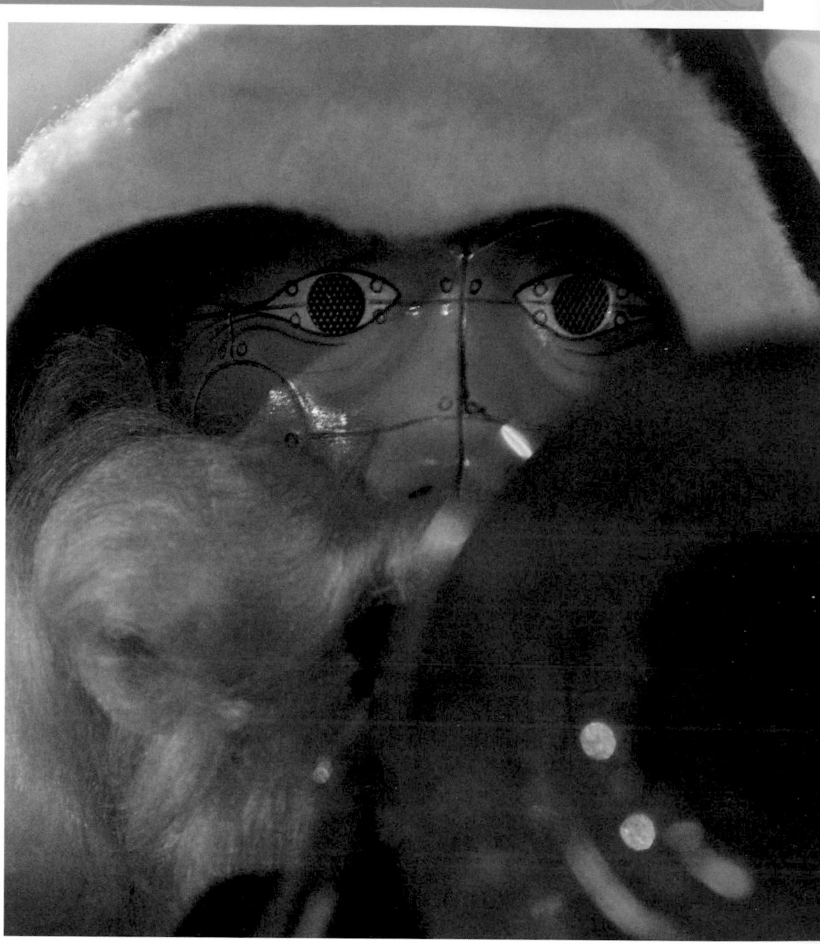

PLANET OF ORIGIN
Unknown

APPEARANCE
Hidden under Santa Claus outfits

WEAPONS
Flame throwers, missile launchers, machine guns – disguised as brass instruments; remote-controlled Christmas trees

TECHNOLOGY
Scavenged and stolen

OTHER SIGHTINGS
London, 2007

21ST-CENTURY BRITAIN

BIG BEN

More accurately the Clock Tower at the north-eastern end of the Palace of Westminster. The tower houses five bells, the largest of which is the Great Bell. This was nicknamed Big Ben, which became the title by which the entire structure – bell, clock, tower and all – became popularly known. The 96.3-metre Clock Tower was partially destroyed by a wing of the Slitheen spaceship, with two clock faces being smashed.

Among the witnesses to the spaceship crash was Elton Pope, who later counted this as part of the series of alien encounters that led him to join L.I.N.D.A. in 2007.

Incoming Prime Minister Harriet Jones ordered the rebuilding of the Clock Tower to begin soon after she took office, and this work was still under way when the Sycorax spaceship arrived over London on Christmas Day.

10 DOWNING STREET

When First Lord of the Treasury Sir Robert Walpole accepted 10 Downing Street as his official residence in the 1730s, he stipulated that the property should be held for the exclusive use of Britain's heads of government after him. Fifty Prime Ministers followed him over the next 270 years, before the building was destroyed by the Doctor and Mickey Smith. Among the house's most famous rooms is the Cabinet Room, the largest room in the building, located on its north-west side and weekly Cabinet meetings were held there from 1796. In 1991, an unsuccessful terrorist attack prompted the government to install three-inch thick steel walls, making the Cabinet Room one of the safest rooms in the country. The protective walls helped the Doctor, Rose and Harriet Jones to survive the missile attack. As Prime Minister, Harriet Jones ordered that the house should be rebuilt exactly as it was. This work was still ongoing when the Sycorax attacked at Christmas.

TOWER OF LONDON

William of Normandy began the construction of what he named the Tower of London in 1078, and many of the monarchs who succeeded him extended and added to the tower over the centuries that followed. The end result is the present arrangement of buildings standing inside two concentric defensive walls and a moat. At an unrecorded date, the top-secret international defence force UNIT established a high-tech base beneath the monument. It is from here that UNIT and the Prime Minister monitored events on Christmas Day after the first Sycorax broadcast was received from *Guinevere One*. When the Sycorax activated their blood control, one-third of the UNIT staff made their way to the top of the Tower.

THE GHERKIN

This structure is the sixth-tallest building in London and has a 360-degree view over the city. Construction work on the tower was completed in 2004, including the fitting of 24,000 square metres of glass – a high-profile casualty of the sonic shockwave that heralded the Christmas Day arrival over London of the Sycorax spaceship.

LOCATION
30 St Mary Axe, London

HEIGHT
180 metres

FLOORS
40

ROALD DAHL PLASS

Located in the Cardiff Bay area of the Welsh capital, this oval area houses the Wales Millennium Centre, the Senedd building of the Welsh Assembly, and a 21-metre water tower sculpture. The water tower marked the epicentre of the earthquake that struck Cardiff, being at the centre of the spatio-temporal Rift.

UNIT

Established to investigate the unexplained and defend Earth from extraterrestrial intervention, the top secret international intelligence taskforce enjoyed a resurgence of influence in the wake of the Slitheen offensive. Initially, these events proved a setback – some of UNIT's most senior personnel were among those gathered and murdered in Downing Street by the Slitheen. By the end of the year, however, UNIT was operating at full capacity from a high-tech base concealed beneath the Tower of London. In concert with Harriet Jones, Major Richard Blake, the base's commanding officer, oversaw Britain's response to the Sycorax incursion on Christmas Day. UNIT was able to track the alien craft's approach to Earth, intercept Sycorax messages, broadcast replies and utilise translation software to determine the aliens' demands. Major Blake drafted in Professor Daniel Llewellyn from the British Rocket Group and assigned a UNIT operative, Alex Klein, as the Prime Minister's assistant for the duration of the emergency. The three men accompanied Harriet Jones when she boarded the Sycorax ship, and both Blake and Llewellyn lost their lives. Like the rest of the world, the UNIT headquarters suffered the temporary loss of about a third of its staff when the Sycorax initiated their blood control – among the operatives affected were: Sally Jacobs, Systems Analyst; Luke Parsons, Intelligence Officer; and Geoffrey Baxter, Data Cypher.

CAPTAIN JACK HARKNESS

REPORTED SIGHTINGS #6 & 7 CONFIRMED

ESTIMATED AGE: 35

LOCATION: Cardiff; Raxacoricofallapatorius, 2006

AVAILABLE INFORMATION: Captain Jack was with the Doctor and Rose Tyler when the TARDIS stopped to refuel at Cardiff's Rift. He helped capture Blon Fel Fotch Pasameer-Day Slitheen, and was alone in the TARDIS when the Extrapolator opened the Rift. When she reverted to an egg, the TARDIS took Blon Fel Fotch to the hatcheries on the Slitheen homeworld. An older version of Jack Harkness (aged approximately 172) was simultaneously present in Cardiff at this time, leading Torchwood Three.

TORCHWOOD

The 127-year-old Torchwood Institute remained a closely guarded secret, kept from much of the UK government and the United Nations, although senior UNIT officers were unofficially aware of its existence. Prime Minister Harriet Jones also knew of Torchwood, and she turned to the Institute to help defend the world from the Sycorax attack. Torchwood had shot down a Jathaa sun glider ten years earlier, and, on Jones's order, used its weaponry to destroy the retreating Sycorax vessel.

Torchwood Three, based in Cardiff and led by Captain Jack Harkness, had previously sent one of its operatives – Toshiko Sato – to work undercover in London's Albion Hospital during the Slitheen crisis.

CHRISTMAS

The defeat of the Sycorax brought what seemed to be a white Christmas (although the 'snow' was debris from the destroyed spaceship), and Londoners resumed their celebrations. Many visited Trafalgar Square, where the Doctor was photographed by Ursula Blake. Her publication of the photo on her website would lead directly to Elton Pope meeting her and joining L.I.N.D.A.

The separate attacks in London by the Roboforms and the Sycorax were not the only attempts to ruin Christmas this year. One Cardiff family found their celebrations under threat when a Graske began to kidnap them and replace them with changelings. The first victim was the mother of the family, who was transported to Griffoth, while her replacement allowed the Graske to capture her husband too. With both father and mother replaced, the two children were prevented from playing with the videogames and camera they'd been given as presents, with their visiting grandparents utterly helpless in the face of this seemingly unstoppable menace. Fortunately, intervention on the planet Griffoth by the Doctor and an unknown associate reversed the Graske's processes and returned all the captives to their points of origin. Back together – and unaware of the fate that had briefly befallen them – the family was able to get on with enjoying Christmas and its traditional songs.

(See also: 1883)

Some traditional Christmas songs

God Rest Ye Merry Gentlemen – traditional (1833)
One Horse Open Sleigh (Jingle Bells) – James Lord Pierpont (1857)
Rockin' Around The Christmas Tree – Brenda Lee (1958)
Another Rock 'n' Roll Christmas – Gary Glitter (1984)
Song For Ten – Tim Phillips (2005)

2007

UFO ACTIVITY

As the Krillitanes arrived in Deffry Vale, residents saw strange lights in the sky and there were reports of unidentified flying objects over the local high school. While the government refused to confirm or deny extraterrestrial activity in the area, a local man named Joe Brandon insisted to the press and public that Deffry Vale was being visited by aliens; local newspaper reports attributed this to his fondness for the local pubs – a rumour that seems to have coincided with activity in the area from the Torchwood Institute. Interest in the strange lights subsided when press attention turned to the sudden turnaround at the town's secondary school. And that press attention attracted the interest of a freelance investigative journalist named Sarah Jane Smith. Meanwhile, Mickey Smith's online attempts to hack into government Defence Special Projects websites to follow up the stories surrounding Deffry Vale were blocked by Torchwood, so he called the Doctor and Rose Tyler back to Earth. While Rose posed as a school dinner lady, the Doctor joined the High School as a supply teacher, replacing a Physics teacher who had won the lottery courtesy of a winning ticket posted through her door at midnight.

SCIENCE AND TECHNOLOGY

THE SKASAS PARADIGM

Also known as the 'God Maker', the Skasas Paradigm is a mathematical equation, which requires both genius and imagination to solve. The solution to this equation would give control of all time, space and matter. These building blocks and energies of the universe could then be harnessed to shape and improve any and all things throughout history.

2007

PLANET OF ORIGIN
Unknown

APPEARANCE
Varies – currently resemble giant bats, with tough wings, sharp teeth, and clawed hands and feet

ABILITIES
Morphic transformation; flight

WEAKNESSES
Loud noise; Krillitane Oil

KRILLITANES

A race of carnivorous warriors able to absorb and amalgamate the physical traits and abilities of any race they conquer. As a composite race, their appearance had changed over time and, at one stage, they were long-necked humanoids. Their current form was bat-like and had been for ten generations, thanks to their subjugation of the planet Bessan, whose inhabitants were winged. They had also gained the mildly telepathic powers necessary to generate a morphic illusion, disguising their true forms.

Under the leadership of Brother Lassar, a thirteen-strong group of Krillitanes developed a plan to manipulate and train human schoolchildren and use them as a huge supercomputer to solve the Skasas Paradigm and become gods. They selected a secondary school in a small town in Greater London and began their infiltration in late 2006. Brother Lassar took on human form and posed as Mr Finch, a school headmaster, while his twelve comrades used morphic illusion to disguise themselves as seven teachers, four dinner ladies and a school nurse. The Krillitanes slept – in bat form – in the school each night, hanging from the ceiling of the headmaster's office. Sometimes, they ate human victims – an Ofsted inspector, the occasional orphaned pupil that wouldn't be missed – but they largely fed on vacuum-packed rats, which they stored in the Maths department stationery cupboards.

An unexpected side effect of the Krillitanes' physiological change was that their own oil became toxic to them. Even small quantities had an acid effect on their skins and could cause their bodies to explode. The oil was vital to their plan, so they stored it in large, deadlock-sealed barrels in the school kitchens, and wore protective clothing whenever they had to use it.

SOCIETY AND EDUCATION

DEFFRY VALE HIGH SCHOOL

The High School took pupils aged 11 to 16 from throughout the town, including children from Ambrose Hall, Deffry Vale's home for orphaned children. After the disappearance of the school's headmaster in the autumn of 2006, the swift appointment of Hector Finch as his replacement seemed to transform Deffry Vale High School's fortunes. At first, the bad news continued as, within a day of Mr Finch's arrival, all seven of the school's Mathematics teachers were suddenly taken ill. Mr Finch immediately brought in seven new teachers and imposed a new school curriculum. At the same time, he replaced the school canteen staff with four new dinner ladies and devised a new school dinner menu, designed, he said, to improve concentration and performance.

Promoted throughout the school with posters declaring 'Eat More Chips', the new menu did just that – it was centred on chips cooked in Krillitane Oil, which acted as a conducting agent to accelerate the children's learning power. School dinners were made compulsory and were provided free to all schoolchildren. Within three months, Deffry Vale High School was attracting headlines for its hugely improved results. Its pupils were unusually well behaved and enthusiastic, and the cleverest of them had gained knowledge beyond anything currently known on Earth.

Mathematics and Science – Advanced

Questions

1. Two identical strips of nylon are charged with static electricity and hung from a string so they can swing freely. What would happen if they were brought near each other?
2. I coil up a thin piece of nichrome wire and place it in a glass of water. Then I turn on the electricity and measure to see if the water temperature is affected. How do I measure the electrical power going into the coil?
3. The greater the damping on a system, the quicker it loses energy to its surroundings. True or false?
4. What is non-coding DNA?
5. What is 65,983 x 5?
6. How do you travel faster than light?

Answers

1. They would repel each other, because they have the same charge. **2.** Measure the current and PD using an ammeter and voltmeter. **3.** False. **4.** DNA that does not code for a protein. **5.** 329,915. **6.** By harnessing a quantum tunnel with an FTL factor of 36.7 recurring.

K-9 MARK III

The Mark I K-9 was created in the 50th century, but the third version of the robot dog was built by the Fourth Doctor as a gift for his former travelling companion Sarah Jane Smith in the early 1980s. A quarter of a century later, K-9 was rusty and in poor repair, and Sarah was unable to keep him running. The Doctor managed to get K-9 operational again, but his depleted power sources proved limiting. He was able to analyse a sample of Krillitane Oil, and then fought off a dozen Krillitanes long enough for the Doctor, Rose, Mickey and Sarah to escape, but this left his power levels dangerously low. He sacrificed himself when he fired a single laser blast at a vat of Krillitane Oil, so destroying the Krillitanes and blowing up Deffry Vale High School.

Before leaving Earth with Rose and Mickey, the Doctor built a new and updated K-9 model, the Mark IV, as a parting gift to Sarah. This unit had improved systems with new omniflexible hyperlink facilities.

PARALLEL 2007

PARALLEL UNIVERSE

A parallel universe is another version of our universe and co-exists with it, two of many realities separated by the Void, a realm of nothingness. When the TARDIS fell through a hole in the Vortex, it plunged through the Void and onto another Earth. The TARDIS could not refuel here, since it needed its power to come from its own universe. The variant Earth shared the same laws of physics and laws of nature, but it was not identical to the world that the TARDIS had just left. The parallel Earth's timeline ran a little ahead of Rose Tyler's reality, and the two versions had many differences, large and small...

PARALLEL EARTH

('PETE'S WORLD')

The continent of Europe included a country called New Germany. The countries of South America had been unified as New South America. Great Britain was a republic, headed by a President.

Airships were a major form of transport. There were pronounced differences between the rich and successful upper classes – who lived on the airships or in country mansions – and the lower orders. Ordinary people were constrained by army-enforced curfews, and there were extremely high levels of homelessness, although this was being reduced by the regular abduction of dispossessed people from the streets.

The international economy was dominated by the power and influence of Cybus Industries, notably in its monopoly over communications and broadcasting, with almost all citizens wearing Cybusnet earpods and the BBC having been abolished. Cybus also controlled the arms trade, computing and medical research, and its CEO, John Lumic, was believed to hold sway over the British government. Even Lumic, however, was theoretically constrained by the decisions of the Ethics Committee and Britain's President, as well as by the Geneva Bio-Convention.

Battersea Power Station was still in operation, although it had been taken over by Cybus Industries and converted from a generating station to a manufacturing plant.

Low-level resistance to the state and to Cybus Industries operated around the world, such as the Free Information Collectives in Europe and, in London, the Preachers. This group did not use Cybus earpods and hoped to bring Lumic down. Their leader was Ricky Smith – the parallel version of Mickey Smith. Ricky had the same family background, but his grandmother, Rita Anne, was still alive (Mickey's grandmother had died some years earlier after tripping and falling down the stairs).

The Preachers received anonymous inside information on the activities of Cybus Industries from a source code-named Gemini. This was Pete Tyler, who had not died in a car accident in 1987 as in our world. A hugely successful businessman, Pete Tyler had been married to Jackie for 20 years, but the couple had had no children. Instead, Jackie had a pet terrier named Rose.

SOCIETY AND INDUSTRY

CYBUS INDUSTRIES

✦ **1982** Established by John Lumic ✦ **1985** Co-founder dies mysteriously ✦ **1991** Cybus products flood markets ✦ **1996** Cybus swallows all competitors ✦ **2001** Worldwide profits reach $78 billion ✦ **2004** New South America reports 265,000 missing ✦ **2007** Ultimate Upgrade project begins

Company divisions and subsidiaries

Cybus Airships ✦ Cybus Earpods Cybus Finance ✦ Cybus Fitness Cybus FM ✦ Cybus Network Cybus Property

IE24

Britain's main broadcaster, following the closure of the BBC. On 1 February, IE24 News reported on Lumic's return to London ('good news for Great Britain'), and the Cybus chief's denial of ill health. Cybus Industries shares had doubled in price. Lumic pledged more support for the homeless of South America. And the Torchwood Institute had published a study on the Barren Earth Scenario, claiming that male fertility rates were declining while the average lifespan throughout the West was decreasing.

INTERNATIONAL ELECTROMATICS (IE)

Apparently a leading supplier of domestic and corporate electrical systems with manufacturing bases in New South America and offices across Britain, IE was in fact a dummy company set up by Cybus Industries. Cybus used IE lorries to transport abducted homeless people and to transport Cybermen, presumably intending to divert attention from the parent company.

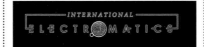

VITEX

The company set up by Pete Tyler to market his Vitex health drinks, Vitex was bought up by Cybus Industries in 2005. Pete became a Cybus executive as well as the public face of Vitex, appearing on ads with his catchphrase 'Trust me on this!' Marketing for Vitex made extraordinary claims for the health drinks' beneficial effects.

Vitex flavours

✦ **Cherry –** Cherries! Water! Reduces wrinkles! ✦ **Pineapple –** Probiotic – Prevents hair loss ✦ **Sunrise –** Berries – Antioxidants – Lengthens life ✦ **Violet –** Melts fat – Vitamin C boost – Blackcurrants ✦ **Water-Lite –** Same look – Same taste – Better 4 U

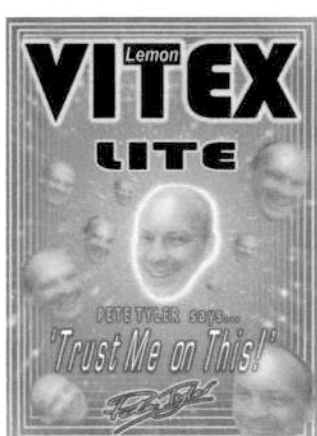

SCIENCE AND TECHNOLOGY

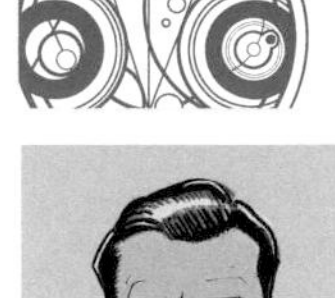

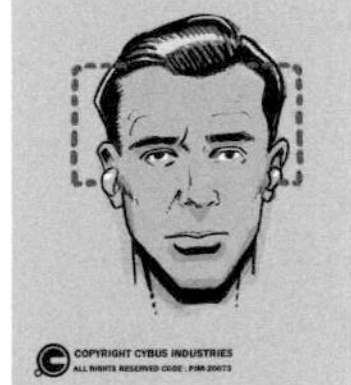

EARPODS

Almost every citizen across the world wore a pair of earpods, connecting them directly to the Cybus Network and to each other. The earpods could function as mobile communication devices, and also received an automatic Daily Download from Cybus Industries, which was fed directly into the brain of the wearer.

The Daily Download

News ✦ International News Sport ✦ Weather ✦ TV Schedules Lottery Numbers ✦ Joke

MOBILE PHONES

The Cybus Network broadcast signals that located mobile phones and connected them to the network. This provided access to global communications, including the internet, and also allowed the phone user to receive the automated Daily Download.

ELECTROMAGNETIC BOMB

Generally used to disable computers, the Preachers' Mrs Moore found one of these just as effective in destroying an attacking Cyberform.

CYBERMEN (1)

The Cybermen were John Lumic's greatest creation. Seeking ways to prolong life, he had theorised that the human brain was the only important element and should be preserved. He had already invented a steel-based high-contact metal, which combined strength with durability, and devised a method of extracting and preserving the intact brain from a human body and bonding its cyber-kinetic impulses with a metal exo-skeleton containing gears and servos. An artificially grown central nervous system of flesh was then threaded throughout the Cyber suit and, in the process, the subject's emotions were suppressed by an inhibitor installed in the Cyberform's chest unit. Feelings had to be suppressed in this way to prevent the Cybermen going insane from the sight of themselves or the pain of the conversion process. The chest unit itself was fronted by the Cybus Industries logo. The Cyber suits could also function without any human content. Lumic's test subjects were drawn from among the world's homeless, and he used the same resource to construct armies of Cybermen once his experiments had successfully concluded. Cybus Industries had factories across seven continents, dedicated to building new armies of Cybermen.

PLANET OF ORIGIN
Parallel Earth

APPEARANCE
2-metre-tall steel humanoids

ABILITIES
Lethal electrical discharge through their hands

WEAKNESSES
Electomagnetic pulse; emotions

PREVIOUS ENCOUNTERS
There were Cybermen in our universe, although they did not originate on Earth. They were created on Earth's twin planet of Mondas, and the Doctor prevented a number of their invasion attempts during the 20th century and in the future, also encountering them in the ice tombs on their adopted homeworld of Telos.

GREAT LIVES

JOHN LUMIC

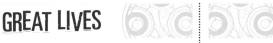

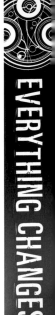

Co-founder of Cybus Industries and inventor of high-contact metal, Lumic was dying. Confined to a motorised wheelchair and sustained by his automated life-support system, Lumic was concentrating his efforts on his plans for the Ultimate Upgrade. Having concluded that the weaknesses of flesh and blood were holding humanity back from its potential and that it was wrong to allow the human brain to die, he developed the next level of mankind: Human-point-2, or Cybermen. His intention was that at his dying breath he would be converted into Cyberform, enabling his mind to live on for ever. When his right-hand man, Mr Crane, attacked his life-support system, however, the first of his Cyberforms judged that he should be upgraded immediately. Lumic was converted and became their Cybercontroller.

THE ULTIMATE UPGRADE

When the British President refused permission for the continuation of the Cybus Industries upgrade project, Lumic ordered the conversion and deployment of a new squad of Cybermen. These attacked and murdered the President at Pete Tyler's country estate during Jackie Tyler's 40th birthday party, then rejected the party guests as incompatible and began to delete them all. With the President out of the way, Lumic then broadcast a signal through the Cybus Network, which hypnotised almost the entire population of London. He directed the Cybermen to convey the subjugated humans to his conversion factories, the chief of which was at Battersea Power Station, where they would all be converted to Cyberforms, the first step to converting all humanity. The Doctor, Rose Tyler, Mickey Smith, Pete Tyler and the surviving Preachers made a three-pronged attack on the power plant, where they disabled the signal transmitting to the Cybermen's emotional inhibitors. The Cybermen went mad, and were overcome, and their Controller perished in the destruction of the Battersea plant.

TORCHWOOD

The Torchwood Institute had a higher public profile on the parallel Earth, although the scientific reports that it published were in part a smokescreen to prevent scrutiny of their real activities. Mickey Smith had remained on Pete's World to help in the fight against the thousands of Cybermen that Lumic had left in factories around the world. The Cybermen were not defeated, yet one day they simply vanished, seemingly without trace.

In the years that followed Lumic's attempted takeover, a parallel Harriet Jones became President of the Republic of Great Britain, and under her the country entered a new Golden Age. The new republican forces discovered that Torchwood had been operating its own agenda. The People's Republic took over Torchwood.

The Cybermen were sealed in the remaining Cybus factories around the world, but many people felt that they had the same rights as other living creatures, and they were not destroyed. After three years, the Cybermen found breaches in the Void between universes and infiltrated the Torchwood in our universe. They disappeared from the parallel Earth. Experimenting with alien technology, Torchwood had developed transporter technology capable of travelling from one Earth to another, but this coincided with escalating environmental problems. Global temperatures rose by two degrees, and the polar ice caps were melting increasingly rapidly. With predictions that London would be flooded within two years, Pete Tyler began to realise that these problems were connected with the Cybermen's use of the breaches in the Void. He sent first Mickey Smith and then Jake Simmonds and a squad of armed troopers through the breach in pursuit of the Cybermen...

L.I.N.D.A.

Each Tuesday, a small group met in basement unit 4b beneath a library on London's Macateer Street to talk about a shared interest. Colin Skinner, Bridget, Ursula Blake and Bliss had each noticed that a man called the Doctor had been at the heart of many of the strange things that had been happening to the Earth in recent years. They researched him, and discovered that his involvement stretched back many years – Bridget identified representations of a blue police box throughout history, while Mr Skinner theorised that 'the Doctor' was in fact a name for a number of different men, each fulfilling the same role. Bliss created sculptures representing the Doctor, while Ursula maintained a website – My Invasion Blog – with a picture of the man himself on its front page. It was that picture, taken at Christmas in 2006, that made Elton Pope contact Ursula, who introduced him to the rest of the group. With Elton accepted as a new member, he suggested that they should adopt the name L.I.N.D.A. – London Investigation 'N' Detective Agency.

The Tuesday meetings gradually lost focus on the hunt for the Doctor, as cookery, novel-writing and music took over. That all changed when Victor Kennedy arrived in March. Kennedy was actually the alien Abzorbaloff in disguise, and he too wanted to locate the Doctor, hoping to steal the TARDIS. He had found L.I.N.D.A.'s *Who Is The Doctor?* website and tracked the group down to Macateer Street, where he set them to work hunting for the Doctor and Rose Tyler.

Musical L.I.N.D.A.

✦ *Daniel* – Elton John (Elton Pope was named after Elton John) ✦ *Mr Blue Sky* – Electric Light Orchestra (Elton Pope's favourite band) ✦ *The Riddle Song* – traditional (Bliss sang this at a L.I.N.D.A. meeting) ✦ *Brand New Key* – Melanie (Bliss and Ursula sang this at a L.I.N.D.A. meeting) ✦ *Don't Bring Me Down* – Electric Light Orchestra (L.I.N.D.A. were practising this when Victor first appeared) ✦ *Regresa A Mi* – Il Divo (Playing in Jackie Tyler's flat as she and Elton moved towards Step Five...)

HOIX

Nasty, brutish and exo-skeletal, little is known about these creatures, except that they have low intelligence, an aversion to certain warm fluids and a voracious appetite – basically, they live to eat, and will consume almost anything. The Doctor and Rose Tyler encountered a Hoix in a dockside warehouse in Woolwich where, witnessed by Elton Pope, the Doctor distracted the creature with a pork chop while Rose attempted to fend it off with buckets of chemicals.

PLANET OF ORIGIN
Unknown

APPEARANCE
Brown-skinned humanoid, with sharp teeth and exposed gums

WEAKNESS
Unspecified chemicals

CLOM

The twin planet of Raxacoricofallapatorius.

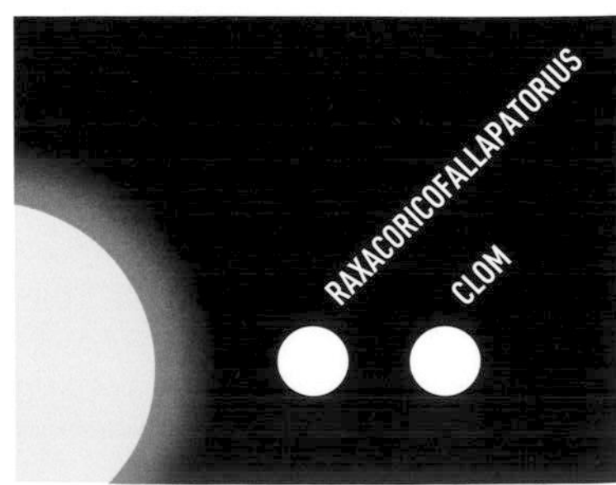

ABZORBALOFF

This is not actually the name of the dominant life form on the planet Clom, whose species designation is known only to themselves and the Shadow Proclamation. They have the same greenish, living calcium skin as their Slitheen neighbours, but they are squatter and have manes of black hair resembling a Mohican and running the length of their backs. Like the Slitheen, they are able to disguise themselves as other life forms. They feed by absorption, and both the Doctor and Elton Pope noted this ability and suggested the name 'Abzorbaloff'.

The Abzorbaloff that infiltrated L.I.N.D.A. in the guise of Victor Kennedy absorbed people through his skin with just a single touch, and so claimed to have a skin complaint (eczema) that prevented him from having physical contact with anyone. The absorption process took the entire victim, including his or her thoughts and memories, personality and even clothes. The face of each victim then protruded through the Abzorbaloff's skin all around his body.

A limitation field, a form of compression technology controlled via a cane that the Abzorbaloff held at all times, prevented the creature from being stretched to bursting whenever he absorbed another victim. When Elton destroyed the cane, the limitation field was destroyed, causing the Abzorbaloff to explode and be absorbed in turn into the ground. The last of his victims, Ursula Blake, was partially saved by the Doctor, who managed to recombine enough of her life essence to preserve her head in a slab of paving stone.

Victims of the Abzorbaloff

- **Victor Kennedy's secretary:** Discovered the Abzorbaloff in Victor Kennedy's office
- **Bliss:** Absorbed after a L.I.N.D.A. meeting
- **Bridget:** Absorbed after a L.I.N.D.A. meeting
- **Colin Skinner:** Absorbed after a L.I.N.D.A. meeting
- **Ursula Blake**: Absorbed during a confrontation with the Abzorbaloff

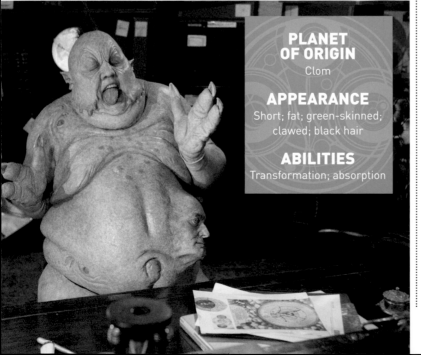

PLANET OF ORIGIN
Clom

APPEARANCE
Short; fat; green-skinned; clawed; black hair

ABILITIES
Transformation; absorption

HOMEWORK

VICTOR KENNEDY'S BASIC SURVEILLANCE AND ESPIONAGE STRATEGY

- **Step 1:** Engage your target. Find some excuse to start a conversation.
- **Step 2:** Without provoking suspicion, get on first-name terms with the target.
- **Step 3:** Ingratiate yourself, with a joke or some humorous device.
- **Step 4:** Find some subtle way to integrate yourself into the target's household.
- **Step 5:** Infiltration.

TORCHWOOD

As Victor Kennedy, the Abzorbaloff managed to access Torchwood's files on the Doctor to build up a detailed profile of him. Among the resources he'd gathered were video and audio files of the Doctor and Rose Tyler entering the TARDIS, and the time machine dematerialising. The Torchwood files on the Doctor's companion Rose Tyler were corrupted by a computer virus named Bad Wolf.

NEWS MEDIA

In March, the UK press's attention was focused on the political fortunes of Harold Saxon. The *Daily Telegraph* reported that Saxon's popularity in the wake of his unveiling of the Archangel communications network at the start of the year was now earning him 61 per cent support in the latest opinion polls. Before long, an unpopular Prime Minister was forced to announce that the government's new defence minister would be Harry Saxon.

The Daily Telegrap
Saxon leads polls with 61 per cent

2007

LEFT TURN

At 10.01am on Monday 25 June, Donna Noble decided to accept an agency contract for temp work at the City-based security firm H.C. Clements. Ignoring her mother Sylvia's argument that she should take another job, she drove her car left out of Little Sutton Street, leading onto Ealing Road, and headed for Chiswick High Road. On her first day at H.C. Clements, the company's personnel officer Lance Bennett made her a cup of coffee, and the two quickly became close friends.

RIGHT TURN

At 10.01am on Monday 25 June, Donna Noble decided to turn down an agency contract for temp work at the City-based security firm H.C. Clements. Accepting her mother Sylvia's argument that she should take another job, she drove her car right out of Little Sutton Street, leading onto Ealing Road, and headed for Griffin's Parade. She was introduced to Jival Chowdry by Sylvia's friend Suzette and took a £20,000 secretarial job at his photocopying business on Merchant Street.

SKARO

The birthplace of the Daleks. Their creation by Davros countless millennia ago was almost averted by the Doctor, who was acting on the orders of the Time Lords. Many historians count the Time Lords' pre-emptive strike as the first action of the Time War.

DALEKS (3)

THE CULT OF SKARO

During the Time War, the Emperor of the Daleks established a secret order that would operate above and beyond even him. This Cult of Skaro comprised four Daleks, and their purpose was to imagine, to think like the Daleks' enemies, and so to find new ways of killing and new means of survival. Daleks do not have names, but the Emperor decreed that the members of the Cult of Skaro should break with this practice. Three bronze Daleks were named Caan, Jast and Thay, while their leader was called Sec and given a black casing. The Cult fled the Time War during its closing stages, taking with them something called the Genesis Ark.

The Genesis Ark

This was a stolen Time Lord prison ship. Externally it was not much larger than a Dalek, but it was bigger on the inside and contained millions of captive Daleks. Aside from the Doctor and his TARDIS, the Ark was all that survived of the Time Lords and their technology. It could be activated only by the touch of an organic time traveller, so the Daleks were unable to open it themselves. Once activated, it needed to be in an open area of 30 square miles before it could release the imprisoned Dalek armies it held.

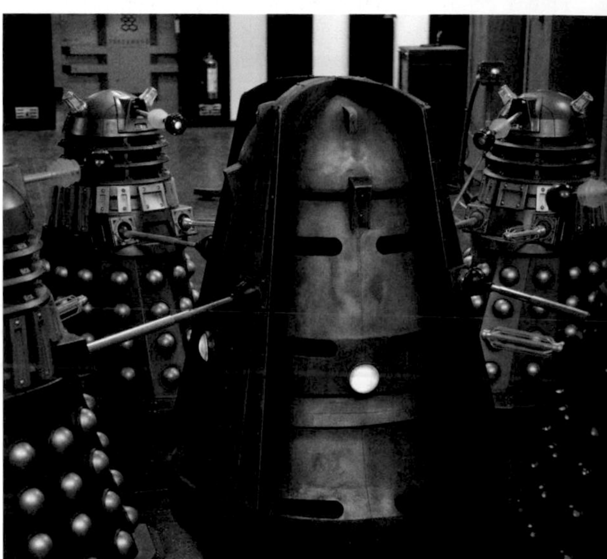

THE VOID

With billions of parallel universes existing alongside each other, the space in-between the universes is an area of absolute nothing – no light or dark, no up or down, no life, no time. The Time Lords called it the Void, and the Eternals called it the Howling, but it has also been known as Hell. As the Time War drew towards its closing stages, the Cult of Skaro constructed a spherical Void Ship and escaped into the Void. The four Daleks waited in the Void, planning their return and protecting the Genesis Ark, inside which the Time Lords had imprisoned millions of Daleks. The Cult of Skaro eventually selected 21st-century London as the place where they were most likely to find the time traveller they needed to open the Ark, and punched a hole in reality through which the Void Ship could enter our dimension.

21ST-CENTURY LONDON

CANARY WHARF

Having detected a radar black spot some 240 metres above sea level in the Docklands area of London, the Torchwood Institute discovered a spatial disturbance and initiated the design and construction of Britain's tallest building around it. The Torchwood Tower, constructed between 1987 and 1991, was a 50-storey skyscraper, known to the general public as One Canada Square or the Canary Wharf Tower. The spatial disturbance was the way into this reality for the Cult of Skaro's Void Ship. Torchwood secured the Void Ship in a specially constructed Sphere Room, and established what became known as the Lever Room at the top of building, from which they operated the Ghost Shifts.

LOCATION
One Canada Square, London
HEIGHT
244 metres
FLOORS
50

GHOST SHIFT

After the arrival of the Void Ship, Torchwood discovered that firing particle engines at the sphere's point of entry reopened the breach. The Void Ship had splintered the surface of this dimension as it entered, in effect opening the barrier between Earth and its parallel version, and ghostly humanoid figures began to transpose themselves across the globe. Reopening the breach not only forced more of the Ghosts into existence on Earth, it was also a potential source of energy to free Britain from its dependence on Middle Eastern oil supplies. Torchwood named this process the Ghost Shift, and operated it twice a day, at 12pm and 7pm, with Ghost activity peaking at twelve minutes past the hour, and measuring energy levels up to 5,000 gigawatts.

At first, the public panicked, as more and more Ghosts began to appear across the planet. Soon, however, people began to associate the Ghosts with deceased friends, relatives and colleagues, and the daily Ghost Shift was widely welcomed. After a couple of months, the Ghosts had become part of everyday life.

MEDIA

THE EXAMINER

As more and more Ghosts appeared throughout the summer, national newspaper *The Examiner* paused in its coverage of the apparitions to celebrate another year of excellent GCSE results for the country's 16-year-olds. The day before this story was published, however, the paper's editor had been visited by an agent from the Torchwood Institute and two white-coated men. These men removed a journalist called Atif from the building, also taking his files on a story he had been researching, and providing the editor with a new front page for the next day's edition. Atif had been attempting to uncover details about the Torchwood Institute, and claimed to know the truth about the Ghost Shift. He was never seen again.

GHOST IMAGES

✦ *Ghostwatch* (BBC One, 12pm and 7pm daily) and *Ghostwatch Update* (BBC Three, 11.15pm), presented by Alistair Appleton, reported that some Ghosts had started to talk, and noted a regular formation of Ghosts around Westminster Bridge. Appleton was on air when the Ghosts materialised fully as Cybermen – he became one of the Cybermen's first victims, as his studio was invaded.

✦ Weather reports included predictions of Ghost activity.

✦ The *Trisha Goddard* show spoke to Eileen, a 22-year-old who had fallen in love with a Ghost, in an edition called 'I Married a Dead Man'.

✦ Derek Acorah complained in an interview that the arrival of the Ghosts had made both him and his talents as a spiritualist medium redundant.

✦ One enterprising company advertised Ectoshine, a household cleaning product that stops domestic Ghosts looking pale and grey.

✦ Over images of Ghosts in the vicinity of the Eiffel Tower, French television covered a presidential announcement that the Ghosts were not eligible for the Legion D'Honneur.

✦ In India, visitors to the Taj Mahal were warned to treat the Ghosts as sacred guests.

✦ Japanese TV reported that the country had gone crazy, with everyone wanting to be a Ghost and interviewed three excited teenage girls in Ghost T-shirts to make the point.

✦ BBC One's *EastEnders* took the opportunity to resurrect its Den Watts character once again, as Peggy Mitchell ordered his Ghost to clear off out of her pub.

✦There were press reports that a Ghost had been elected Member of Parliament for Leeds in a by-election.

TORCHWOOD

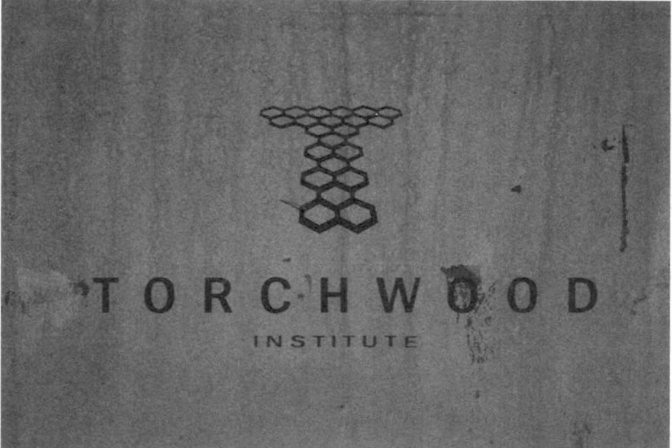

✦ **Established:** 1879 by Queen Victoria under the Torchwood Foundation Charter.
✦ **Motto:** 'If it's alien, it's ours'.
✦ **Headquarters:** One Canada Square, London. The Lever Room was at the top of the tower, with the heavily protected Sphere Chamber several floors down. There were numbered staircases at each corner of the building, connecting every level, and lifts running from the Lever Room through every floor down to the Loading Bays.
✦ **Chief Executive Officer:** Yvonne Hartman.
✦ **Senior operatives:** Matt Crane, Gareth Evans, Adeola Oshodi, Dr Rajesh Singh.
✦ **Precepts, purposes and mode of operation:** Keeping Britain great and fighting the alien horde. The Charter identified the Doctor as an enemy of the Crown. Dedicated to the restoration of the British Empire. Retained use of Imperial system of weights and measures, refusing to adopt the metric system. All staff had a basic level of psychic training. Any alien craft infringing British airspace was shot down. Any recovered alien technology and weapons would be stored and examined, in the hope that they could contribute to the restoration and strength of the British Empire.

VOID SHIP

Torchwood scientists quickly found that the Sphere, as they knew it, defied analysis – it weighed nothing, had no quantifiable age, emitted neither heat nor radiation, and had no atomic mass. By all normal measures, the Sphere did not exist. The Doctor identified it as a Void Ship, itself a theoretical impossibility, being designed to exist outside space and time and travel through the Void. When the final Ghost Shift reached 100 per cent, the Void Ship became active and the Sphere Chamber instruments instantly detected weight, mass and an electromagnetic field. This triggered an automatic quarantine measure, which sealed Rajesh Singh, Mickey Smith and Rose Tyler in the Sphere Chamber as the Void Ship opened and the Cult of Skaro emerged.

SPECTROMETER

Torchwood's Research & Development department developed a new spectrometer, which could detect the heat of a single protozoa through half a mile of steel. Even this was unable to penetrate the Void Ship.

LEVER ROOM

The centre of Torchwood's Ghost Shift operation, Yvonne Hartman had based her office here and supervised the regular opening of the breach. These Ghost Shifts were organised and monitored by a team of nine operatives, controlled from a network of four computers and initiated by the manual operation of two large levers. When the levers were fully engaged, the breach was opened 100 per cent.

BAZOOLIUM

Rose Tyler bought a small jar made of Bazoolium at an asteroid bazaar, bringing it back to Earth as a gift for her mother. Bazoolium grows cold when it's about to rain, and becomes hot when it's going to be sunny.

SCIENCE AND TECHNOLOGY

3-D GLASSES

The coloured filters in the lenses superpose a composite image of the right component of a viewed object in one colour onto the left component in a contrasting colour to produce an anaglyphic image of the object. This allows the wearer to view two-dimensional objects with a three-dimensional effect. It also reveals particles of background radiation – Void stuff – that surround any object or life form that has travelled through the Void.

TRIANGULATION DEVICE

Connected to the TARDIS console, when its three cones activated a scanner screen displayed the data needed to pinpoint the Ghosts' point of origin. The device caused an excitation of the Ghost field, which Torchwood were able to trace to the TARDIS.

JATHAA SUN GLIDER

A spacecraft shot down over the Shetland Islands in 1997, and stripped of its technology and armaments by Torchwood. The Jathaa weapon was used in 2006 to destroy the Sycorax spaceship.

PARTICLE GUN

Another item of scavenged alien technology, and one which Torchwood's scientists had spent eight years analysing before they discovered how to operate it.

MAGNA-CLAMPS

Several of these were found in an alien spaceship buried at the base of Mount Snowdon in Wales. They cancel the mass of any object to which they are attached, so that up to two tons of weight could be lifted with a single hand.

EARPIECES

Standard communications devices issued to all Torchwood Institute operatives. These were very similar to the Earpods developed by Cybus Industries on the parallel Earth. The Cybermen captured and killed three Torchwood operatives then reanimated and controlled them with replacement earpieces that fed nervous tissue through the ear and directly into the brain.

REMOTE TRANSMITTER

The Cybermen had installed a transmitter in a cordoned-off area of the Torchwood Tower, using it to direct the controlled Torchwood operatives and hijack the Ghost Shift. This allowed them to instigate an unscheduled Ghost Shift and open the breach 100 per cent, so that the Ghosts could fully materialise. Five million Cybermen achieved full transfer across planet Earth.

TRANSPORTER DISCS

Devised by Torchwood on the parallel Earth, these enabled Mickey Smith, Jake Simmonds and a squad of troops to cross the Void into our world. Each time a disc was used, however, it ripped a hole in the universe and raised the global temperature of the parallel world. With continued use, both planets would eventually start to boil and then fall into the Void. The discs stopped working when the Doctor sealed the breach.

CYBERMEN (2)

When the Dalek Void Ship created the breach in the barrier between the Earth and its parallel, an advance guard of Cybermen followed it through and infiltrated Torchwood Tower, where they installed Cyber-conversion units and their remote transmitter and began to abduct and control Torchwood operatives. By now the Cybermen had moved on from using electrical discharge as their main means of defence and attack and had incorporated arm-mounted laser weaponry into their design. They had also developed a rudimentary hierarchy, each troop of Cybermen directed by a single Cyberleader. If that Cyberleader was terminated, its shared files were downloaded into another Cyberman, which then became the new Cyberleader.

THE BATTLE OF CANARY WHARF

Although the human armies attempted to repel the invading forces, the simultaneous full transfer of five million Cybermen across the planet gave the invaders an instant victory. With Cybermen in millions of homes, people could do nothing but watch as the Cyberleader announced humanity's fate through their TV screens. The Cybermen would remove fear, sex, class, colour and creed to make humans identical. Humans would become like Cybermen.

Victory was short-lived, as the Cybermen almost immediately found themselves facing the Daleks, and their weapons had little effect on the Daleks' protective force fields. The Cult of Skaro forced their way through Torchwood Tower to a loading bay, where Dalek Sec overrode the roof mechanism and led the Daleks and the Genesis Ark into the London sky. There the Ark – already activated by the handprint of Mickey Smith – opened to release the millions of Daleks it contained. As the Daleks flew across London, exterminating all life forms below, Cyberleader One was forced to abandon the conquest of Earth and call all Cyber units to Torchwood to fight them. He also initiated emergency upgrading of captured humans, converting them into sometimes rudimentary Cyberforms.

While the Daleks and Cybermen fought, and Torchwood's military forces attempted to hold back the aliens, the Doctor managed to reprogram and reboot the Lever Room systems to reverse the Ghost Shift process. This opened the breach and sucked back anything that had travelled through the Void, including all the Cybermen and all the Daleks. Since the breach itself was part of the Void, it too was soaked in Void stuff, so it eventually closed itself, closing off both universes. The Cult of Skaro initiated an emergency temporal shift and escaped to 1930s New York. The Doctor used a magna-clamp to stop himself being pulled into the Void, but Rose Tyler and her family and Mickey Smith were all sealed in the universe containing the parallel Earth, seemingly for ever. Their names were included on the official list later compiled of London's casualties.

WEEPING ANGELS

At one time known as the Lonely Assassins, the Weeping Angels were the only race in the galaxy that killed people nicely. With one touch, they would send their intended prey back in time to live their lives in full. The Angels then fed off the potential energy of the lives that their victims would otherwise have led. They moved exceptionally quickly, seeming to vanish from one spot and reappear in another in the blink of an eye. They could only move, however, if they remained unobserved. If they were seen by anything or anyone, they were quantum-locked, becoming immobilised solid stone – the perfect defence mechanism.

Four Weeping Angels encountered the Doctor and Martha Jones in Wester Drumlins, an abandoned and dilapidated house in London, and despatched them to 1969. The TARDIS, and its key, remained in 2007.

PLANET OF ORIGIN
Unknown

APPEARANCE
Stone statues

ABILITIES
Highly rapid movement; transportation of victims through time

WEAKNESS
Being seen

MISSING PERSONS

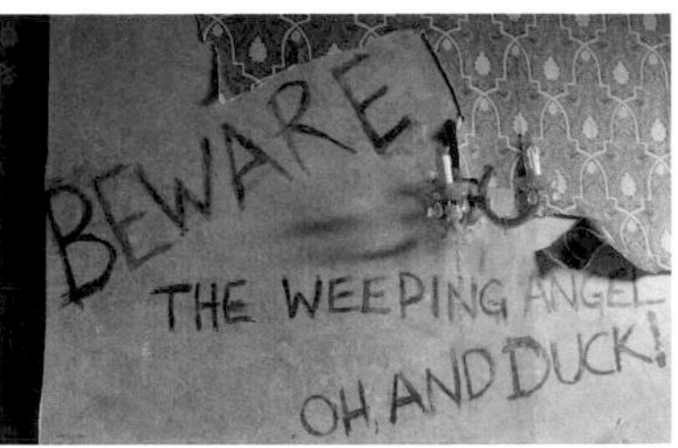

Between 2005 and 2007, Wester Drumlins was the scene of a series of disappearances. The victims' cars were often found nearby, sometimes with the engines still running and personal items inside. The cars were all stored in a car park beneath the local police station, alongside a locked replica police box, also recovered from Wester Drumlins. Detective Inspector Billy Shipton was the police officer in charge of the ongoing investigation, although he had no leads to follow until he too was sent back in time (to 1969) by a Weeping Angel, the same one that had previously despatched the Doctor and Martha Jones.

Sally Sparrow met Shipton when she decided to report the disappearance from Wester Drumlins of her friend Kathy Nightingale (sent to 1920). Sally had been exploring the old house and had found a message that the Doctor had left her in 1969, written on one of the walls. She had also discovered the TARDIS key in the hand of one of the four statues, and the Angels had followed her to the police station. The Angels took the TARDIS back to Wester Drumlins.

2007

WIBBLY-WOBBLY TIMEY-WIMEY STUFF

2008 The Doctor meets Sally Sparrow, who gives him her notes on Wester Drumlins and the Weeping Angels

2005 The Weeping Angels begin to take victims at Wester Drumlins ✦ Police led by DI Billy Shipton investigate the disappearance

2007 The Doctor and Martha Jones are attacked at Wester Drumlins

1969 Following Sally's notes, the Doctor leaves messages for her at Wester Drumlins

2008 Sally and Lawrence take over Banto's DVD store ✦ Sally meets the Doctor and gives him her notes on Wester Drumlins and the Weeping Angels

2007 Sally explores Wester Drumlins and finds the messages from the Doctor ✦ Sally and Kathy Nightingale investigate Wester Drumlins ✦ Kathy is attacked

2007 Sally meets Billy, now an old man, in hospital ✦ Sally and Lawrence watch the Easter Egg at Wester Drumlins ✦ The Weeping Angels attack Sally and Lawrence but they escape into the TARDIS ✦ The TARDIS departs for 1969, leaving Sally and Lawrence surrounded by Weeping Angels ✦ The Angels, left looking directly at each other when the TARDIS dematerialised, have frozen for ever

1920 Kathy arrives in Hull

1969 Billy arrives in 1969 and meets the Doctor and Martha ✦ The Doctor gives Billy the Easter Egg film

2007 Kathy's grandson delivers Kathy's letter to Sally at Wester Drumlins ✦ Sally contacts Lawrence Nightingale at Banto's DVD store ✦ Sally meets DI Billy Shipton, who is attacked by the Angels

1987 Kathy writes a letter to Sally

MEDIA

DVDs

Developed in the 1990s, digital versatile discs quickly replaced video cassettes as the predominant medium for domestic TV and film viewing and recording. For some years, computer games had frequently contained hidden extra features, which the player would have to search for using clues in the game menus, and the DVD format followed this lead. The hidden extras soon became known as Easter Eggs. Having found himself in an England a decade before he would even be born, Billy Shipton spent his new life working in publishing – first books, then videos and finally DVDs. Following the Doctor's instructions, Billy placed Easter Eggs on the masters for 17 commercial DVD releases. These represented Sally Sparrow's complete DVD collection, and the Easter Eggs contained a filmed recording of the Doctor and Martha Jones in 1969, apparently engaged in one side of a two-way conversation. When Sally Sparrow realised that a list of these discs coincided with her own DVD collection, she met Kathy Nightingale's brother Lawrence at Wester Drumlins, where the pair watched the Doctor's film. With Sally providing her side of the conversation, and Lawrence making a transcript of the complete exchange, the Doctor was able to explain the situation to Sally. Billy also placed a second message on the DVDs, this one intended for the TARDIS. This activated Security Protocol 712, which showed Sally and Lawrence a hologram of the Doctor stating that they were carrying an authorised control disc. The DVD carried instructions for the TARDIS to follow the Doctor and Martha to 1969, leaving Sally and Lawrence in 2007.

Available at Banto's DVD store

Breakfast in the Rain ✦ Dance of Days ✦ Civilization Zero
Angel Smile ✦ Falling Star ✦ One Oak Country
My Best Friend's Boyfriend ✦ Mean Teens
Shooting the Sun

BAD WOLF

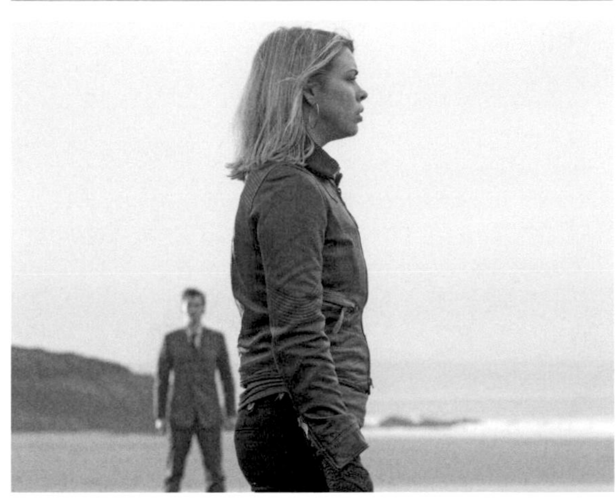

Several months after being trapped on the parallel Earth, Rose Tyler had a dream in which she heard the Doctor calling to her. She, Jackie, Pete and Mickey drove hundreds of miles through Europe and into Norway, eventually reaching a beach fifty miles from the city of Bergen.

This was Dalig Ulv Stranden, which translated as Bad Wolf Bay. There Rose spoke to a hologram of the Doctor, who was harnessing the power of a supernova to send his image through the last tiny gap between the universes before it closed. He could not come through properly without fracturing the gap and causing the collapse of both universes, and they had only two minutes to talk and say goodbye, it seemed, for ever.

TORCHWOOD

In 1984, the Torchwood Institute acquired the locksmith and security firm H.C. Clements. They established an underground research laboratory complex beneath the Thames Flood Barrier, accessed via a secret level of the H.C. Clements headquarters through an extensive tunnel system. Over the next 22 years, their experiments in particle extrusion led Torchwood to the discovery and manufacture of Huon particles in Lab 003. At the same time, Torchwood laser-drilled a shaft from their laboratories more than six thousand kilometres below the Earth's surface and all the way to the planet's inner core.

LEFT TURN

After a six-month relationship, Donna Noble and Lance Bennett held their wedding at St Mary's Church, Haven Road, Chiswick on Christmas Eve. As Geoff Noble led his daughter up the aisle, she was enveloped by a strange glow and vanished from the church. She materialised moments later inside the TARDIS.

RIGHT TURN

After six months working at Jival Chowdry's Capital Copies, Donna had been promoted to a £23,000 per annum position as Chowdry's Personal Assistant. Still single, she was spending Christmas Eve in a pub with six mates, including Veena, Mooky and Alice, when the Racnoss Webstar appeared over London.

RACNOSS

A perpetually hungry, omnivorous race. Born starving, the Racnoss travelled the cosmos in their Webstars, devouring whole planets, until the Fledgling Empires of the Dark Times waged war against them and the species became almost extinct.

Just two Webstars escaped the war. One, piloted by the Empress of the Racnoss, fled to the edge of the galaxy, where the Empress hibernated for 4.6 billion years.

The second – the *Secret Heart* – contained the eggs for a new generation of Racnoss, and it drifted into Earth's nascent solar system, where it became the single rock around which the rest of the planet was formed.

When Torchwood drilled down to the Earth's inner core, they awoke the children of the Racnoss, whose call was heard by the Empress, drawing her Webstar towards the Earth. Following the destruction of the Torchwood Institute in the Battle of Canary Wharf, the Empress took over both H.C. Clements and the underground research facility, continuing to manufacture Huon energy and devising a plan to unlock the *Secret Heart* and release her children.

PLANET OF ORIGIN
Unknown

APPEARANCE
Red-skinned; half-humanoid, half-arachnid; six eyes; sharp teeth; eight legs; two arms with razor-sharp spears

TECHNOLOGY
Webstars; teleportation

SCIENCE AND TECHNOLOGY

HUON PARTICLES

This lethal energy form was created by the Time Lords in the Dark Times as an element of their time-travel technology. When they discovered that Huon energy unravelled the atomic structure and was therefore lethal, the Time Lords eradicated all traces of it from the universe, although traces remained in the hearts of their TARDISes. The Torchwood research labs used water from the River Thames to extrude new Huon particles in liquid form through a flat hydrogen base. But these particles were inert and needed something living to catalyse inside. The Empress of the Racnoss instructed Lance Bennett to dose Donna Noble with liquid Huon particles, and after six months her body was saturated with Huon energy. The chemical war of adrenalin and acetylcholine in her system caused by the excitement of her wedding to Lance produced an endorphin rush that was sufficient to activate the particles. Donna became a living key – purging the particles from her body and sending them down the shaft would unlock the Racnoss Webstar at the heart of the Earth. However, the Huon energy in the Doctor's TARDIS magnetised the particles inside Donna as they reached boiling point and drew her into his time machine.

BIODAMPER

With the Racnoss's Roboforms able to track Donna, the Doctor gave her a biodamper, in the form of a ring, intended to conceal her biochemical traces from them. A biodamper could not hide Huon energy though, so the device was useless.

ROBOFORMS (2)

Having fled from the Doctor shortly before the Sycorax invasion twelve months earlier and escaped the destruction of the Sycorax ship, the Roboforms encountered the Empress of the Racnoss when she first arrived on the planet Earth. She installed remote-control technology that responded to voiced commands, and the Roboforms became servants instead of scavengers. When the TARDIS removed Donna from her Christmas Eve wedding to Lance, the Roboforms were despatched to London to retrieve her, once again disguised as a troupe of Santas playing 'God Rest Ye Merry Gentlemen' on their brass instruments. Another, also in Santa guise, abducted Donna in a taxi, but the Doctor rescued her. A larger group of robot Santas surrounded Donna's wedding reception and attacked the guests with exploding Christmas tree decorations, until the Doctor used amplified sonic vibrations to destroy them. The Racnoss still had several more Roboforms at her disposal, and used them to protect the shaft to the Earth's core. These were remotely incapacitated by the Doctor, and were later destroyed by the flood that killed the newborn Racnoss children.

APPEARANCE
Featureless golden robots

WEAPONS
Flame throwers, missile launchers, machine guns – disguised as brass instruments; remote-controlled Christmas trees and decorations

WEAKNESS
Ultrasonic vibration

OTHER SIGHTINGS
London, 2006

THE CHRISTMAS STAR

The first London knew of the second Christmas-time alien attack in two years was when a huge, star-like object appeared in the sky over the city. As Christmas shoppers gazed up at this Christmas Star, the Empress of the Racnoss commanded her Webstar to harvest the humans and reduce them to meat. Bolts of energy were released from the Webstar, striking down at London as thousands of onlookers began to flee. Defence minister Harold Saxon immediately sent tanks onto the city streets, with orders to destroy the threat. The Webstar was destroyed with the Empress of the Racnoss on board.

21ST-CENTURY LONDON

THAMES BARRIER

LOCATION
A 520-metre-wide stretch of the River Thames between Newham and Greenwich in London

HEIGHT
20 metres (four largest gates)

WEIGHT
3,700 tonnes (four largest gates)

Constructed between 1974 and 1984, this flood barrier consists of ten movable gates positioned end-to-end across London's River Thames, which can seal the river off from the sea in the event of dangerously high tides. The Doctor detonated explosions in the chambers beneath the Barrier, flooding the secret base and flushing the newborn Racnoss children back down the shaft. The required water completely drained the Thames.

WEDDING MUSIC

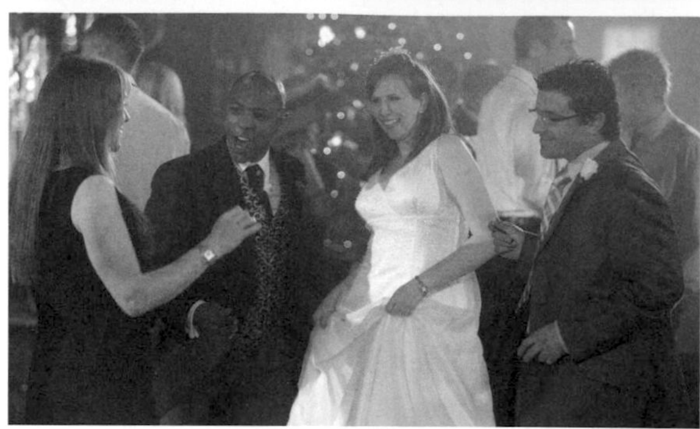

✦ *The Wedding March* from *A Midsummer Night's Dream* (Op. 61) – Felix Mendelssohn (1842)
✦ *Merry Xmas Everybody* – Slade (1973)
✦ *Love Don't Roam* – Neil Hannon (2006)

CAPTAIN JACK HARKNESS

REPORTED SIGHTING #13 CONFIRMED

ESTIMATED AGE: 174

LOCATION: Cardiff, 2008

AVAILABLE INFORMATION: Having waited 139 years for the arrival of a version of the Doctor that coincided with his own timeline, Captain Jack finally heard the TARDIS engines as the time machine arrived at the water tower in Cardiff Bay for a 20-second refuelling stop at the Rift. He left the Torchwood Hub, taking with him the Doctor's severed hand in a jar, and ran across Roald Dahl Plass. Clinging to the TARDIS exterior, Captain Jack was transported 100 trillion years through the Vortex to the planet Malcassairo...

LEFT TURN

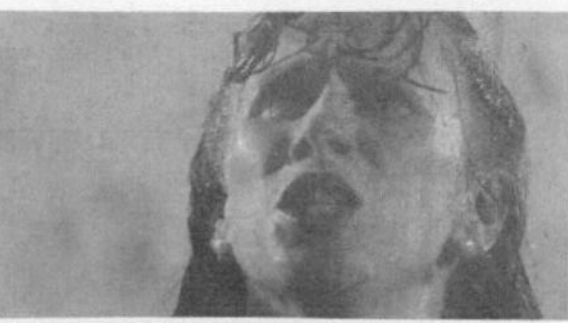

As the Doctor watched the floodwaters from the Thames fill the shaft and slaughter the Racnoss children, Donna convinced him that he'd done enough and they should leave. They climbed to the top of the Thames Barrier before Donna returned to her parents' house in Chiswick.

RIGHT TURN

As the army shot down the Racnoss Webstar, Donna watched UNIT soldiers retrieve the Doctor's corpse from the base below the Thames Barrier, which he had blown up and flooded. Donna was approached by Rose Tyler, who asked her about the dead man, then vanished.

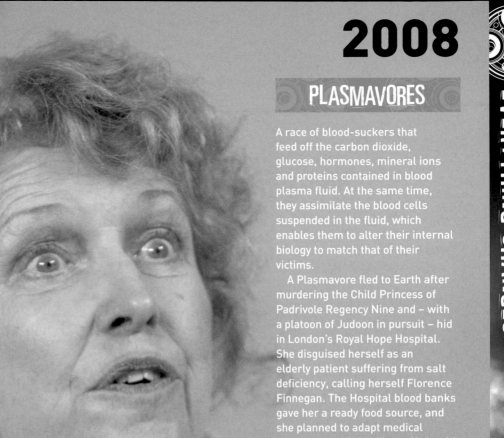

2008

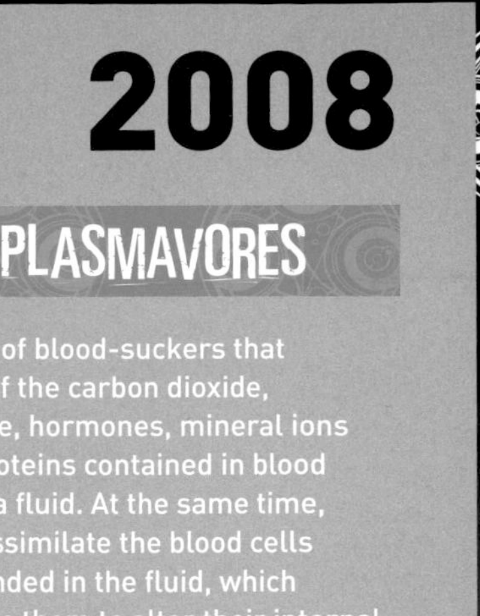

PLASMAVORES

A race of blood-suckers that feed off the carbon dioxide, glucose, hormones, mineral ions and proteins contained in blood plasma fluid. At the same time, they assimilate the blood cells suspended in the fluid, which enables them to alter their internal biology to match that of their victims.

A Plasmavore fled to Earth after murdering the Child Princess of Padrivole Regency Nine and – with a platoon of Judoon in pursuit – hid in London's Royal Hope Hospital. She disguised herself as an elderly patient suffering from salt deficiency, calling herself Florence Finnegan. The Hospital blood banks gave her a ready food source, and she planned to adapt medical equipment to defend herself should the Judoon locate her. The Judoon were able to identify her as non-human, however, when the Doctor tricked her into assimilating his Gallifreyan blood.

PLANET OF ORIGIN
Unknown

APPEARANCE
Humanoid

WEAPON
A little straw

SLABS

The Plasmavore also hired a couple of Slabs as bodyguards. Slabs are composed entirely of leather, function as basic slave drones and always come in pairs. The Doctor destroyed one with an enormous dose of Röntgen radiation from an X-ray machine, while the second was disintegrated by Judoon blaster fire.

PLANET OF ORIGIN
Unknown

APPEARANCE
Leather-clad, helmeted humanoid

WEAKNESS
Radiation

2008

THE ROYAL HOPE TRUST

A leading London teaching hospital, the Royal Hope stands on the south side of the Thames Embankment within sight of the Houses of Parliament. It was at the centre of an extraordinary news story when the hospital vanished at 12.20pm, in the midst of a thunderstorm, leaving only a huge crater. Sixty-three minutes later, the Royal Hope reappeared, its staff and patients all telling police and reporters the same story – that the whole hospital had been transported to the moon by alien space police, who had catalogued them all and then left.

Guide to the Royal Hope Hospital

✦ **Level G:** Foyer, reception, little shop
✦ **Level 1:** Café, paediatric cardiac surgery, paediatric therapies, paediatric wards, pharmacy, special care baby unit, treatment rooms
✦ **Level 2:** Academic department, paediatric medical day unit, parents' accommodation
✦ **Level 3:** Blood banks
✦ **Level 4:** Cardiac catheter lab 1, mortuary, operating theatres, pathology wards, recovery room, rheumatology wards, X-ray department, theatre staff changing rooms
✦ **Level 5:** Consultants' offices 1, MRI room 1
✦ **Level 6:** Breast clinic outpatients unit, breast screening unit, delivery suites, female wards, orthopaedic department, recovery room, seminar rooms
✦ **Level 7:** Cardiac catheter lab 2, cardiovascular research, colcoscopy, consultants' offices 2, intensive care unit, male wards, MRI room 2, obstetrics theatre, outpatients department, patients' lounge, staff kitchen, staff locker room, smoking area (balcony), treatment rooms, ward stores

THE MOON

Earth's only natural satellite orbits the planet once every 27.3 days at an average speed of 1.022 kilometres per second. The closest to Earth its elliptical orbit brings it is 363,104 kilometres, and it is slightly more than a quarter of the Earth's size, with a diameter of 3,476 kilometres. Its atmosphere is too thin to allow humans to exist there without pressurised protective clothing and an oxygen supply. By 2008, humans had visited the moon seven times – six of these in manned *Apollo* missions between 1969 and 1972, and a seventh when the Judoon used an H_2O scoop to transport the Royal Hope and all its staff and patients to the lunar surface.

JUDOON

Race of interplanetary police-for-hire. Unintelligent but honourable, the Judoon accept any properly authorised commission to track down and punish criminals. They act as police, judge and jury, believing that justice should be swift. Galactic Law prohibits them from operating on Earth and they have no jurisdiction over human crime, so when their hunt for the Plasmavore led them to London they set up plasma coils around the Royal Hope and used an H_2O scoop to transport the hospital to the neutral territory of the moon. Landing on the moon in their vast, cylindrical battleships, the Judoon platoon took over the hospital, locking down its computers and wiping its patient records before beginning a methodical search for their prey. They scanned each life form to identify it as human or non-human, reasoning that the Plasmavore would be the only non-human present. Having located and executed the Plasmavore, they left the moon and returned the Royal Hope to Earth.

PLANET OF ORIGIN
Unknown

APPEARANCE
Bipedal, twin-horned pachyderms; helmeted and armoured

WEAPON
Blaster

WEAKNESS
Stupidity

OTHER SIGHTINGS
Shadow Proclamation, 2009

SCIENCE AND TECHNOLOGY

H_2O SCOOP

Using plasma coils installed around the Royal Hope, the H_2O scoop sucked the entire building and the 1,023 people inside it up to Earth's moon. In the process, it created electrical storms around the hospital, with the atmospheric disturbance it caused dragging the resultant rain upwards. The process took three minutes, at the end of which the hospital stood inside a protective force field, which prevented the hospital's air being lost in the thin atmosphere of the moon. The air contained within the hospital was sufficient to support a thousand people for only one hour.

JUDOON EQUIPMENT

Each Judoon trooper is issued with a hand-held blaster, able to burn through glass and evaporate any life form, as well as a language identification and assimilation scanner, and a species scanner incorporating a marker pen. The Judoon uniform includes a utility belt to hold this equipment.

X-RAY MACHINE

Standard Earth hospital equipment, which utilises electromagnetic radiation in medical imaging. It uses Röntgen radiation, which is lethal to many life forms in sufficient quantities. The Doctor increased the radiation output of an RHT X-ray machine by 5,000 per cent to kill a pursuing Slab.

MRI SCANNER

Magnetic resonance imaging uses magnetic fields to reconstruct an image of the body that is being scanned for medical diagnosis. The Plasmavore rewired it and increased its main field strength from the standard setting of 1.5 tesla to 50,000 tesla, so that it could fry the brain stem of any life form within 250,000 miles. The Doctor reset and disabled the machine before it could destroy all life on the side of the Earth facing the moon.

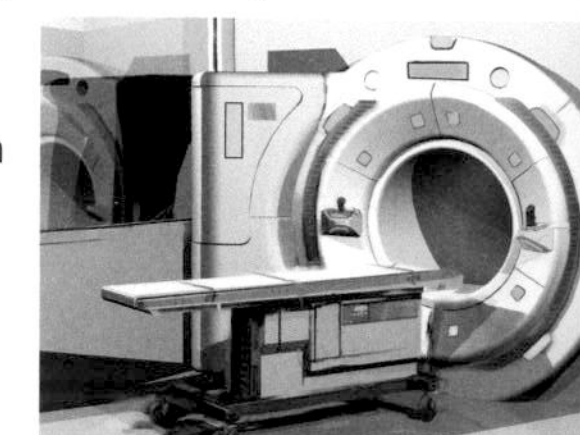

ELECTION COUNTDOWN

MONDAY: 3 DAYS TO GO

Former defence minister Harold Saxon was by now standing as an independent candidate and campaigning to become the nation's Prime Minister in the general election to be held three days later. 'Vote Saxon' posters had appeared across the country during the first few months of the year, and he had been making political capital out of the government's failure to protect the country from alien incursions or to inform them of what had been happening. Many people saw the Royal Hope incident as further proof of the truth of his claims.

LEFT TURN

While Donna Noble was beginning to search for the Doctor, the Royal Hope Hospital was returned to Earth by the Judoon. There had been two casualties – a patient who had attacked a Judoon trooper, and the senior consultant Mr Stoker, a victim of the Plasmavore. Having saved the Doctor's life, medical student Martha Jones began to travel with him in the TARDIS.

RIGHT TURN

While Donna Noble was being sacked from her job as Jival Chowdry's Personal Assistant, the Royal Hope Hospital was returned to Earth by the Judoon. There was only one survivor – medical student Oliver Morgenstern, whose life was saved by Martha Jones before she died. Among the casualties was a freelance investigative journalist, Sarah Jane Smith, who had died after disabling the MRI scanner.

ELECTION COUNTDOWN

TUESDAY: 2 DAYS TO GO

Professor Richard Lazarus of Lazarus Laboratories held a televised press conference to announce that evening's unveiling of the results of his lifetime's work – an experiment that would change the future of the human race. By his side was Letitia Jones, LazLabs' new head of public relations, appointed thanks to the intervention of would-be Prime Minister Harold Saxon. Saxon was also behind the funding of LazLabs' work, acting through his intermediary Lady Thaw, and he arranged Tish's appointment to ensure the presence at the LazLabs event of several members of her family – her mother Francine, her brother Leo, and her sister Martha, a medical student at the Royal Hope and current travelling companion of the Doctor. Saxon sent an unidentified agent to the LazLabs launch, who quickly tried to make the Jones family suspicious of the Doctor.

THE LAZARUS EXPERIMENT

The Genetic Manipulation Device developed by Professor Richard Lazarus was a sonic microfield manipulator which used hypersonic soundwaves to create a state of resonance that would destabilise its subject's cell structure. The subject – Lazarus himself – was placed inside the device and a metagenic program manipulated the coding of his protein strands, instructing his genes to rejuvenate. Although there was a system overload during the procedure, with the Doctor narrowly averting an explosion, the 76-year-old Lazarus emerged from the GMD restored to a physical age of 40.

The process left Lazarus with a huge appetite, due to an energy deficit, which he had expected. He had not, however, predicted that his DNA would continue to fluctuate, or that he would be unable to control the mutation of his body. The GMD had changed his molecular patterns, activating a dormant aspect of his DNA that quickly became dominant. This was an evolutionary possibility that had been rejected millions of years earlier, when the human race had developed in its stead. The potential remained, inert and locked away in humanity's genes, until the GMD reactivated it in Lazarus, causing him to mutate into a gigantic, exo-skeletal creature that resembled a scorpion three times the size of a man. He retained his sentience, memories and speech, but periodically transformed into the creature. In this form, he rampaged through LazLabs, feeding on the life essence of its human victims and reducing them to dried-out husks.

The Lazarus creature trapped the Doctor and Martha Jones inside the GMD and switched it on, but the Doctor was able to reverse the machine's polarity. This caused the capsule to reflect not receive energy, which the Doctor directed at the creature in an attempt to destroy it. Lazarus, however, proved resilient and escaped to nearby Southwark Cathedral.

21ST-CENTURY LONDON

SOUTHWARK CATHEDRAL

A place of Christian worship had been established at this location on the south side of the River Thames by 1086, making it one of the oldest churches in London, although it did not become a cathedral until the early 20th century. The building itself was constructed between 1220 and 1420, and it survived everything from the Great Fire of London to the Second World War. During the Blitz in the early 1940s, Southwark Cathedral became a place of refuge from the nightly bombing raids, with locals including the young Richard Lazarus regularly sheltering in the crypt.

When Lazarus returned to the sanctuary of the Cathedral 66 years later, the Doctor, Martha and Tish followed him and lured him to the top of the building's bell tower. As the Lazarus creature attacked the two sisters, the Doctor played the Cathedral organ, using the sonic screwdriver to maximise its volume. The resonance of the sonic vibrations from the Cathedral bell overpowered the creature and sent it tumbling to its death at the bottom of the bell tower.

T.S. ELIOT

Lazarus's poet of choice, Eliot (1888–1965) was a leading member of the early 20th-century Modernist movement in English literature. Lazarus quoted from his 1925 work *The Hollow Men*, while the Doctor also mentioned Eliot's allusion to the biblical figure Lazarus in *The Love Song of J. Alfred Prufrock* (1915).

RED HATCHING

As the Doctor and Martha Jones raced to prevent Red Hatching – armed with just a bow and arrows and with only twenty minutes left – the Doctor met Sally Sparrow outside her shop. Sally gave him notes she had kept on what had happened to her the year before, and which would happen to the Doctor in his future. Thanks to the Doctor and Martha, humanity would never know the danger it had faced from Red Hatching.

ELECTION COUNTDOWN

WEDNESDAY: 1 DAY TO GO

In the months and weeks leading up to Britain's general election, Harold Saxon quickly amassed overwhelming public backing – some reports suggest he had the votes of as much as 98 per cent of the population. Leading politicians from all sides abandoned their political parties to join his campaign, among them Conservative Member of Parliament Anne Widdecombe, whose message of support was posted on the Saxon website in the run-up to the election. Other media figures keen to display their enthusiasm for Saxon included Sharon Osbourne and boy-band McFly. The Saxon website also offered biographies of Saxon and his wife Lucy, and a number of uplifting political messages that were short on content but – everyone agreed – sounded good.

THURSDAY: ELECTION DAY

As the nation attended the polling booths to give Harold Saxon a landslide majority, anonymous members of his team were concentrating their efforts on 'the Jones Plan' – a strategy to locate and entrap Martha Jones and the Doctor through Martha's family. Martha's calls to her mother were bugged and intercepted by Saxon personnel, while Francine Jones herself was fed disinformation about the Doctor and encouraged to betray her daughter. The phone calls proved untraceable, however, because Martha was calling from a 42nd-century spaceship via Universal Roaming...

FRIDAY: RESULTS

"... what this country really needs, right now, is a Doctor – *Harold Saxon (London, 2008)*

With the votes all counted, Harold Saxon was driven to Buckingham Palace and invited by the Queen to form a new government. Returning to Saxon headquarters with his wife, Lucy, the country's new Prime Minister made a brief speech announcing that a sick country needed healing. He was then driven to the newly rebuilt and freshly reopened 10 Downing Street, where he was given finance reports, military protocols, EC directives, budget papers and policy recommendations, and chaired his first Cabinet meeting. His first act was to assassinate the members of his Cabinet. Saxon had also arranged for Tish Jones to be recruited to his office staff.

FIRST CONTACT?

In a live television address to the nation, the new Prime Minister condemned the previous government for its silence over recent alien incursions – the Slitheen, the Sycorax, the Cybermen, the Racnoss Webstar. He announced that a new alien race, the Toclafane, had made contact with him and offered great benefits to humanity. Diplomatic relations with this new species would begin the next day, and would be broadcast live on television. The UN went into emergency session, while the US Houses of Congress held a joint session and demanded that the US President take control of the situation.

President Winters then flew to Britain on Air Force One, insisting that he take over from Saxon as the Earth's representative and UNIT forces replace the British Army for the operation. Under policy directives drawn up by the UN Security Council forty years earlier, First Contact could not take place on any one country's territory, so the televised meeting with the Toclafane would take place on board the aircraft carrier *Valiant*.

At dawn on the Saturday morning, the US presidential mission, Saxon and his officials, UN representatives and UNIT operatives began to assemble on the *Valiant*'s flight deck and prepare for the global broadcast – by 7.58am, tehy had confirmed that Europe was online, confirmation was awaited from South America and they were tracking Japan. At 7.59am, all armed personnel left the flight deck, and television crews began to broadcast events from eight o'clock as President Winters began his speech of welcome to the Toclafane. When the Toclafane arrived, they killed Winters but, two minutes later, the watching world saw Harold Saxon gunned down by his wife. The Toclafane had vanished, UNIT was back in control and the crisis was over.

GREAT LIVES

HAROLD SAXON

A graduate of Cambridge University, Harold Saxon's achievements extended beyond academia. He was a former Rugby Blue who had also excelled in Athletics. He had published a bestselling novel, *Kiss Me, Kill Me*, and met his wife Lucy when she worked on his autobiography. At the peak of his business success, he established the Archangel communications network and moved into politics. As defence minister, Saxon ordered the destruction of the Racnoss Webstar on Christmas Eve 2007, helped design the *Valiant*, and quickly became the most likely candidate to be Britain's next Prime Minister. A day after achieving a record-breaking election landslide, he was fatally shot by Lucy Saxon, moments after murdering the US President live on TV. But Harold Saxon did not exist.

ARTHUR COLEMAN WINTERS

The elected President of the United States of America. Since the Master had disregarded UN protocols for dealing with extraterrestrial contact, Winters took the opportunity to assume the leading role in the negotiations, intending to brand the event as a US-led rather than UN operation, so securing his own place in history. Welcoming the Toclafane to the planet Earth and its associated moon, Winters described himself as the designated representative of the United Nations. He was promptly disintegrated by the Toclafane, under the direction of the Master.

THE MASTER

Reaching 21st-century Earth at the end of 2006, the Master assumed the guise of Harold Saxon. He met and married Lucy Cole, and took her to Utopia at the end of the universe, where they discovered the eventual fate of the last members of the human race. The Master returned to Earth with Lucy, where he set up the Archangel network and cannibalised the TARDIS to create a Paradox Machine. Within 18 months, he was Prime Minister and immediately established himself as the new ruler of the Earth, using the Paradox Machine to bring the Toclafane 100 trillion years back in time to control and enslave the people of the Earth. The Master built a huge fleet of war rockets, intending to wage war on the universe and found a new Gallifrey. After a year of misrule, he was fatally shot by Lucy Saxon.

TOCLAFANE

When the Master and Lucy Saxon reached Utopia 100 trillion years in the future, they discovered that the last surviving humans had conducted experiments on themselves in an attempt to outlive the universe. These last humans had dispensed with bodies and limbs, retaining only their heads which they installed into technologically advanced metal spheres. The spheres were heavily armed with blades and laser weapons and could fly, while the human remains contained inside them had a species-wide telepathic link. This self-mutilation had sent them mad, leaving them with

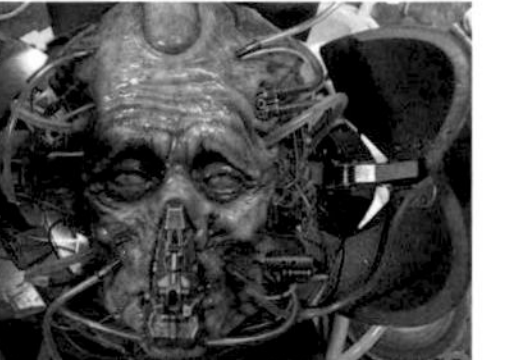

no purpose beyond survival and destruction – they killed because it was fun. The Master devised a plan to transport the spheres, which he named Toclafane after a Gallifreyan fairy tale, to 21st-century Earth, where they could establish a new empire that would last another 100 trillion years. There they killed more than 600 million people, and enslaved the rest, acting as the Master's mobile and seemingly invulnerable security force. Over the next twelve months, just one Toclafane was destroyed – in South Africa – by a random lightning strike with a current of 58.5 kiloamperes transferring a charge of 510 megajoules. Martha Jones used these readings to attack and capture a second sphere.

ARTS AND MEDIA

PRESS

Vivien Rook of the *Sunday Mirror* managed to talk her way into Downing Street to interview Lucy Saxon, revealing that she'd discovered that Harold Saxon did not exist – his entire biography had been faked. Saxon admitted to Rook that he was in fact the Master, then summoned some Toclafane to murder her. Before going to Downing Street, however, the journalist had sent her evidence to Torchwood.

BROADCASTING

BBC News 24 provided constant coverage of the general election through to Saxon's return from Buckingham Palace and his first speech as Britain's new Prime Minister. Later the same day, all UK television channels carried Saxon's announcement of first contact with the Toclafane. There was also news of a government-ordered nationwide hunt for a group of dangerous terrorists – the Doctor, Martha and Captain Jack (or 'the Captain', as News 24 labelled him). On the CBeebies channel, normal service continued with the *Teletubbies*.

By the evening, News 24 was telling viewers that the eyes of the world were on Great Britain and that US President Arthur Winters had been invited by the Prime Minister to receive the new species – the presidential plane *Air Force One* had been seen over British airspace.

On AMNN, Trinity Wells told Americans that the USA would be assuming control, with President Winters flying to Britain to take charge. According to AMNN, Winters had been chosen to lead the world into a new age. In China, state television announced that it would be illegal for the country's citizens to view the broadcast from Britain, and any that did so would be arrested.

'YOUR LORD AND MASTER, PLAYING...'

- *Voodoo Child* – Rogue Traders
- *I Can't Decide* – Scissor Sisters

SCIENCE AND TECHNOLOGY

ARCHANGEL

A network of 15 satellites orbiting the planet Earth, Archangel provided mobile communications for much of the population and carried signals for all the other service providers. The network constantly broadcast a second, hidden signal to all users, which affected the subconscious of 98 per cent of the population of Great Britain – layers of code contained in a low-level hypnotic rhythm. This signal effectively convinced everyone that the Master was Saxon, made them blind to his invented history and convinced them to vote for him. As a result, even the Doctor had been unable to detect the Master's presence on Earth during the previous 18 months.

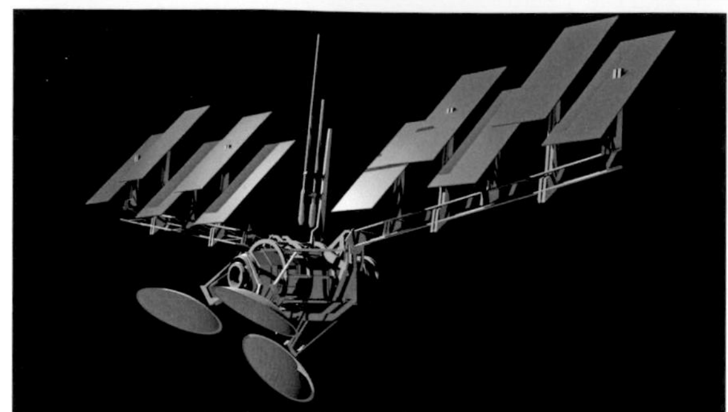

PERCEPTION FILTERS

Adapting the hypnotic signal from Archangel and the perception properties of the TARDIS, the Doctor constructed perception filters for himself, Martha and Captain Jack using TARDIS keys and components from a mobile phone and a laptop computer. The perception field he produced prevented people from noticing them – so long as they didn't draw attention to themselves – by shifting observers' awareness slightly. The Master, however, was unaffected by this perception field.

THE VALIANT

An airborne aircraft carrier, flying through the skies above Earth as the planet's first line of defence against alien attack. As defence minister, Harold Saxon had helped design the *Valiant*, equipping it with the most advanced technology available. The vessel was armed with the Jathaa weapon that Torchwood had used against the Sycorax in 2006. When the *Valiant* was selected as the scene for official contact with the Toclafane it was airborne, located at 58.2 degrees north, 10.02 degrees east. Having taken control of the Earth, the Master remained on the *Valiant*. He had already brought the TARDIS on board, and now intended to use the craft both as prison and headquarters. UNIT subsequently repossessed the *Valiant*, and a year later they took it into battle against the Sontarans.

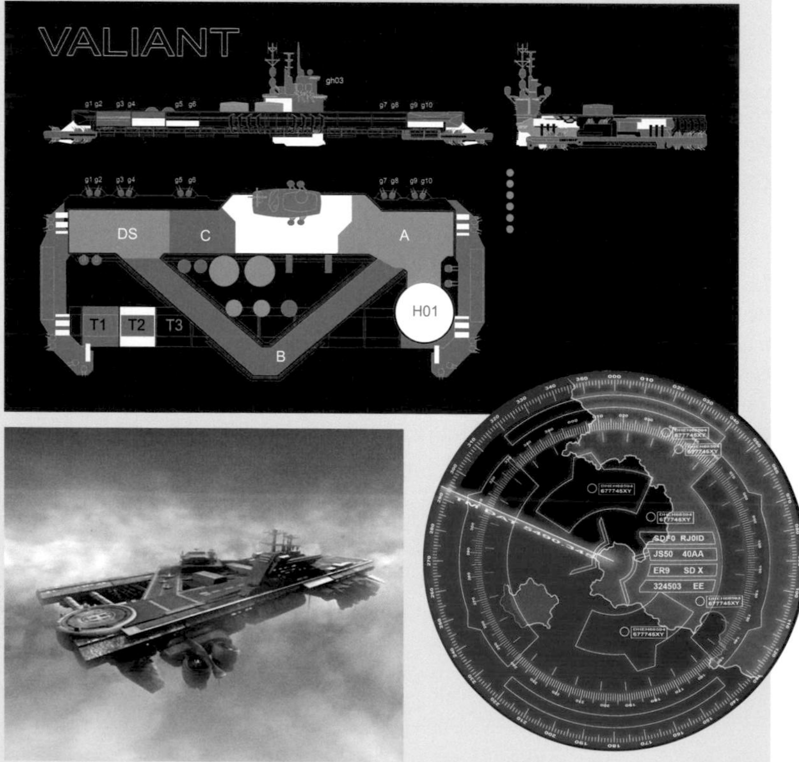

LASER SCREWDRIVER

A tool devised by the Master as a lethal equivalent to the Doctor's harmless sonic screwdriver. It was equipped with a laser beam that could kill or simply disable, and its controls were isomorphic – they responded only to the Master. It also contained a variation on the genetic manipulation technology devised by Professor Richard Lazarus. By inputting details of the Doctor's genetic code, the Master was able to suspend the Doctor's ability to regenerate and physically age his body, initially by 100 years and later to its full 900 years.

PARADOX MACHINE

By his own assessment, the Paradox Machine was the Master's greatest technical achievement. He had cannibalised the TARDIS to create the device, operating it to cause a tear in the fabric of space and time, through which the Toclafane could travel to 21st-century Earth and destroy their own ancestors.

CAPTAIN JACK HARKNESS

REPORTED SIGHTING #15 CONFIRMED

ESTIMATED AGE: 174

LOCATION: London, 2008

AVAILABLE INFORMATION: Using his Vortex Manipulator, Jack returned to Earth from Malcassairo with the Doctor and Martha in time to see the results of Britain's general election. Soon afterwards, the new government announced that the group were wanted terrorists. All three teleported onto the *Valiant* and attempted to stop the Master, but they were unable to prevent the arrival of the Toclafane.

TORCHWOOD

While Captain Jack accompanied the Doctor and Martha, the new Prime Minister sent the rest of the Cardiff-based Torchwood team to the Himalayas.

THE YEAR THAT NEVER WAS

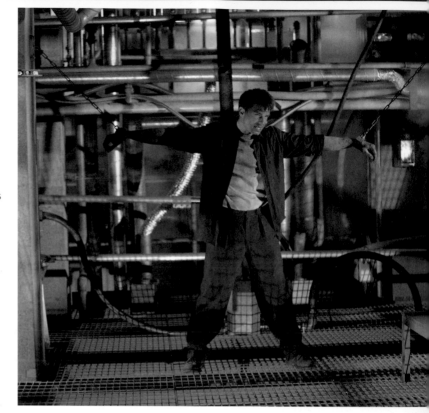

For twelve months, the Master and the Toclafane ruled the Earth. The population was decimated on that first morning and many more deaths followed, beginning with the Great Celebrity Purge of Week One. Famous victims of the Master's purges included billionaire software chairman Bill Gates and TV presenters Des Lynam and Des O'Connor. Millions more were killed when the islands of Japan were burnt, and again when New York was destroyed.

Some survived and resisted. Others survived and cooperated – the Master used human troops to enforce night-time curfews, and there were informers like Professor Allison Docherty, who worked unwillingly to betray the Resistance in the hope that she could save her son. The paediatrician Dr Tom Milligan was among those who appeared to cooperate with the Master, but he used his medical status as cover to allow him to travel and work against the new regime.

Huge statues of the Master were erected all over the Earth, and his image replaced the granite presidential memorial carved into Mount Rushmore in America's South Dakota. The planet's surviving population was rounded up and enslaved. At night, 100 people were packed into each house, with water but no food; each morning, they were put to work in enormous factories and shipyards built all over the planet. These shipyards stretched across the south coast of England, as well as much of Russia, from the Black Sea to the Bering Strait, designated Shipyard No. 1. Some 200,000 war rockets were built and equipped with black hole converters to attack and devastate the universe. They were powered by energy created in the Fusion Mills of China and the Radiation Pits of Europe.

Then, twelve months after he had taken control, the Master's plans reached fruition. A final three-minute countdown to the alignment of the black hole converters and the launch of the war rockets began. During that year, however, the Doctor had tuned his mind to the Archangel network and integrated with its matrices, which allowed him to draw on the psychic energy of the entire human race as they all chanted his name at the same moment. The network's satellites bound together their thoughts in

a telepathic field, and the Doctor reversed the Master's ageing effect. Shedding the 900 years that had been added to his physical form, the Doctor overpowered the Master, while Captain Jack attacked and destroyed the Paradox Machine. With the paradox broken, time ran backwards by a year and a day to the moment just after the death of President Winters. The Toclafane were returned to the end of the universe, while the population of the Earth lost all knowledge of a year that, for them, had never happened.

Only those aboard the *Valiant* knew anything of these events. Lucy Saxon had been driven mad by her trip to Utopia, by her husband's brutal treatment of her and by the year's events. She shot the Master. Martha Jones's family – Francine, Clive and Tish – had all experienced a year's slavery on the *Valiant* and would always remember the devastation and destruction. Captain Jack had been chained up and tortured, killed several times for the Master's amusement. Meanwhile, the Doctor had undergone a year's humiliation at the hands of the only other survivor of his race.

GREAT LIVES

MARTHA JONES

Having saved the Doctor's life in the Royal Hope Hospital on the first day she met him, Martha would end her travels with the Doctor having saved both the Time Lord and the world. As the Master assumed control of the Earth, Martha used Captain Jack's Vortex Manipulator to teleport back to the surface of the planet. Once there, she spent 365 days walking through every country, protected only by a perception filter. As she travelled, she met all the enslaved people that she could find, and talked to them.

Legends grew around Martha Jones – the only woman to escape the destruction of Japan, and the only one that could kill the Master. The stories told of a specially constructed gun, loaded with four specific chemicals, its parts hidden in San Diego, Beijing, Budapest and London. This gun, it was said, had been developed by Torchwood or UNIT as a defence against Time Lords like the Doctor and the Master and was the only thing that could kill a Gallifreyan and prevent him regenerating. When she returned to London after a year, she needed just one final chemical, stored, she said, in an old UNIT base in North London.

This story was a decoy for the Master, designed to lure him into taking Martha back to the *Valiant*. Martha had also told the people of the world about the Doctor – the man who had already saved them more times than they could ever know, and who would do so again. She instructed everyone to think of the Doctor, to say his name at the same time – the moment at which the countdown to the launch of the Master's war rockets would complete.

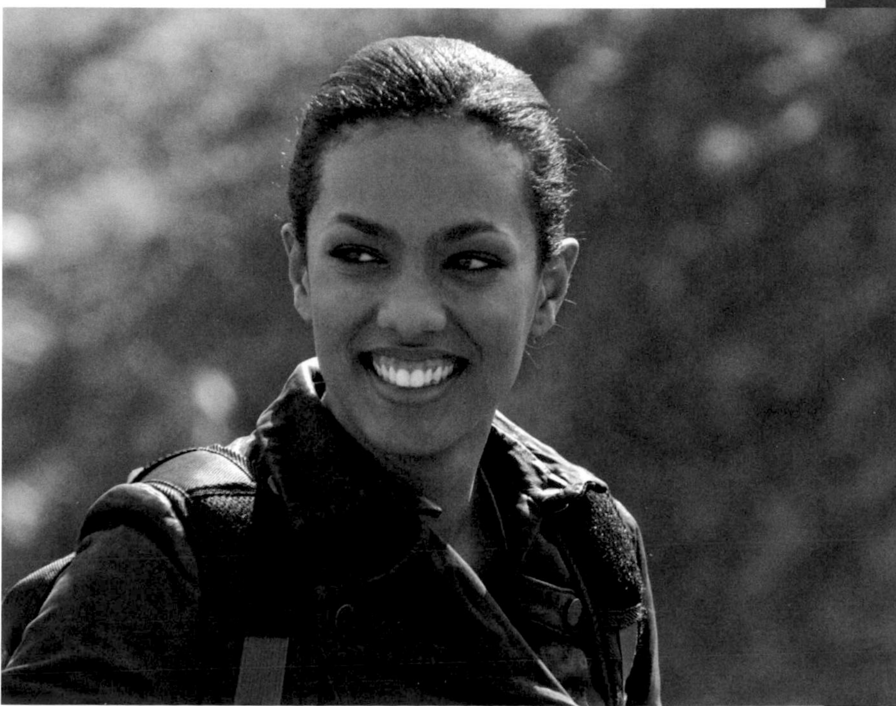

2008

TIME CRASH

In the wake of the destruction of the Master's Paradox Machine, the Doctor began to repair his TARDIS but forgot to put its shields up. Without protection in the Vortex, the TARDIS suffered a temporal collision – with an earlier version of itself. The two identical TARDISes merged with each other, their two different time zones both existing at the heart of the time machine and generating a paradox that threatened to blow a hole the size of Belgium in the space-time continuum within five minutes. With each passing moment, the emergency became more serious, the TARDIS's alert status rising from Level 5 to Level 10 in 55 seconds before the ship's cloister bell signalled the imminent creation of a black hole big enough to consume the entire universe.

Each TARDIS had, however, been carrying its own version of the Doctor – in his fifth and tenth bodies. The Tenth Doctor found that he already knew the solution to the problem, because he remembered being his fifth self watching his later self carrying it out. By venting the TARDIS's thermo-buffer, flooring the helmic regulator and frying the zeiton crystals, he managed to generate a supernova at exactly the same moment as the creation of the black hole, the explosion of the former cancelling out the implosion of the latter. Matter remained constant and the end of the universe was averted for another 100 trillion years.

The two versions of the TARDIS then separated, leaving the Tenth Doctor alone in his own TARDIS. Before he had time to restore the ship's shields, it crashed once again – this time into the prow of the starship *Titanic*.

THE FIFTH DOCTOR

The two TARDISes collided at a point in the Fifth Doctor's life when he was travelling with two companions, Nyssa of Traken and Tegan Jovanka. Together, they had averted a plot by the Cybermen to destroy 26th-century Earth during a peace conference, before preventing the return to this universe of a renegade Time Lord called Omega, and defeating the Mara, a mind-controlling entity, on the planet Manussa. When the time crash occurred, the co-existence of the two Doctors shorted out the time differential between them, temporarily causing the Fifth Doctor to look older than he had in his own timeline.

CAPTAIN JACK HARKNESS

REPORTED SIGHTING #16 CONFIRMED

ESTIMATED AGE: 175

LOCATION: Cardiff, 2008

AVAILABLE INFORMATION: With time reset to 8.02am two days after Britain's general election, the Doctor and Martha Jones dropped Captain Jack off in Cardiff and he returned to Torchwood.

BBC PROMS

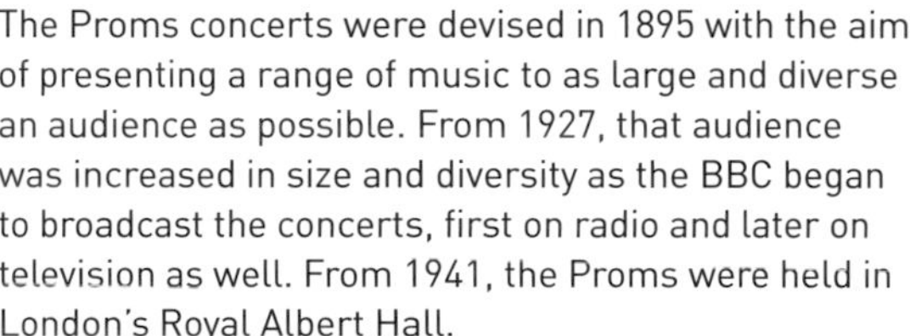

The Proms concerts were devised in 1895 with the aim of presenting a range of music to as large and diverse an audience as possible. From 1927, that audience was increased in size and diversity as the BBC began to broadcast the concerts, first on radio and later on television as well. From 1941, the Proms were held in London's Royal Albert Hall.

On Sunday 27 July, during the thirteenth concert in the 114th season of the Proms, a portal opened between the Albert Hall and the TARDIS. The Doctor took the opportunity to premiere *Ode to the Universe*, his own composition, which he had just completed. He passed the music through the portal to the BBC Symphony Orchestra, which began to play a piece that, the Doctor explained, had been inspired by the Music of the Spheres – the gravity patterns of the rotation of every planet, every sun and every galaxy in the cosmos, all fed through the TARDIS's harmonic filter to produce the sound of the universe. The Doctor drew his first symphony from this beautiful sound and produced what turned out to be an awful noise.

While both orchestra and audience took the opening of a hole in space in front of them fairly calmly, they were rather more surprised when a Graske managed to get through the portal from the TARDIS and started to run around the Albert Hall, attacking people with a water pistol.

Fortunately, the Doctor was able to reverse the polarity and teleport the Graske back inside his TARDIS. He then reverse-flipped the Graske's teleport and sent him to the other side of the universe, before closing the portal and allowing the Proms concert to continue.

STO

Sto is an Earth-type planet located in the Cassavalian Belt. It is home to a number of species, although its dominant life form is humanoid, having evolved to be very similar to human beings. Their civilisation is considerably more technologically advanced than Earth's – interstellar travel is now common enough for Sto to have a thriving interplanetary cruiseliner industry.

Society is highly stratified on Sto. There is an underclass of cyborgs, part organic and part machine, who have long been denied equal rights and have had to live in the Cyborg Caravans, separated from the rest of society. There have recently been moves to grant cyborgs the rights that they had previously been denied, allowing them to begin to integrate – even inter-species marriage has now been permitted in law. Generally, however, Sto society despises cyborgs. Some, like Bannakaffalatta and Max Capricorn himself, are forced to accept cybernetic augmentations through accident or ill health and old age, and they go to great lengths to disguise the fact.

At the next level of Sto society are its poor majority, who carry out menial labour, such as robotics maintenance, for very low wages – for Milk Market workers Morvin and Foon Van Hoff, for example, it would take 20 years to earn enough to pay off a vone bill of only 5,000 credits, while Bayldon Copper, a former travelling salesman, had never earned enough to buy his own home.

CURRENCY CONVERSION

- 1 Sto credit = UK £0.017857125
- 56.000056 Sto credits = UK £1.00
- 5,000 Sto credits = UK £89.285
- 56,000,056 Sto credits = UK £1,000,000.00

ZOCCI

While humanoids and robots dominate Sto society, other species do co-exist. Among these are the Zocci, a diminutive race with distinctively red and spiky skin and a vocabulary almost entirely free of verbs.

HEAVENLY HOST

An example of Sto's highly developed robotics technology, this particular android variant was designed to resemble the angels of Earth's Christian mythology, making them suitable staff for the *Titanic*'s cruise of primitive cultures as it took in an Earth Christmas. Extremely powerful, they had the strength of ten and were also able to fly, although their most basic function was simply to supply information to the passengers. Like most robots across the cosmos, they were programmed to assist and never harm the organic life forms they served but, also like most robots across the cosmos, it was quite easy to reprogram them to attack the survivors of the meteoroid strike that crippled the starship.

PLANET OF ORIGIN
Sto

APPEARANCE
Tall, metal, statue-like; golden faces and hands; folding wings; haloes supported above heads on metal struts

WEAKNESSES
An electromagnetic pulse wrecks their robotics

THE FASTEST, THE FURTHEST, THE BEST

Max Capricorn had been running his company for 176 years. By this time, age had taken its toll on his body – all that really remained of Max Capricorn was his head, sustained by a mobile life-support system. As a cyborg, he now had to hide himself away and had been running the business by hologram for several years before the company board voted him out. As the share price fell and Max Capricorn Cruiseliners began to fail, Max devised an elaborate plan to combine revenge with retirement. The 60-year-old captain of the *Titanic*, Hardaker, had only six months to live, and Max offered to provide financial support for his family if he scuppered the starship and caused it to crash into the Earth. The loss of the ship and its passengers and crew would cause the company's shares to collapse in value; the destruction on the planet would lead to the board being jailed for mass murder. Max himself would hide in an Omnistate Impact Chamber on the Host Storage Deck (Deck 31) of the cruiseliner, from where he could control the Host and ensure the success of his plan, and had arranged for employees to collect him from the wreckage on the Earth. He would then retire to the beaches of the planet Penhaxico Two, where the ladies were very fond of metal...

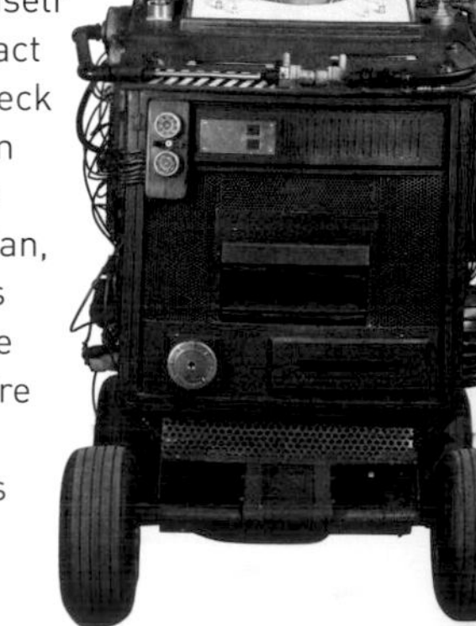

MAX CAPRICORN CRUISELINERS

THE STARSHIP TITANIC

LENGTH
912.4 metres

CONSTRUCTION
Nitrofine metal

DECKS
31

ENGINES
4 nuclear storm drives

The final voyage of the Starship *Titanic* offered its wealthy passengers the chance to experience primitive cultures, culminating in a Christmas-time visit to the planet Sol 3, also known as Earth. The cruiseliner was a replica of one of Earth's most famous vessels, an ocean liner that had crashed and sunk in the Atlantic Ocean in 1912, and the décor and crew were both designed to provide an authentic early period setting for the trip. With several onboard kitchens supplying Earth-type food and waitresses topping up the drinks, a band supplied a steady stream of traditional Christmas songs and the games tables offered the chance to make a few credits, while stewards and android Hosts catered for their passengers' every wish.

As the *Titanic* entered Earth orbit, Captain Hardaker took the ship's protective shields offline and magnetised the hull, drawing a nearby meteoroid storm onto a devastating collision course. With the starship's port side turning towards the planet, the meteoroids approached starboard from west 0 by north 2. As small chunks of burning stone preceded the main impact and began to shatter the starship's windows, the vessel's oxygen membrane remained in place, but the real meteoroid strike crippled the *Titanic* and immediately slaughtered all but 50 or 60 of its passengers and crew. The few survivors were then systematically murdered by the reprogrammed Heavenly Host. The ship's nuclear storm drive began to cycle down, leaving only minutes until the *Titanic* would lose orbit and hit the planet below, threatening massive destruction and loss of life on Earth in the resultant nuclear explosion.

The ship's internal communications were still operating, and the Doctor was able to talk to the only surviving crewmember on the Bridge, Midshipman Frame. He instructed Frame to fire up the engine containment field and feed it into the core, which temporarily kept the engines running. But Max Capricorn could control the engines remotely from Deck 31. He deactivated them shortly before waitress Astrid Peth forced him off the deck and into the heart of the nuclear storm drive, also sacrificing herself.

SCIENCE AND TECHNOLOGY

TELEPORT

Passengers on the *Titanic* were offered the chance to take shore leave and experience Christmas for themselves – a visit via teleport to London on Christmas Eve. Each passenger taking shore leave was given a teleport bracelet that connected them to the controls in one of the starship's Reception areas as their constituent molecules were beamed down and reassembled on the planet below.

The teleport had an emergency setting: in the event of accident, the user's molecules were automatically suspended and held in stasis. By triggering the shift feedback on the molecule grid and boosting it with the restoration matrix, it was possible to link up the surface suspension and restore the user to full health.

OMNISTATE IMPACT CHAMBER

An indestructible survival chamber – with its shielding at 100 per cent it could protect its occupant from anything up to and including a supernova. Max Capricorn concealed one on Deck 31 of the *Titanic*, draining the ship's own power to maintain his protection.

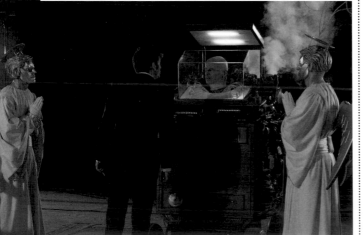

GREAT LIVES

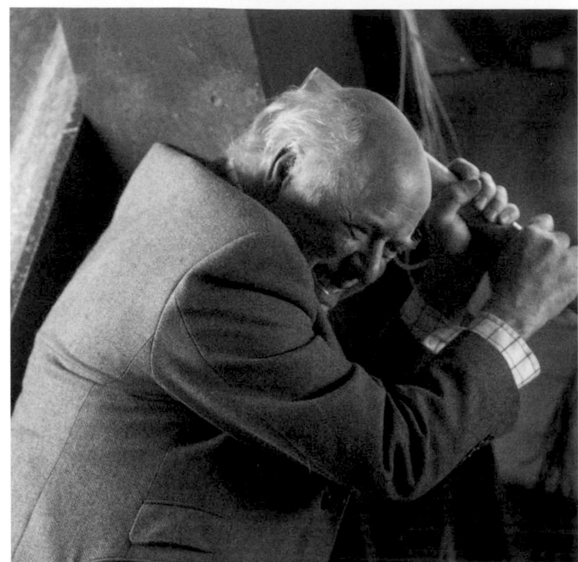

MR COPPER

Formerly a travelling salesman, when Bayldon Copper retired from selling robotics components such as electromagnetic pulse transmitters he took a degree in Earthonomics at Mrs Golightly's Happy Travelling University and Dry Cleaners. He exaggerated his academic qualifications and experience in order to secure the position of Ship's Historian aboard the *Titanic*, in which capacity he conducted brief tours of the primitive cultures that the ship visited. Mr Copper was one of just three survivors of the *Titanic*'s final voyage, but was worried that his falsified qualifications would earn him a ten-year prison sentence when the rescue ships reached the stricken cruiseliner. The Doctor used the ship's teleport to take Mr Copper to Earth. There, they discovered that Mr Copper's company credit card would make him a rich man. For the first time in his life, he had money and would be able to afford his own home. Mr Copper bought himself a house – with a garden and a door and a kitchen, with chairs and windows and plates. Having bought himself a home, he still had change from his million pounds. Inspired by his experiences with the Doctor, he used the money to set up the Mr Copper Foundation. The Foundation funded and created the Subwave Network, a piece of sentient software. Programmed to locate former associates and travelling companions of the Doctor at times of emergency, the Subwave Network was further developed by former Prime Minister Harriet Jones and would be used for the first time just months later...

HISTORY

MR COPPER'S HISTORY OF CHRISTMAS

The Earth continent of Yooropee includes the countries Great France, Great Germany and, separated by the British Channel, Great Britain, also known as Yookay, and they are all at war with the continent of Hamerica. Yookay's capital city is Old London Town, and the country is ruled over by Good King Wenceslas. The people of Earth are a barbarous, warlike race, who worship the great god Santa, a creature with fearsome claws. Their celebration of Christmas is a festival of violence, by the end of which the only survivors are those who have been good. Each year, the people of Yookay go to war against the country of Turkey; they then eat the people of Turkey for Christmas Dinner, which makes a change from the usual Earth delicacy – 'beef'. Soon afterwards, the Earth people start boxing.

LEFT TURN

Its engines failing, the *Titanic* began to fall towards London. The Doctor managed to pilot the ship as it fell, using the heat of entry into the Earth's atmosphere to ignite the secondary storm drive. Uncertain whether he would manage to steer clear of Buckingham Palace, he phoned a secure number, identifying himself and giving the emergency code 771, before warning officials to evacuate the Palace. He then managed to clear the building and fly the craft back out into space. Among the few non-Royals that had remained in London was Wilfred Mott, a newsvendor and the grandfather of Donna Noble. He briefly met the Doctor who had joined a party on shore leave from the *Titanic*.

CHRISTMAS AND THE ARTS

CHRISTMAS FAVOURITES

- *One Horse Open Sleigh (Jingle Bells)* – James Lord Pierpont (1857)
- *Winter Wonderland* – Felix Bernard (1934)
- *I Wish It Could Be Christmas Every Day* – Wizzard (1973)
- *The Stowaway* – Yamit Mamo (2007)

VONE-IN COMPETITION

Morvin and Foon Van Hoff won their tickets for the *Titanic*'s Christmas voyage by calling a competition hotline. The successful entrant had to name all five husbands of Joofie Crystalle in *By the Light of the Asteroid*, a popular TV show widely known as 'the one with the twins'.

UK TV NEWS

On Christmas Eve, BBC News 24 concentrated on the mass desertion of London. After alien attacks over two successive Christmases, many people thought that the city would suffer again on 25 December. Royal correspondent Nicholas Witchell told viewers that the Queen was remaining in Buckingham Palace to show people that they had nothing to fear. On Christmas morning, newsreader Jason Mohammad reported that the country had escaped alien intervention, just as the *Titanic* was plunging towards Buckingham Palace...

RIGHT TURN 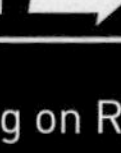

Acting on Rose Tyler's advice, Donna Noble used a winning raffle ticket for a luxury break in a country hotel to take her mother, Sylvia, and grandfather, Wilfred Mott, away from London for Christmas. On Christmas morning, a hotel maid told Donna that she had something on her back, and she caught a glimpse of a black, insect-like creature in the mirror. But the creature seemed to vanish, and she was quickly distracted by television news reports of a replica of the *Titanic* plunging towards Buckingham Palace. The spaceship's nuclear storm drive exploded and destroyed London. Southern England was flooded with radiation and seven million people were left homeless.

2009

PLANET OF ORIGIN
Various Adiposian breeding worlds

APPEARANCE (NEWBORN)
Approximately 15 centimetres tall; white; undeveloped arms and legs (two of each); black eyes; single fang

ADIPOSE

The Adipose are a race of creatures entirely composed of fat. They reproduce asexually, seeding other life forms and absorbing fat from their bodies until a single kilogram has been amassed to form a tiny, self-sustaining body. The child Adipose then separates from its host. It feeds on fat, but can also convert bone, hair and internal organs, although these elements make the child feel sick. A fully grown Adipose is 4.5 metres tall.

Their last breeding planet was Adipose 3, but the planet had been stolen by the Daleks as part of a plan to create an ultimate weapon – the Reality Bomb. Galactic law prohibits the Adipose from seeding developed planets, but the loss of Adipose 3 forced the Adiposian First Family to seek a new breeding planet. They hired a wet nurse, Matron Cofelia of the Five-Straighten Classabindi Nursery Fleet, Intergalactic Class, to foster a new generation of Adiposian children. Matron Cofelia illegally selected a Level Five planet called Earth, planning to use its human occupants as surrogates.

LEFT TURN

More than a year after meeting the Doctor, Donna Noble was still searching for signs of him. She had set out to travel the world, but had found the tourist trek round Egypt unfulfilling after battling a giant red arachnid in a secret base below a major London landmark. She'd taken a secretarial job with the Health and Safety Executive, but walked out after two days. Donna had then moved back to her mother's house and devoted herself to tracking down the Doctor, following up strange stories in the press or on the internet, and looking into UFO sightings, crop circles, sea monsters, a series of bizarre events in Cardiff and internet reports of the disappearance of the world's bees. Eventually, an online report led her to Adipose Industries. Pretending to represent the HSE, Donna got into the Adipose offices to investigate...

RIGHT TURN

In the aftermath of the destruction of London and with millions of the survivors from across southern England homeless, Britain had an Emergency Government and was under martial law. France closed its borders, and those left in Britain were living in wartime conditions. Having lived in a hostel since Christmas, Donna, Sylvia and Wilf were allocated housing in Leeds. They were billeted in a small terraced house, but they were not alone: the seven-strong Merchandisi family had the upstairs rooms, while Rocco Colosanto, his mother and his wife, his wife's sister and her husband and all their children occupied the front and back rooms on the ground floor. The Nobles took up residence on camp beds in the kitchen. The country's best and only hope was a promise of £50 billion financial aid from the USA...

ADIPOSE INDUSTRIES

'The fat just walks away'

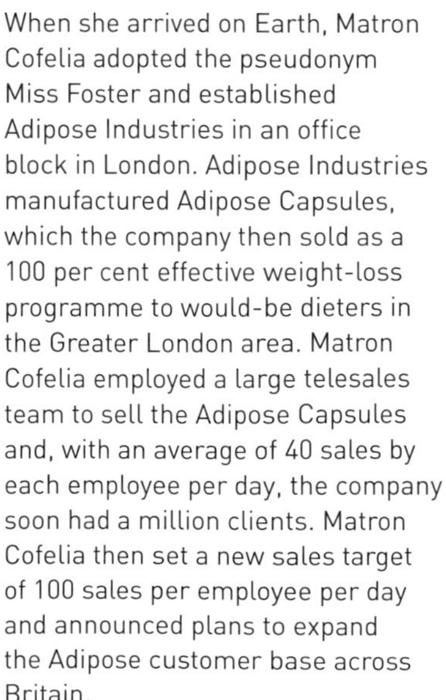

When she arrived on Earth, Matron Cofelia adopted the pseudonym Miss Foster and established Adipose Industries in an office block in London. Adipose Industries manufactured Adipose Capsules, which the company then sold as a 100 per cent effective weight-loss programme to would-be dieters in the Greater London area. Matron Cofelia employed a large telesales team to sell the Adipose Capsules and, with an average of 40 sales by each employee per day, the company soon had a million clients. Matron Cofelia then set a new sales target of 100 sales per employee per day and announced plans to expand the Adipose customer base across Britain.

For £45, each client was supplied with a box containing 21 Adipose pills (one capsule for each day of a three-week course), alongside an information pack and a free gift: an 18-carat gold pendant. The complete package was delivered by registered post within three working days of receipt of payment. Every customer reported a steady loss of exactly one kilogram of excess fat per night for the duration of the course.

Adipose Client Base (extract)

Stacey Campbell, 23 Marsley Street, Haringey, London N4 5DB ✦ Melanie Darforth, 12 West Vaughn Street, Haringey, London N8 2TC ✦ Roger Davey, 16 Candleford Street, Haringey, London N4 5DE ✦ Colin Stretton, 41 Clement Street, Barnet, London N12 7GG ✦ Ciaran Thompson, 9A Dartmore Road, Tower Hamlets, London E9 9FZ ✦ Ellen Highbury, 45C Juniper Avenue, Tower Hamlets, London E2 3LA

SCIENCE AND TECHNOLOGY

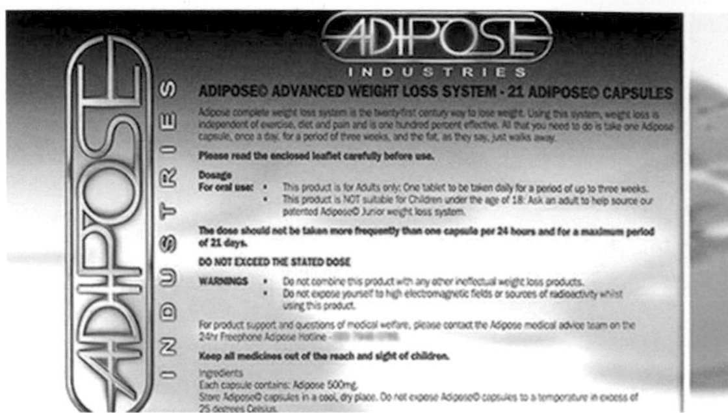

ADIPOSE CAPSULES

According to Adipose Industries, the Capsule was composed of a synthesised mobilising lipase, bound to a large protein molecule. The mobilising lipase broke up the triglycerides stored in the adipose cells, which then entered the bloodstream and were flushed away. In fact, the Adipose Capsule bound the excess fat together to form an Adipose child. This parthenogenetic process was triggered by a bioflip digital stitch contained in the gold pendant given to each customer, and the capsule contained in each pendant bio-tuned itself to its user after a single touch. Matron Cofelia was able to regulate and monitor parthenogenesis in each customer, although the introduction of a second raw capsule that had not been bio-tuned could induce unscheduled parthenogenesis, which Donna inadvertently triggered for Stacy Campbell. Matron Cofelia induced full parthenogenesis, and Stacy died as her entire body converted.

LEVITATION POST

Matron Cofelia wired up the entire Adipose Industries office block to convert it into a levitation post to assist herself and the Adipose children in their ascent to the Adipose Nursery Ship.

THE ADIPOSE NURSERY SHIP

A huge, brightly illuminated black disc that revolved on a central spindle and had numerous spokes along its radii. The Nursery Ship arrived to collect the Adipose children, but the Adiposian First Family, aware of the illegality of using a Level Five planet as a breeding world, let Matron Cofelia fall to her death. The spaceship was later intercepted by the Shadow Proclamation and the children were taken into care.

MEDIA

THE OBSERVER

A national Sunday newspaper, its science correspondent Penny Carter also had her suspicions about Adipose Industries and its miracle weight-loss programme. Having discovered that the Adipose test results had all been faked, Penny attempted to conceal herself in the building and search through the company records but was discovered and held prisoner.

LEFT TURN

With her plans under threat from the Doctor, Matron Cofelia decided to advance the birthplan and trigger Emergency Parthenogenesis – all users of Adipose Capsules would be entirely converted. This would cause the deaths of a million people across London as their skeletons and internal organs were converted into Adipose tissue. The Doctor was able to override and cancel Matron Cofelia's signal, halting the breeding programme. Ten thousand Adipose had been born, but there had been no further human deaths.

RIGHT TURN

In their kitchen-home in Leeds, Donna, Sylvia and Wilf watched AMNN's news of millions of deaths across America. Trinity Wells reported that sixty million Americans had simultaneously dissolved into fat. Countless Adipose children were marching through the streets of every major city in the United States of America. Enormous Adiposian Nursery Ships hovered over each city, transporting the Adipose children up through the air and on board before flying away. The crisis in America ended hopes of US aid for Britain.

PLANET OF ORIGIN

Sontar

APPEARANCE

Humanoid; 1.5 metres tall; grey-brown skin; bulbous head, resembling baked potato; three fingers on each hand; armoured

WEAKNESS

A blow to the probic vent at the back of the neck stuns or kills

BATTLE CRY

Sontar-Ha!

SONTARANS

Devoted to a life of warfare, the Sontarans are the finest soldiers in the galaxy. They reproduce through cloning, with batches of millions grown in each hatching. They have been at war with the Rutans, a race of shape-shifting amphibians, for 50,000 years, a war which will continue for millennia. Their one significant weak point is the probic vent at the back of each warrior's neck, which means that every Sontaran must always face his foe, and Sontaran officers think it an honour to be permitted to remove their helmets and enter battle openskinned. They have no fear of death, which makes them even more formidable opponents.

The Sontarans were aware of the Last Great Time War between the Time Lords and the Daleks, and they considered it the finest war in history. They were not, however, allowed to join it, perhaps because they have only the most rudimentary time-travel technology based on osmic projection.

As part of their ongoing war effort, the Sontarans have conquered or destroyed thousands of worlds across the galaxy, converting some into clone worlds on which to breed new armies. This was the intended fate for the Earth. To this end, General Staal devised a plan to take over the Earth by stealth, converting its atmosphere to one composed of clone feed by ensuring that hundreds of millions of atmospheric conversion devices were spread across the planet...

Sontaran Officers

- General Staal of the Tenth Sontaran Battle Fleet ('Staal the Undefeated')
- Commander Skorr of the Tenth Sontaran Battle Fleet ('Skorr the Bloodbringer')
- Lieutenant Skree of the Tenth Sontaran Battle Fleet

GREAT LIVES

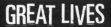

LUKE RATTIGAN

A child prodigy, Luke Rattigan was already demonstrating advanced skills and development for his age by the time he attended his local primary school in 1990. Identified as gifted in mathematics and science, within two years he had been moved to a specialist school, where he proved able to understand elementary quantum physics. At the age of twelve, he invented the Fountain Six Search Engine, which made him a millionaire overnight. In September 2005, Mensa experts pioneering new ratings systems for advanced IQ gave him a rating of 174 (Exceptionally Gifted). The following year, he used his wealth to purchase a mansion on Templeford Road in the Greater London borough of Richmond. There he founded a private school, the Rattigan Academy, established to make advances in science and technology. Handpicking 100 of the finest young academic minds and brightest talents from around the world, Rattigan quickly turned his Richmond-based Academy into one of the world's most productive and creative think tanks.

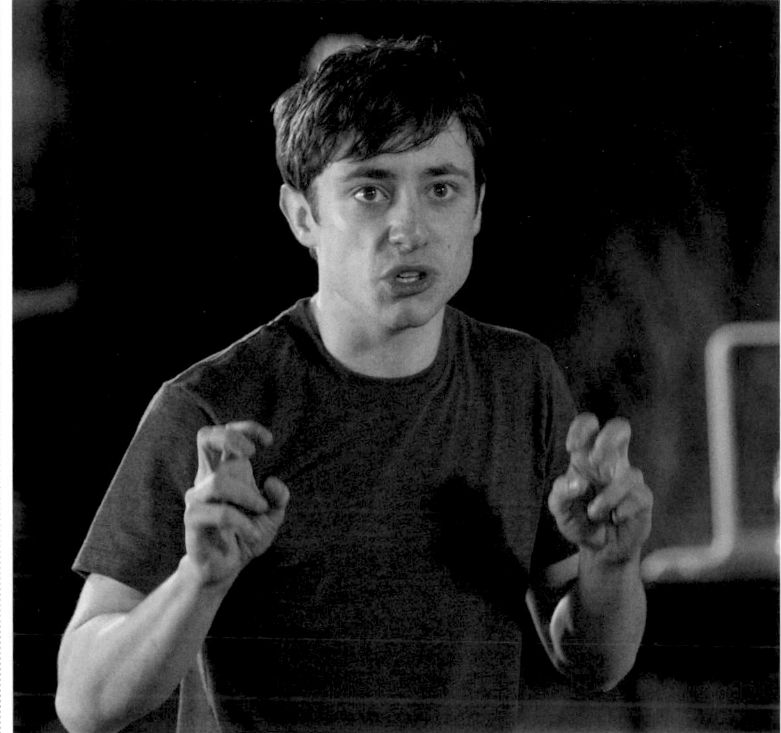

Luke's scientific advances eventually attracted the attention of the Sontarans, who saw an opportunity to turn the Earth into a new clone world. Capitalising on Luke's feelings of alienation, the Sontarans guided his experiments and inventions towards a goal of taking the Academy members to a new planet and making it habitable for a new race of intellectually superior humans. The Sontarans told him that they had identified a suitable planet – beyond Alpha Geminorum, the second-brightest star in the constellation Gemini, lay Castor 36, a planet suitable for colonisation. With Sontaran help, Luke developed the Atmospheric Omission System (ATMOS) and made plans for 'Planetfall' – the colonisation of Castor 36 – even devising a breeding programme for his hundred pioneering geniuses.

When Luke revealed his plans to the Academy students, they all thought he was mad and walked out. Discovering that he had been tricked by the Sontarans and Castor 36 did not exist, Luke was inspired by the Doctor to do something clever with his life. He saved the Doctor and sacrificed himself to destroy the Sontaran Warship orbiting the Earth.

MEDIA

JO NAKASHIMA

A freelance investigative journalist, whose suspicions of ATMOS led her to the Rattigan Academy. She confronted Luke Rattigan, whose students threw her out. Realising that what was at stake was too important to leave to the national press, she attempted to contact Colonel Mace at UNIT, ordering her ATMOS SatNav to take her to Tower Bridge. Instead, it drove her into the river, where she drowned, trapped inside her car.

TELEVISION

Once again the rolling television news services provided constant coverage of the situation once ATMOS had been triggered. Kirsty Wark was on BBC News 24, announcing the state of emergency declared by the British government and advising people to stay away from all ATMOS-fitted cars. AMNN's Trinity Wells brought the same message to American viewers. This was followed by a United Nations directive to the world's urban populations to stay indoors, as News 24 brought pictures of New York, Istanbul and Sydney shrouded in toxic fumes and Wark gave reports of thousands of people in Europe attempting to escape the gas on foot and of thousands more attempting to flee America's East Coast by boat into the Atlantic. Wells had similar stories – America's freeways were blocked by abandoned vehicles and hordes of people were walking across the country to escape what some saw as a Biblical plague signalling Armageddon.

UNIT

UNIT's Tower Bridge headquarters was alerted to the dangers of ATMOS by the concurrent deaths of 52 people in their cars and by the telephoned warning from journalist Jo Nakashima. Operating under the command of Colonel Mace, UNIT's Operation Blue Sky raid took over the ATMOS factory and established an on-site field base in a pantechnicon with computer connections to the world's information and communications resources, satellite and radar monitoring and nuclear arsenals. Mace also gave the go-ahead for Dr Martha Jones to summon the Doctor back to Earth.

Key Personnel

✦ Colonel Alan Mace (call sign: Trap 1)
✦ Captain Marion Price
✦ Dr Martha Jones (call sign: Greyhound 6)
✦ Private Carl Harris (call sign: Greyhound 15)
✦ Private Steve Gray (call sign: Greyhound 16)
✦ Private Ross Jenkins (call sign: Greyhound 40)

SCIENCE AND TECHNOLOGY

ATMOS

The Atmospheric Omission System was marketed as the means by which the Earth's 800 million cars could continue to be used without producing environmentally harmful emissions. With ATMOS fitted, a car's carbon emissions were reduced to zero, while purchasers were rewarded with a free satellite navigation system and £20 of shopping vouchers – the invention was enthusiastically taken up in every country, with half the world's cars fitted with ATMOS. There were 17 factories around the world with a central depot in London, and their hypnotised workforces managed 24-hour production of the devices.

On receiving a trigger signal from the Sontaran Warship, all 400 million ATMOS devices began to discharge clouds of a gaseous compound. This compound was 90 per cent carbon monoxide, hydrocarbons and nitrogen oxides, but the remaining 10 per cent was a Sontaran clonefeed called Ceasofine Concentrate, made up of one part Probic 5 and two parts Bosteen. By releasing this gas, the Sontarans intended to convert the Earth's atmosphere to create a ready-made clone world, at the same time wiping out humanity when the gas achieved 80 per cent density and became lethal to humans. Almost ready to begin the subjugation of Earth, the Sontarans tested ATMOS by sending their signal to 52 cars in different time zones across the globe at exactly the same moment.

ATMOS SATNAV

ATMOS offered the free installation of an in-car satellite navigation system to every customer. The SatNav received signals from orbital satellites to determine a car's position and guide its driver to a destination via both onscreen and spoken instructions. The ATMOS SatNav could be directed from the Sontaran Warship, enabling General Staal to override the system and take complete control of any vehicle fitted with the device. In this way, he killed an investigative journalist, Jo Nakashima, trapping her inside her car and driving it into a river. He attempted to do the same to the Doctor and UNIT driver Ross Jenkins, but the ATMOS SatNav had been programmed to disregard the Doctor's orders. By commanding it to drive them into a river, the Doctor was able to confuse the machine, which then exploded.

RATTIGAN ACADEMY INNOVATIONS

The Rattigan Academy was responsible for several technological advances, in areas including:
✦ biospheres ✦ ecoshells ✦ gravity densification ✦ gravity simulation ✦ hydroponics ✦ terraforming ✦ nano-tech steel construction ✦ single-molecule fabric

CORDOLAINE SIGNAL

A means of rendering projectile weapons ineffective: copper excitation causes the shell of a bullet to swell, jamming it inside the barrel of the gun. UNIT overcame the Sontarans' use of a Cordolaine Signal by using bullets coated in rad-steel, which prevented the expansion of the copper, allowing the UNIT troops to fight back effectively.

TELEPORT

The Sontarans installed a teleport pod in their cloning room inside the ATMOS factory depot in London, allowing Commander Skorr to lead an Attack Squad into battle against UNIT without having to fly scoutships into Earth's airspace. There was a second pod at the Rattigan Academy, and General Staal and Luke Rattigan used this to travel between the mansion and the Sontaran Warship. The Warship itself held several teleport pods, including one in the Sontaran War Room at the heart of the craft.

THE VALIANT

UNIT deployed its airborne carrier ship over the London ATMOS factory, initially using its huge fan-engines to disperse the Sontaran gas, before blasting the Sontarans inside the factory with the Jathaa laser weapon retrieved from the Torchwood Institute after the Battle of Canary Wharf.

LEFT TURN

When the Sontarans triggered the ATMOS devices, the Earth began to choke. As the gas released from the ATMOS devices reached 60 per cent density, UNIT became aware of the Sontaran Warship orbiting the Earth and initiated DefCon One, instigating a global nuclear assault – the nuclear weapons of China, France, India, North Korea, Pakistan, the UK and the USA were coordinated and targeted on the alien craft. The Sontarans were able to prevent the missile launches by using a clone of Martha Jones to access the NATO defence system via a remote link to UNIT's live mainframe, wiping the launch codes each time the countdown reached zero. The Doctor found and freed the real Martha, causing the clone to die, then teleported them all to the Rattigan Academy. With input from the Sontarans, Luke Rattigan had developed an Atmospheric Convertor, which the Doctor recalibrated to ignite and burn the Sontarans' clonefeed compound and restore the Earth's atmosphere. General Staal immediately ordered the initiation of Sontaran Stratagem One – ravaging the planet and wiping out all life. Resetting the Convertor again, this time to burn up Sontaran air so that it would destroy the aliens' Warship, the Doctor teleported into the War Room. General Staal refused the chance to withdraw his forces but, before the Doctor could activate the Convertor, Luke Rattigan teleported onboard, sent the Doctor back to Earth and blew up the Sontaran Warship.

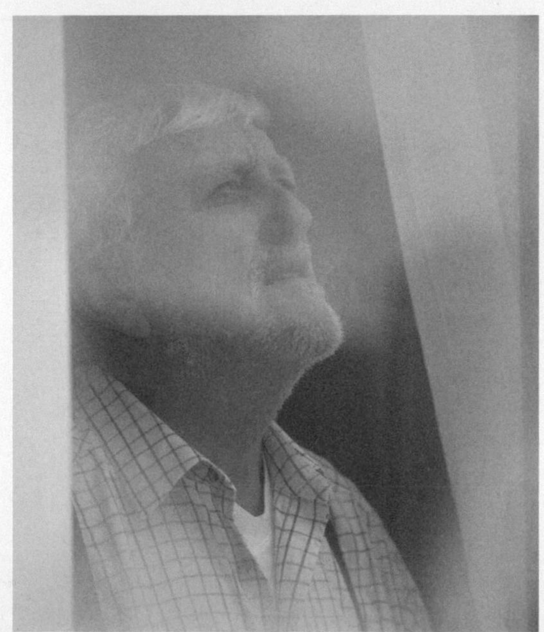

RIGHT TURN

When the Sontarans triggered the ATMOS devices, the already devastated Britain was relatively unaffected – the country was too poor to afford much petrol, so the majority of vehicles affected were military. But the rest of the planet began to choke in the clonefeed fumes. A soldier in Leeds, retreating from his gas-emitting jeep, thought he saw something black and insect-like on Donna's back, but when she turned around there was nothing there. Soon afterwards, Donna encountered Rose Tyler once again, who said that the last members of Torchwood were on the alien Warship, trying to stop the Sontarans. Moments later, Earth's poisoned skies began to clear as the Sontaran Warship exploded with the Torchwood team still on board, but not before Torchwood's leader, Captain Jack Harkness, had been transported to Sontar. Rose told Donna that the loss of Torchwood meant that Earth had no more heroes to defend it, and explained that the planet should have had a defender – the man whose corpse she had seen taken from the Thames Barrier on Christmas Eve 2007. She said that Donna should have been with the Doctor that night to save his life but that, in this version of the world, she had never met him – this made Donna the most important woman in creation. Something even worse was coming and, three weeks later, Donna would go with Rose to save the world – and would die.

2009

RIGHT TURN

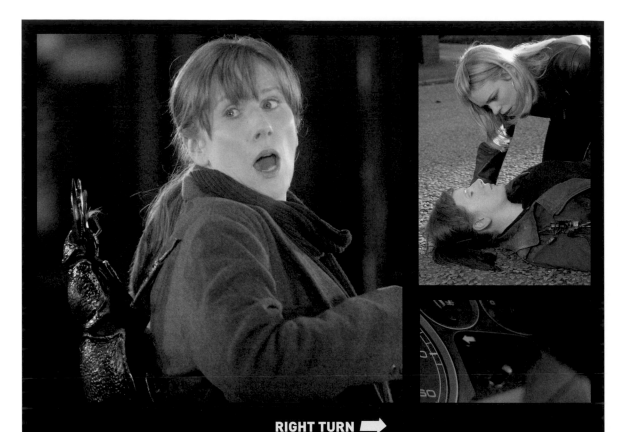

Following the ATMOS emergency, Britain's Emergency Government retrenched still further, pursuing a policy of England for the English and introducing new laws that apparently consigned all foreign-born residents to labour camps. The foreign families sharing the Leeds house with Donna, Sylvia and Wilf were shipped away on army trucks. With Wilf becoming ill and with no jobs available, even with the army, Donna was reduced to stealing soup to feed her family. And then the constellations disappeared from the sky...

With every version of Earth in danger, Rose Tyler had been pulled into this version of the world, where the only hope lay with Donna. She took Donna to a UNIT base and showed her the dying TARDIS, rescued from beneath the

Thames Barrier after the Racnoss attack. Revealing a huge black beetle on Donna's back that was feeding off the time energy caused by the disruption to Donna's timeline, Rose told her that the creature had made her take a single decision in 2007 that had prevented her from meeting the Doctor. Without Donna, the Doctor had died saving the Earth from the Racnoss, and without the Doctor there had been no one to protect the Earth from every subsequent alien incursion. The whole world had changed around Donna.

The TARDIS had identified the crucial moment and took Donna back to Monday 25 June 2007 to prevent herself from making the wrong choice. Unable to reach the right place in time, Donna sacrificed herself – she ran in front of a lorry that ran her down. In the ensuing traffic jam, Donna and Sylvia's car was unable to turn right out of Little Sutton Street to head for Griffin's Parade. Donna ignored her mother's protests and decided to...

TURN LEFT

DALEK CAAN

The last surviving member of the Cult of Skaro escaped Manhattan in 1930 using an emergency temporal shift. This took Dalek Caan back into the Time War, a journey that should have been impossible, since the whole War was timelocked. Travelling unprotected, Caan saw the whole of Time and was driven insane, but he managed to reach the Gates of Elysium in the War's very first year, where he rescued Davros from the jaws of the Nightmare Child. Davros's new race of Daleks kept Caan's remains – an opened, melted and warped Dalek casing, gutted of most of its innards but still holding all that was left of the Dalek mutant, an insane creature with a single blind eye – which they referred to as the Abomination. They listened to his prophecies and planned a final, devastating assault on the universe. But Caan had seen and understood the effect of his race throughout ime and space. He manipulated the timelines to bring the Doctor and his friends and Davros and his creations together in the right place at the right time to ensure the final end for the Daleks.

DALEK CAAN'S PROPHECY

He is coming. The threefold man, the Doctor, is coming... And death is coming. Everlasting death for the most faithful companion... So cold and dark and hot, fire is coming, the endless flames... The Doctor will be here as witness at the end of everything... The Doctor and his precious Children of Time... And one of them will die at the time of ending... The Doctor's soul will be revealed... The Children of Time will gather, and one of them will die.

2009

DAVROS

Rescued from the Time War by Dalek Caan, Davros immediately began to engineer a new race of Daleks. Each Dalek creature was grown from a single cell that Davros extracted from the remains of his own body. As they had before, his creations outgrew him and turned on him, imprisoning him in the Vaults of their Crucible ship. There he waited for the fulfilment of Dalek Caan's prophecies and the destruction of all things. He was last seen in the Vaults of the Crucible, as the Dalek ship was destroyed around him...

PLANET OF ORIGIN
Skaro

APPEARANCE
Half humanoid, half Dalek; dried-up skin; crystalline blue eye on forehead; single metal hand; black leather tunic; encased in the lower half of a Dalek casing

WEAPONS
Arcs of electricity shot from his artificial hand

MIGRANT BEES

Some of Earth's bumble bees were in fact from the planet Melissa Majoria. Perhaps sensing that the walls of the universe were breaking down, these migrant bees had abandoned the Earth and made their way home on the Tandocca Scale – a series of infinitely small wavelengths that the bees used as a carrier signal.

THE STOLEN EARTH

At eight o'clock London time, an ordinary Saturday morning sky was suddenly transformed into night, as a worldwide tremor on a scale greater than any earthquake left the whole planet in darkness. Above the Earth, in place of the usual starscape of the Milky Way, 26 planets could be seen. A cross-dimensional spatial transference had transported the Earth through space to a new galaxy. Surrounded by an artificial atmospheric shell that kept the planet's atmosphere intact, the Earth was now in the Medusa Cascade, part of a massive web of planetary orbits, at the heart of which lay a massive Dalek spaceship. Before long, a battle formation of 200 Dalek saucers was heading for the Earth, broadcasting a message for the human race: 'Exterminate!'

The Dalek fleet shot down UNIT's carrier ship *Valiant*, drove the air force out of the skies above North Africa, landed in Japan, destroyed the plane carrying the UK Prime Minister and targeted military bases across the globe. As they landed in each country, the Daleks began their Human Harvest, ordering humans to accompany them on board the saucers, exterminating anyone that refused or resisted.

MEDIA AND TV

Until the Dalek fleet arrived, the world's broadcasters continued much as usual. Continuous coverage of the latest worldwide emergency was brought to America by AMNN's Trinity Wells, who had news of a United Nations edict asking people not to panic. She had no explanation for the sudden appearance of 26 planets in the sky, but Professor Richard Dawkins correctly suggested on the BBC's all-channels news programme that all the evidence indicated that the planet itself had moved to an entirely new sector of space. Channel 4's *Paul O'Grady Show* went ahead despite the emergency, with O'Grady managing to make light of events. Shortly afterwards, 200 Dalek ships were spotted heading for Earth. News reports of the approaching alien fleet were the last things to be broadcast until the emergency was over.

THE SUPREME DALEK

The new race of Daleks that Davros had fashioned replaced their creator with a new leader, who directed the operation to destroy reality from the Command Deck of the creatures' new flagship, the Crucible. The Supreme Dalek was distinguished by its predominantly red casing. It was destroyed by Captain Jack Harkness with the Defabricator gun that he had first used against the Daleks in 200,100.

THE MEDUSA CASCADE

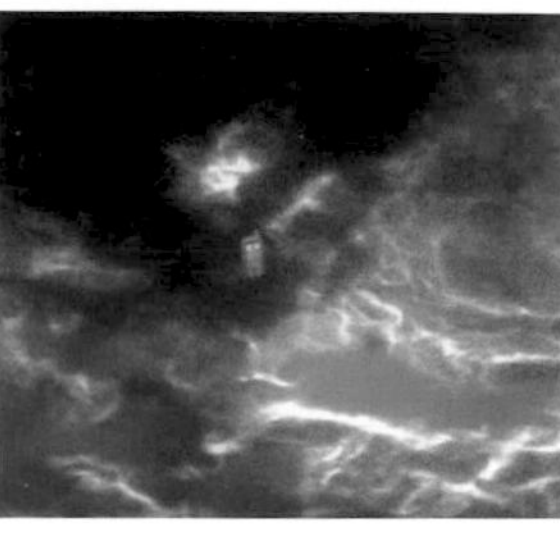

The Doctor first visited the Medusa Cascade when he was just 90 years old. An area of blue and gold gas clouds, it was the centre of a Rift in time and space which, according to the Master, the Doctor had once singlehandedly sealed.

The Daleks piloted their Crucible ship to the Cascade, and then began transporting whole worlds there to form an immense array.

THE PLANETARY ARRAY

A total of 27 worlds were transported across space to the Medusa Cascade and reassembled, like the pieces of an engine, to form a huge planetary array, one second out of sync with the rest of the universe. Of these planets, 24 had disappeared at exactly the same time, among them:

✦ Callufrax Minor ✦ Clom ✦ Earth
✦ Flane ✦ Griffoth ✦ Jahoo
✦ Shallacatop ✦ Strepto ✦ Woman Wept

Three others had been removed from other time periods:

✦ Adipose 3 ✦ The Lost Moon of Poosh ✦ Pyrovillia

The planetary array was held in perfect balance in an optimum moving pattern of slow orbits to form the Daleks' ultimate weapon. The Daleks had moved the planets by transmatting them along the same wavelength as the Tandocca Scale, which left a very faint, dust-like trail through time and space which the Doctor was able to follow to the Medusa Cascade.

THE CRUCIBLE

The Daleks' spherical command ship was many miles in diameter, studded and riveted in bronze and with six metal arms radiating from its centre. It was large enough to hold 200 Dalek saucers. The Supreme Dalek led from the vessel's Command Deck, while the lower levels contained the Vaults, where Davros and Dalek Caan were kept. At the centre of the Crucible was a core of Z-Neutrino Energy and, when the ship reached 100 per cent efficiency, it would become the heart of the Daleks' Reality Bomb. The Daleks tested the weapon on prisoners held in test areas on board the Crucible, and planned to shelter in the ship when they detonated the Bomb.

THE REALITY BOMB

When the Daleks activated the planetary alignment field of the array, the planets began to shine with haloes of Z-Neutrino Energy from the Crucible's core. The configuration of the 27 planets flattened that energy into a single string, as the array combined to form a transmitter that would send the compressed Energy along the Tandocca wavelength and across the universe. This was the Reality Bomb, and its detonation would separate every form of matter into its constituent particles by cancelling out the electrical field that binds atoms together. Those particles would crumble to dust, which would dissolve into nothing. Breaking through the Medusa Cascade's Rift into every dimension and parallel, on full transmission the Reality Bomb would destroy reality itself.

THE SHADOW PROCLAMATION

Staffed by a variety of species including the Judoon, the Shadow Proclamation is recognised as the ultimate authority by the majority of races across much of the cosmos on matters of law and security. Its codes of Articles and Protocols cover diplomatic relations and species categorisation, while its Strictures and Holy Writs empower the Shadow Proclamation to declare war and seize transport and technology.

The Shadow Proclamation is chaired by the Shadow Architect, a female albino dressed in black robes, and she is assisted by albino servants.

The Doctor has referred to the Shadow Proclamation during his attempt to negotiate with the Nestene Consciousness on Earth in 2005, and also expected the Pyroviles he encountered in first-century Pompeii to be aware of it.

When the Earth was removed from its orbit by the Daleks, the Doctor sought the aid of the Shadow Proclamation. Taking Donna there, he discovered that Earth was just one of 27 planets to have vanished from time and space and managed to track them to the Medusa Cascade. He and Donna left to follow the Tandocca trail before the Shadow Architect could commandeer the TARDIS for use in the war that she promptly declared against whoever had stolen all the lost worlds.

2009

ALIEN TECHNOLOGY

PROJECT INDIGO

Earlier in the year, UNIT had salvaged Sontaran technology from the ATMOS factory and the Rattigan Academy. This included the wreckage of the Sontarans' teleport equipment, from which UNIT scientists built their own prototype teleportation device – Project Indigo. Without the ability to input coordinates or stabilise the device, Project Indigo remained experimental, but UNIT ordered Martha Jones to use it to attempt to reach the Doctor once the Daleks began to invade. Project Indigo was an operator-worn harness, activated by pulling two cords, but Martha realised that it was controlled telepathically when it delivered her from New York to where she'd most wanted to go – her mother's house in London. A central panel on the harness – the key element of the salvaged equipment – displayed a string of numbers which UNIT had been unable to decipher, but which Captain Jack recognised as containing a teleport base code (oscillating 4 and 9). This base code not only reactivated Jack's broken Vortex Manipulator, it also gave Martha greater control over Project Indigo. She teleported to a Castle in Germany, the site of Osterhagen Station One.

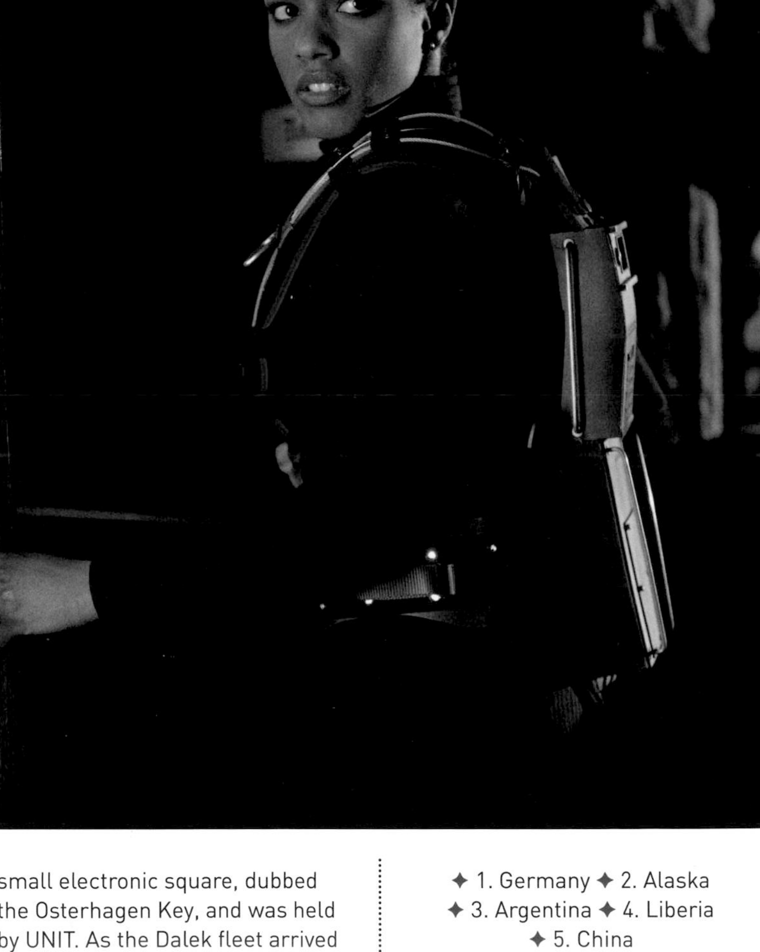

OSTERHAGEN KEY

With at least eighteen examples of alien aggression in just four years, Earth authorities agreed on a top-secret final solution, should the world ever be fatally compromised and the human race left without hope. A chain of 25 nuclear warheads were placed at strategic locations beneath the Earth's crust – their detonation would rip the planet apart. The trigger was a

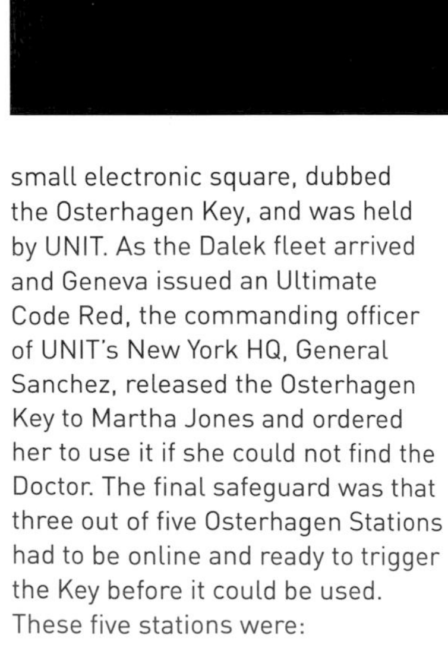

small electronic square, dubbed the Osterhagen Key, and was held by UNIT. As the Dalek fleet arrived and Geneva issued an Ultimate Code Red, the commanding officer of UNIT's New York HQ, General Sanchez, released the Osterhagen Key to Martha Jones and ordered her to use it if she could not find the Doctor. The final safeguard was that three out of five Osterhagen Stations had to be online and ready to trigger the Key before it could be used. These five stations were:

✦ 1. Germany ✦ 2. Alaska
✦ 3. Argentina ✦ 4. Liberia
✦ 5. China

Martha made contact with Stations Four and Five from the German station, and so had authority to detonate the nuclear arsenal. She contacted the Crucible and issued an ultimatum – if the Daleks did not leave the planet, she would destroy it. The Daleks used Defence Zero-Five to transmat her aboard the Crucible, leaving the Osterhagen Key in Germany.

SUBWAVE NETWORK

Former UK Prime Minister Harriet Jones had discovered that the Mr Copper Foundation had devised a Subwave Network, a piece of undetectable sentient software which Harriet developed to locate anyone who might help contact the Doctor during an emergency. The Subwave Network could hack into and even activate computer and communications systems across the world, and Harriet used it to make contact with Torchwood in Cardiff and Sarah Jane Smith and Martha Jones in London; the software also located Rose Tyler at Sylvia Noble's Chiswick home, although she was unable to communicate with the others and could only watch. With the planetary array a second out of sync with the universe, however, none of the Doctor's friends were able to contact him.

They combined forces, boosting their telephone signals with power from the National Grid and the Cardiff Rift, while Sarah's alien computer Mr Smith, running at 200 per cent, linked up with every telephone exchange in the world. With billions of phones calling the Doctor at the same time, the Subwave Network immediately became visible, and the Daleks despatched a saucer to Harriet Jones's house. Having opened the Network to its maximum, Harriet transferred it to Torchwood, while the signal continued to spread out from the Earth. The phone call pulled the TARDIS into sync with the Medusa Cascade and allowed the Doctor to talk to Torchwood, Sarah and Martha, with Rose still looking on. The Daleks were able to interrupt the transmission and Davros broadcast to the TARDIS, the first contact between the two since Davros's apparent death at the beginning of the Time War. The TARDIS then landed in London (Vector 7, grid reference 665).

WARP STAR

A warpfold conjugation locked inside a carbonised shell resembling a minute diamond on a chain, a Warp Star was given to Sarah Jane Smith by a Verron Soothsayer. Captain Jack wired it into the Crucible's mainframe from a test area antechamber and threatened to explode it, destroying the entire Dalek spaceship. The Daleks engaged Defence Zero-Five to transmat them to the Command Deck, leaving the Warp Star in the test area.

DIMENSION CANNON

Developed by Torchwood on the parallel Earth as a means for Rose Dimension Cannon allowed its users to communicate or physically cross from one universe to another by ripping a hole in the fabric of space. As the walls between the universes collapsed and the Void collapsed, these Dimension Jumps became easier, and Rose had already made several shifts when the Trickster's Beetle affected Donna. After the Dalek attack, Rose, her mother Jackie and Mickey Smith all used these yellow pendants to cross into this universe. The pendants also worked as a teleport within a single dimension, but required up to 30 minutes to recharge after each Jump.

TORCHWOOD

Once Harriet Jones had transferred the Subwave Network to Torchwood Three in Cardiff, the Daleks located and attacked the Hub. With Captain Jack in London, only Gwen Cooper and Ianto Jones were left to defend Torchwood, but a defence system developed by their late colleague Toshiko Sato placed the Hub in a timelock, trapping the Daleks in an instant in time as they entered the underground base but also shutting Gwen and Ianto inside the Hub.

UNIT

UNIT's HQ in Manhattan, New York, commanded by General Sanchez, was one of the earliest casualties of the Dalek attack. Martha Jones was able to teleport to London using Project Indigo, but her fellow operatives Jalandra, Wikowsky, DaCosta and Suzanne were all exterminated.

THE CHILDREN OF TIME

ROSE TYLER

Rose Tyler met the Doctor in 2005 during the attempted invasion by the Nestene Consciousness. She travelled with him from then on, witnessing the Coronation in 1953 and the end of the world in the year five billion, defeating assaults on the Earth by the Slitheen and the Sycorax, and fighting Daleks in 2012 and 200,100. Following the Battle of Canary Wharf in 2007, Rose Tyler was trapped on a parallel Earth that ran a little ahead of this one. Having some idea of what was to come, and still desperate to rejoin the Doctor, she used the Dimension Cannon to cross to this universe. She watched the approach of the Dalek fleet on a screen in an abandoned computer shop in London before deciding to track down Donna's family, saving them from capture by a Dalek, which she gunned down. Rose watched the conversation over the Subwave Network from the Nobles' house, unable to participate, but used the Dimension Cannon to lock onto the TARDIS once it was pulled in by the global phone call to the Doctor. She watched as the Doctor was struck down by a Dalek ray, and was with him in the TARDIS when it was brought on board the Crucible.

THE CHILDREN OF TIME

JACKIE TYLER

Jackie also first met the Doctor in 2005, and was terrorised by Autons during a late-night shopping trip. After close encounters with Slitheen and a killer Christmas tree, she took her first brief trip in the TARDIS to the Torchwood Institute just before the Cybermen invaded in 2007. Like Rose, she was then left on the parallel Earth, living with the parallel version of her late husband Pete and having a second child with him, called Tony. Always determined to protect her daughter, Jackie followed Rose back to this universe with Mickey. When she, Mickey and Sarah Jane were taken to the Crucible, Jackie almost became a victim of the Daleks' Reality Bomb tests, but her Dimension Jump pendant had recharged and she was able to teleport out of the test area.

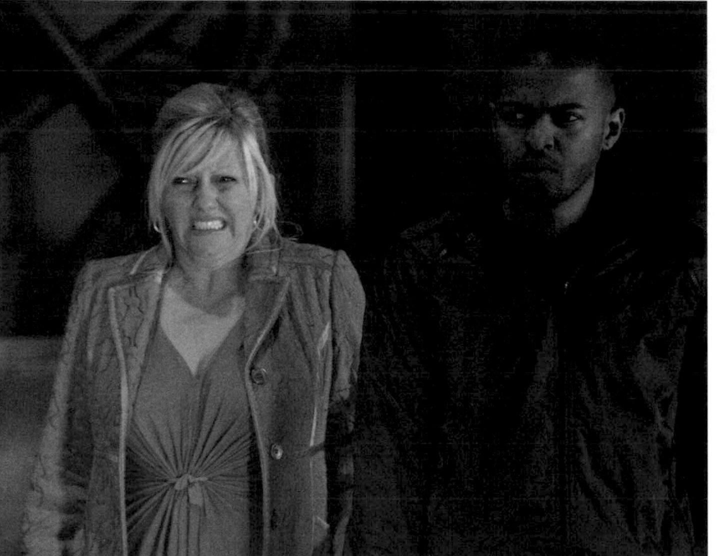

MICKEY SMITH

Having been copied by the Nestene Consciousness and attacked by Slitheen, Roboform Santas and Krillitanes, Mickey was the first to stay on the parallel Earth following the defeat of the Cybermen in 2007. He lived in Pete Tyler's mansion, looking after his Gran and continuing to defend the parallel world from Cybermen and other threats. When the Dalek attack began in this universe, Mickey used the Dimension Cannon to shift to London, arriving just in time to save Sarah Jane Smith from two Daleks. He, Jackie and Sarah Jane surrendered to the Daleks so that they could get inside the Crucible.

HARRIET JONES

After her political downfall at the end of 2006, the former UK Prime Minister retired to an old house in the country, still convinced that she had done the right thing in ordering the destruction of the Sycorax spaceship. She devoted herself to finding and perfecting ways to protect the planet from alien aggressors. One of these was the development of the Subwave Network, but connecting it to the world's telephone networks made the program visible to the Daleks, who tracked her down and exterminated her.

CAPTAIN JACK HARKNESS

REPORTED SIGHTING #17 CONFIRMED

ESTIMATED AGE: 2,065

LOCATION: Cardiff, London, 2009

AVAILABLE INFORMATION: When the Daleks invaded and Harriet Jones made contact with the Doctor's associates, Captain Jack was able to reactivate the teleport function of his Vortex Manipulator using the basecode from Project Indigo and locked on to the location of the TARDIS. Arming himself with the repaired Defabricator gun that he had used on the Game Station in the year 200,100, he teleported to London in time to see the Doctor hit by a Dalek ray. Jack himself was exterminated and almost incinerated on board the Crucible, but came back to life yet again.

THE CHILDREN OF TIME

SARAH JANE SMITH

The Doctor's former travelling companion was still a freelance investigative journalist, living at 13 Bannerman Road, Ealing, London with her adopted son, Luke, and a highly advanced Xylok computer she called Mr Smith. She had recently dealt with two attempts by members of the Slitheen family to exact revenge for their defeat in Downing Street in 2006, helped by Luke and their neighbour Maria, and their schoolmate Clyde, with occasional assistance from K-9. Taken aboard the Crucible with Mickey Smith and Jackie Tyler, Sarah gave Captain Jack the Warp Star and they attempted to hold the Daleks to ransom.

MARTHA JONES

When Martha first met the Doctor, he was one of four alien species that she encountered in the space of an hour. She went on to travel with him, meeting Shakespeare and Daleks, seeing a living sun and the 1969 moon landing, and protecting the Doctor for several weeks as he hid from the Family of Blood in 1913. She saved the entire world from the Toclafane and the Master, and then left the TARDIS, soon gaining her medical qualifications and being recruited by UNIT. Promoted to Medical Director on Project Indigo, Martha was at UNIT HQ when the Earth was stolen. She was the only person in the world with a phone number for the Doctor, but the signal was blocked and there was no way to reach him. UNIT's General Sanchez charged her with triggering the Osterhagen Key if she could not find the Doctor, and she teleported to her mother Francine's house in London and then to Germany before being taken to the Crucible by the Daleks.

DONNA NOBLE

The Dimension Cannon developed on the parallel Earth could measure the timelines of the separate universes, and revealed that they all converged on Donna. This was what had led Rose to find Donna when she was being affected by the Trickster's Beetle. But it was not the reason for the timelines' convergence. When the Daleks used a chronon loop to transfer the TARDIS onto the Crucible, Donna remained inside, drawn by the sound of a single heartbeat resonating back through time...

THE DOCTORDONNA

The Doctor, hit by a Dalek extermination ray, began to regenerate but he did not change his appearance this time. Instead, he healed himself and drained off the excess regeneration energy into the jar containing his severed hand. As he, Rose and Captain Jack entered the Crucible Command Deck, something kept Donna in the TARDIS. The Supreme Dalek ordered the TARDIS destroyed and, with Donna still inside, it was dropped down a metal shaft leading to the Z-Neutrino core of the Crucible. Donna touched the hand-in-the-jar, causing an instantaneous biological metacrisis: a new Doctor, seemingly identical to the original but in fact part human, grown out of Donna. He even shared some of her speech patterns. It was the single heartbeat of the Duplicate Doctor rippling back through time that had drawn Donna to the jar. Neither of them realised that it had been a two-way biological metacrisis – the process had fed back to her, remaining inert and waiting for the spark that would activate the Time Lord brain lying dormant in her mind.

With the original Doctor and Rose in Holding Cells in the Crucible Vaults and Martha, Captain Jack, Sarah, Mickey and Jackie under Dalek guard, the Duplicate Doctor built a Z-Neutrino biological inversion catalyser, planning to lock the Reality Bomb transmission onto Davros's genetic code. This would cause the Reality Bomb to backfire and destroy the Crucible. Their attempt to use it failed, and the Duplicate Doctor was placed in a Holding Cell. Donna was hit by an arc of electricity from Davros, and that provided the spark the Time Lord part of her needed.

The part-human, part-Time Lord DoctorDonna closed all Z-Neutrino relay loops with an internalised synchronous back-feed reversal loop, switching off the Reality Bomb. Davros attempted to kill her, but she activated a bio-electric dampening field with a retrogressive arc inversion to turn his electrical arc back on him. The Daleks fired on her, but she blocked their guns in a self-replicating energy blindfold matrix by macrotransmission of a K-filter wavelength, and then disabled them by using biofeedback shielding to exacerbate the Dalekenium interface, thus inculcating a trip-stitch circuit-breaker in the psychokinetic threshold manipulator throughout the Crucible. This caused the Daleks to lose control, making them vulnerable to all the prisoners that Donna released from the Holding Cells.

The Doctor, the Duplicate Doctor and the DoctorDonna then operated the Daleks' Magnatron together, reversing its settings and returning the stolen worlds back to their home systems. With only Earth left in the Medusa Cascade, the Vaults were attacked. Captain Jack destroyed the Supreme Dalek with his Defabricator gun, but not before it had damaged the Magnatron. Earth had to be towed home by a TARDIS operated by a crew of six: the Doctor, Rose, Martha, Mickey, Captain Jack and Sarah, assisted by Rift power provided by Torchwood

and harnessed around the TARDIS by Mr Smith and K-9.

There had never before been a two-way biological metacrisis between human and Time Lord, because the result was fatal to a human being – Donna's mind could not cope with the knowledge it had gained and it was killing her. The Doctor's only option was to wipe Donna's memory, removing all traces of him and their travels together. If she remembered him for a second, she would burn up. He took her back home to Sylvia and Wilf, and left behind a Donna Noble who no longer had any knowledge of her experiences since Christmas Eve 2007.

DALIG ULV STRANDEN

The Dalek race was, it seemed, entirely wiped out in the Medusa Cascade by the Duplicate Doctor, who maximised Dalekenium power feeds and blasted them back into the Crucible.

After this act of genocide, the Doctor realised that his other, part-human self was too dangerous to be left on his own. But he also realised that there was one person who could make the Duplicate Doctor better, because she had done the same for him. So he took Rose and the Duplicate Doctor, along with Jackie, to the parallel Earth before the universes were sealed off again.

The Doctor's final farewell to Rose once again took place at Bad Wolf Bay in Norway, but this time he was leaving her with a part-human Doctor who would share her life and age alongside her in a universe that also needed defending.

2012

GREAT LIVES

HENRY VAN STATTEN

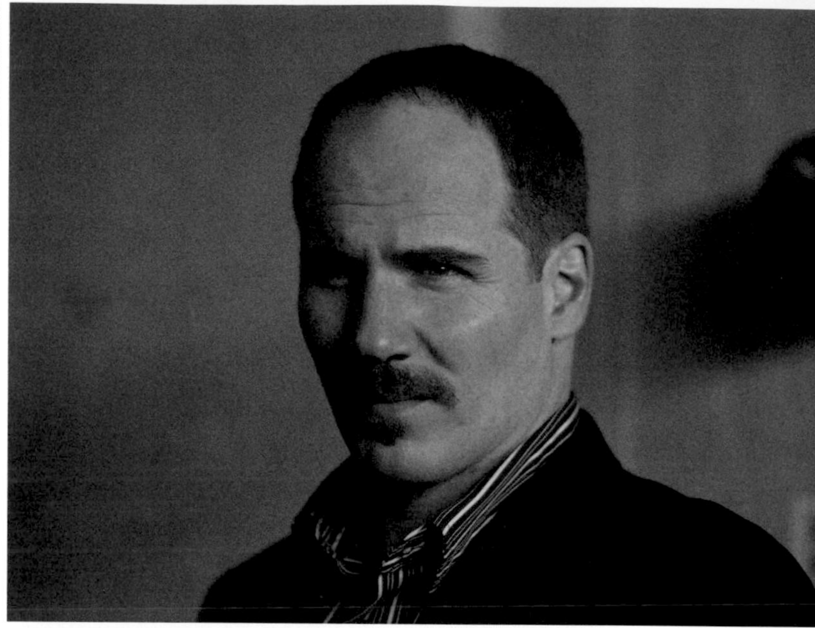

An American multi-billionaire who made his money during the dotcom boom of 1995–2001, Henry Van Statten became almost as well known for his interest in all things extraterrestrial. He founded the IT solutions company Geocomtex, which gradually expanded into every area of cutting-edge technology. Many of the company's technical and medical innovations were derived from recovered and scavenged alien objects. While few knew that Van Statten had become rich enough to secretly buy the entire internet, it was not unknown during the first few years of the new millennium for him to publicly discuss his belief that Earth had been visited by aliens many times. In the latter part of that decade, Van Statten became a recluse, retreating to a 53-storey base near Salt Lake City in Utah on the West Coast of America. From there Van Statten used his wealth to amass the most valuable collection of alien artefacts in the world, stored in the Exhibit Room in the Vault on the lowest level of the base, half a mile below ground, originally designed as a nuclear bunker. His headquarters were on Level 1 at the top of the base, a large oil painting of Van Statten adorning the wall of his private office, which had a lift running all the way down to Level 53. The base was topped by a helipad on which he could land his helicopter, *Bad Wolf One*.

As one of the richest men in the world, Van Statten was able to influence the political direction of America and therefore the world. US Presidents would call to wish him a happy birthday, though he showed no loyalty in return – he would instruct his staff to arrange the replacement of a President whose popularity was slipping, even deciding which political party the next US leader should come from. Such was the secrecy surrounding the activities in Utah, that any staff dismissed by Van Statten would have their minds wiped and be left on the streets of random US cities.

Van Statten disappeared from his Utah base on his birthday, soon after 400 of his employees were massacred by the prize of his collection. An alien creature that Van Statten had called a Metaltron was revived and escaped from its Cage. It was actually the last Dalek in the universe, which rampaged through the Vault, killing everyone it encountered. Geocomtex passed into the hands of Diana Goddard, Van Statten's chief aide, who ordered the entire Utah base closed down and filled with concrete.

Geocomtex

The Utah base was staffed by more than 400 employees – accountants, lawyers, public relations personnel, research scientists and armed security. Among Van Statten's workforce were:

Polkowski – Van Statten's chief aide, dismissed for disagreeing with Van

Statten over the replacement of the President. His mind was wiped and he was dumped on the streets of a US city.
Diana Goddard – Polkowski's replacement, who usurped Van Statten after the death of the Dalek.
Simmons – Given the task of forcing the captive Dalek to talk, he tortured it extensively, drilling into its casing and subjecting it to electric shocks. He was its first victim when it regenerated.
Adam Mitchell – A clever, 20-year-old from England, recruited by Van Statten to locate and purchase possible extraterrestrial artefacts across the world. His latest acquisition was an alien musical instrument for which he'd paid $800,000.
Bywater – A senior guard at the Utah bunker and an early victim of the revived Dalek.
De Maggio – Another senior guard at the bunker, charged with escorting Adam Mitchell and Rose Tyler to safety but also killed by the Dalek.

A selection from the Van Statten Collection

Van Statten: I wanted to touch the stars.
The Doctor: You just want to drag the stars down. Stick them underground. Beneath tons of sand. And dirt. And label them. You're about as far from the stars as you can get.

✦ Ape head ✦ Cyberman head ✦ Guns (various) ✦ Hairdryer ✦ Metal ore ✦ Metal from spacecraft hull ✦ Metaltron (Dalek) ✦ Meteorite chunks ✦ Moondust ✦ Robot ✦ Roswell milometer ✦ Slitheen arm

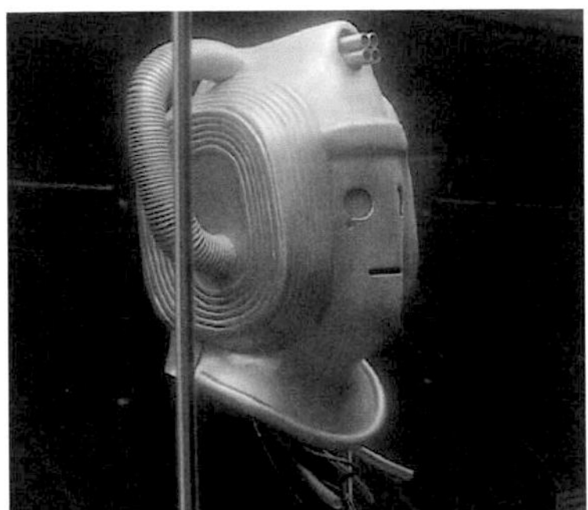

SCAVENGED TECHNOLOGY

Henry Van Statten's research scientists had made some significant scientific advances thanks to the alien technology that he had amassed. The materials recovered from Roswell in 1947 had ended up in the Utah collection and had, Van Statten claimed, allowed the development of broadband internet access. Bacteria from a crater in Russia had been cultivated to produce the cure for the common cold. Geocomtex had kept this cure secret, instead producing and marketing more profitable palliatives.

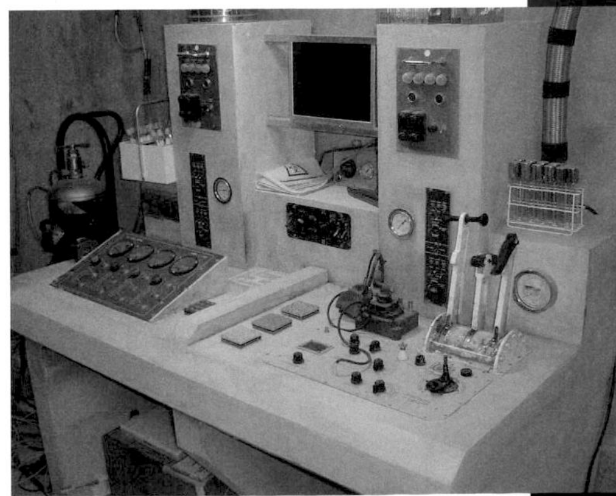

DALEKS (1)

The prize of the Van Statten collection was the Metaltron, an inert and unresponsive metal casing displaying signs of life that indicated that there was a creature inside the shell. It had arrived on Earth during the 1960s, falling like a meteorite and landing in the British Overseas Territory of Ascension Island, St Helena and Tristan da Cunha in the South Atlantic Ocean. On impact, it created a crater and remained inside for three days, burning and screaming, after which it was recovered by the military and concealed, before it passed through the hands of a series of private collectors and eventually ended up as the sole living specimen in the Van Statten collection after he bought it at auction in August 2006. Van Statten's pet was a badly damaged, rusted and insane Dalek, although no one at Geocomtex knew this, and Van Statten's people experimented on it at length, torturing it in a vain effort to force it to communicate. They did not succeed, although they quickly established that the creature was dangerous when a man who touched the Dalek's casing burst into flames.

Aside from broadcasting the distress signal that eventually drew the TARDIS to Utah, the Dalek remained inactive until it encountered the Doctor. He revealed that it was the last surviving Dalek in the cosmos, the only Dalek survivor of the Last Great Time War. It was then revived by Rose Tyler. Realising that Rose was a companion of the Doctor, the Dalek tricked her into touching its casing, which allowed it to feed off her DNA and extrapolate the biomass of a time traveller. This regenerated its casing and all its systems, restoring its eyestalk, sucker and gun to working order and enabling

PLANET OF ORIGIN
Skaro

ABILITIES
Flight; force-field protection; revolving central section; incredibly fast decryption and decoding; absorption of brainwaves

WEAKNESS
Concentrated firepower can damage the eyepiece or eyestalk

WEAPONS
Ray gun and sucker arm

DALEKS (1)

complete cellular reconstruction of the one-eyed tentacled mutant creature inside. A genius that could calculate 1,000 billion combinations in a second, it quickly escaped from the Cage before connecting to the Geocomtex mainframe via its sucker attachment and draining enormous quantities of power – first from the base, then from the whole of Utah and then from the entire West Coast of America. At the same time, it downloaded the entire internet, absorbing the sum of human knowledge and a massive quantity of trivia, gossip and telefantasy statistics. It accessed Earth's satellites and radio telescopes and scanned the galaxy for signs of Dalek life, but found nothing.

The Dalek then proceeded through the base, level by level, exterminating hundreds of men and women. Its force field made it effectively immune to the soldiers' bullets, which melted before they reached its polycarbide casing. Its gun attachment fired a deadly electrical force, and its revolving central section allowed it to gun down attackers on all sides without moving from the spot. The Dalek was able to override equipment such as cameras, doors and lifts and operate them remotely. While its sucker attachment could be used to extract or input electronic data and to scan organic brains and extract their brainwaves, it could also function with lethal force against individual humans, crushing their skulls. The Doctor suggested that the soldiers should concentrate their fire on

the Dalek's eyestalk – probably its weakest point – but they did not have the chance to try this before the Dalek exterminated them all. The creature was also able to fly, floating up the stairs through several levels of the base.

The absorption of Rose Tyler's DNA had contaminated the Dalek's own genetic structure, and the creature began to change. It gained emotions that it had never previously known, feeling pain and loneliness and an empathy with, especially, Rose that left it unable to exterminate her. Initially it had decided to follow every Dalek's primary order and follow the Dalek instinct to destroy and conquer. But the realisation that it had acquired feelings and compassion from Rose and that it was no longer a pure Dalek led the creature to yearn only for freedom and to feel sunlight on its unprotected body. It demanded that Rose order it to self-destruct and, when she did, it elevated a few metres into the air and imploded.

TIME IN FLUX

At this point in their timelines, the Doctor and this Dalek seemed to be the only survivors of the Last Great Time War – the last of their races. The Cult of Skaro were still inside their sphere in the Void and had yet to emerge in the Torchwood Institute and precipitate the Battle of Canary Wharf in 2007. The Empire State Building had been constructed without their interference, and the Earth had never been transported across the universe to the Medusa Cascade. Like Henry Van Statten, most of the human race had no idea what a Dalek was. With the death of the last Dalek, the Doctor was the unwilling victor of the Time War. Or so he thought...

(See also: 200,100; 2007; 1930; 2009)

ISOLUS

The Isolus children are tiny creatures that resemble flowers. They travel as an enormous family of four billion on an endless journey through space that began thousands of years ago in the Deep Realms. As the Isolus mother drifts through the stars, she jettisons fledgling spores by the million. The spores – her children – travel inside individual, very light, five-centimetre, dull grey pods, in which they ride the energy of the solar tides. These billions of brothers and sisters are intensely emotional and have an empathic link. Sustained by their mutual love and need for each other, they cannot be alone, and it takes them thousands of years to grow up. Throughout their travels, they use ionic power to create and animate fantasy worlds, where they play together and feed off each other's love.

Entering Earth's solar system, the Isolus passed too close to a solar flare, and a tidal wave of solar energy scattered their pods. A single Isolus dropped to Earth on Saturday 21 July, and was attracted by the high temperature of some freshly laid tar in a street in East London. Its pod was embedded in the road and began to absorb heat from the streets around it, while the Isolus sought the love it needed to survive. It quickly found Chloe Webber, a 12-year-old girl, whose alcoholic father had crashed his car and died some months earlier after several years of taking out his temper on the girl and her mother, Trish. Recognising in Chloe the same feelings of loss and need for love and company, the Isolus entered her body, in effect possessing her and sharing its powers to create and animate fantasies.

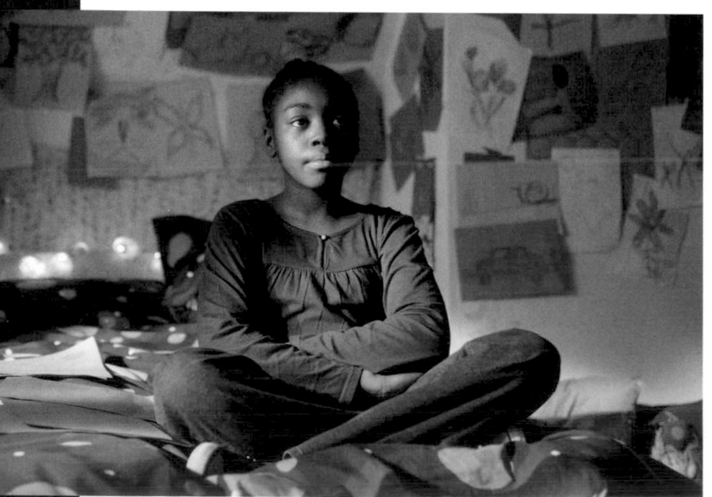

MISSING CHILDREN

Between Saturday 21 and Friday 27 July, three children (and a cat) vanished from Dame Kelly Holmes Close, a street on the approach to the Olympic Park. Danny Edwards had been riding his bike down an alley behind his house. Jane McKillen, 10, went missing on 23 July. Eleven-year-old Dale Hicks was playing football in a front garden on the morning of 27 July when he disappeared in front of his friend Tommy, Tommy's father and an elderly neighbour, Maeve. Police from the East London Constabulary questioned all the residents and put notices on lamp posts appealing for information or witnesses but without success.

XXX OLYMPIAD

OPENING CEREMONY

Held in London between Friday 27 July and Sunday 12 August, the 2012 Summer Olympics featured more than 300 athletes competing in 26 different sports. A specially constructed Olympic Park in the Stratford area of East London included a central stadium which played host to the traditional opening ceremony on the first day. The ceremony began with the raising of the Union Flag as the country's national anthem was performed, before the Parade of Nations, in which teams of participating athletes marched into the stadium, led by the Greek competitors and with the UK, as host nation, entering last. After speeches by the presidents of the organising committees, the Games were declared open and the Olympic Flag was brought into the stadium during the playing of the Olympic Anthem, at the end of which the Olympic Oath was spoken. The final stage of the opening ceremony was the lighting of the Olympic Flame from the Olympic torch, which had been carried around the world over the preceding weeks, the torchbearer making the final approach to the stadium through Central London, along the Strand and then east along the Thames

Embankment towards the streets of Stratford as the ceremony got under way. As the Flame was lit, a large firework display began, and street parties were held around the capital.

The queues for the opening ceremony had started a week earlier, and there was a capacity crowd for the evening's events. The entire occasion was televised live by the BBC, and several million television viewers watched in disbelief as all 80,000 spectators vanished from the stadium, along with hundreds of athletes, press reporters, TV commentators and police. Some minutes later, just as suddenly and without explanation, they all reappeared and the Games continued without further comment. The Isolus had used its ionic power to transform the stadium and everyone in it into the fantasy world of Chloe Webber's drawings. When Rose reanimated the Isolus pod using the heat from the Olympic torch and the euphoria of the watching crowds, the Isolus withdrew from Chloe and returned all the abducted people.

The athlete carrying the Olympic torch had stumbled as the Isolus pod connected with the torch, and some moments later he collapsed to the ground. But the day was saved by the Doctor, who picked up the torch and ran with it to the stadium, lighting the Olympic Flame that signalled the commencement of the Games, and sending the Isolus pod back out into space to rejoin its family.

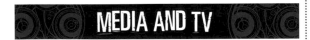

MEDIA AND TV

CRIME CRACKERS

A regional television show dedicated to helping the public help the police to crack down on crime, with the slogan *You CAN make a difference!* On 27 July, shortly after the disappearance of Dale Hicks, the show's producers filmed a short report and appeal for information that might help find the missing children of Dame Kelly Holmes Close. A telephone hotline number was given out by the show's energetic presenter. But by the time it was scheduled for broadcast, all three children had been safely returned to their families.

BBC NEWS 24

The news channel devoted itself to up-to-the-minute continuous live coverage of every stage of the run-up to and start of the Summer Olympics, with news anchor Huw Edwards providing commentary just as he had for royal weddings and state funerals. Edwards' reports followed the progress of the torchbearer through London's streets, and he was on hand when cameras showed a suddenly deserted Olympic stadium. Even his fellow commentator, Bob, had vanished from the stadium's press boxes. With Edwards very nearly but not quite lost for words, 80,000 people were just as suddenly returned to their seats, and the news coverage moved smoothly back to the streets of Stratford as the Olympic torch approached. The day's second disaster promptly struck, as the torch-carrying runner fell to the ground and an already tired and emotional Edwards promptly declared that the Olympic Dream was dead. When a mystery man took up the torch and ran with it to the stadium, Edwards' words must have summed up the nation's mood on seeing the Doctor rescue them from disaster: 'No one wants to stop him.'

SUPERPHONE

The Doctor took Adam and Rose from Utah to Satellite Five in 200,000. While there, Adam used Rose's mobile phone in an attempt to send a record of 197,988 years of technological advances back to his own time. The Doctor quickly discovered what he'd done and returned Adam to his Manchester home, staying long enough to destroy the answer machine that held the data. Adam was left in 2012 with an info-spike chip in his head.

2105

The Doctor: There you go. Step outside those doors it's the 22nd century.
Rose: You're kidding.
The Doctor: That's a bit boring though. Do you want to go further?

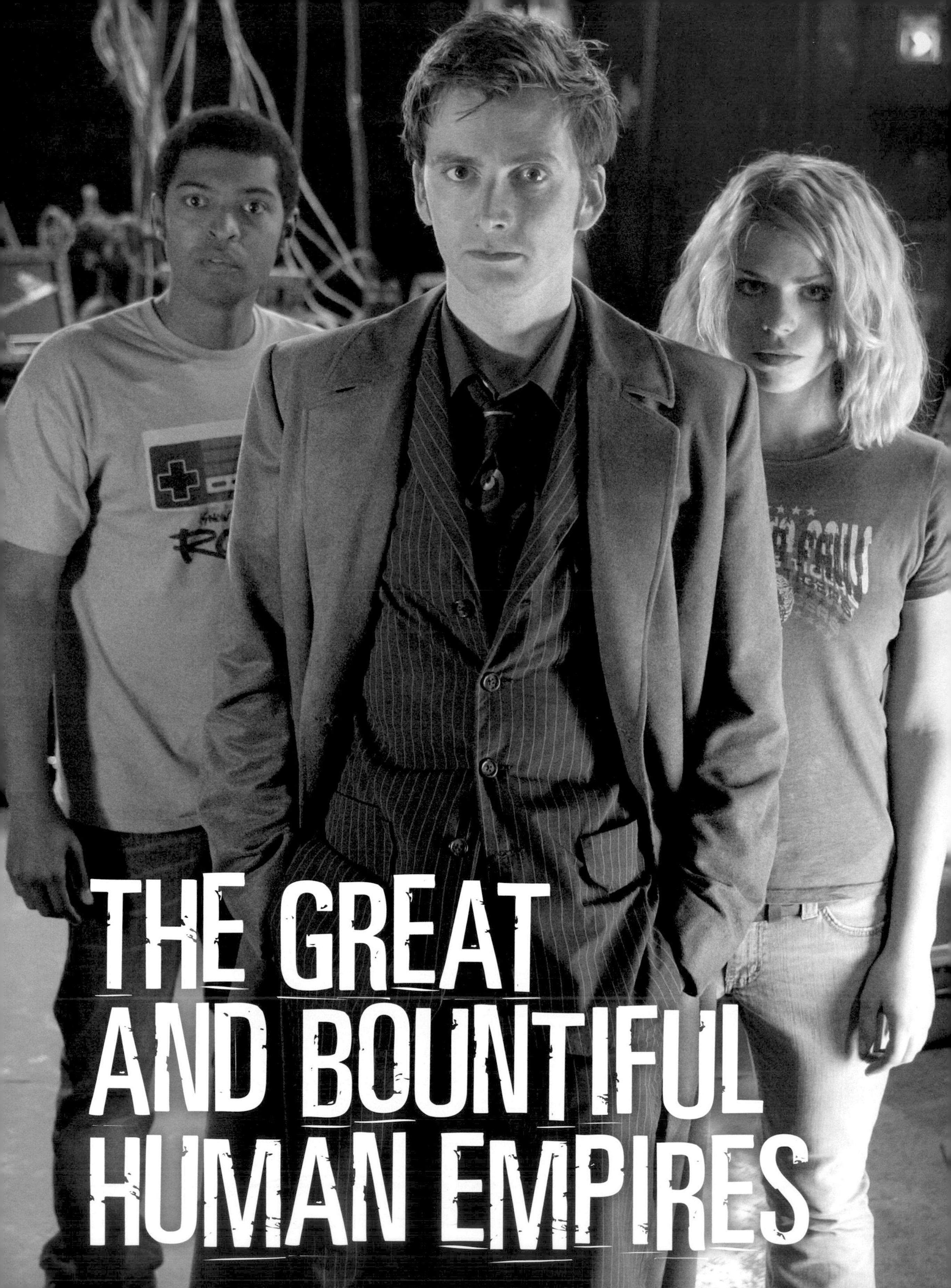

THE GREAT AND BOUNTIFUL HUMAN EMPIRES

NEW WORLDS

As humans developed the technology to reach beyond Earth's moon and then out of the solar system, they explored countless new star systems and planets, and met many new species. Sometimes these encounters led to new alliances; sometimes – as with the Daleks – wars broke out; and sometimes humanity expanded its reach and influence to form great empires. Often, humans were travelling in search of new minerals and natural resources, but, occasionally, they would visit a new world then simply leave again...

JUSTICIA

A solar system whose seven worlds were taken over by an expanding Earth empire. Justicia was the scene of Rose Tyler's first visit to an alien world with the Doctor.

SAN KALOON

According to the guidebooks, San Kaloon was famous for its Glass Pyramid. Also visited by Rose and the Doctor.

WOMAN WEPT

The planet took its name from its major continental landmass which, viewed from space, resembled a woman lamenting. The Doctor took Rose to see this planet's thousand-mile-long beaches, where a freak solar event had frozen the sea in an instant, leaving immobilised waves of ice suspended 30 metres into the air above them. The planet was one of the 27 worlds transported to the Medusa Cascade by the Daleks in 2009.

EXXILON

> **Sarah Jane Smith:** I saw things you wouldn't believe.
> **Rose Tyler:** Try me.
> **... Sarah:** Daleks. *(London, 2007)*

After the Dalek Wars, a space plague hit the Empire's outer worlds. The cure was parrinium, a mineral found on Exxilon. An Earth expedition to Exxilon was followed by a Dalek taskforce determined to prevent humans from securing parrinium. The Third Doctor and Sarah arrived to discover a greater problem: Exxilon's artificially intelligent city had reduced the race that created it to barbarism. It was draining all power from passing spaceships and preventing anyone from leaving the planet. The Doctor, the humans and the Daleks destroyed the city, and the Dalek saucer was blown up as it took off.

MIDNIGHT

The planet Midnight offers a beautiful vista – measureless plains of jagged diamond rocks stretch out beneath a bright sun through the Winter Witch Canyon towards the glacier-sized Sapphire Waterfall. The waterfall rushes towards the edge of the Cliffs of Oblivion on the Multifaceted Coast, where it fragments into a cascade of sapphires that pour a hundred thousand feet down into a crystal ravine. And the planet is deadly to all life.

Midnight is older than the Earth, yet it is a world without a history. It orbits an X-tonic sun in a lifeless star system. The planet has no atmosphere and is bombarded by the raw Galvanic Radiation of its sun's 100 per cent X-tonic rays, which have fused the planet's surface into solid diamonds. In places, great diamond canyons have formed, their shapes changing with every mammoth diamondfall. Any living being that attempted to walk on the surface of Midnight would be instantly vaporised. X-tonic light is inimical to every known form of life, from carbon-based bipeds and gaseous helixes to hydrogen-based micro-organisms and sentient silicates. No one has ever set foot on Midnight.

As the spacefaring pioneers of the human race began to move further and further out beyond their own solar system, they discovered Midnight. This new world had no people to conquer, and it couldn't be colonised or farmed. Its minerals had been poisoned by the X-tonic rays, and Professor Winfold Hobbes theorised that the sapphires of the Sapphire Waterfall were nothing more than a compound silica with iron pigmentation, which left Midnight with no value beyond its beauty. But humans have always found some way to exploit and profit from their discoveries, and eventually the Leisure Palace Company moved in.

27th Century

THE LEISURE PALACE

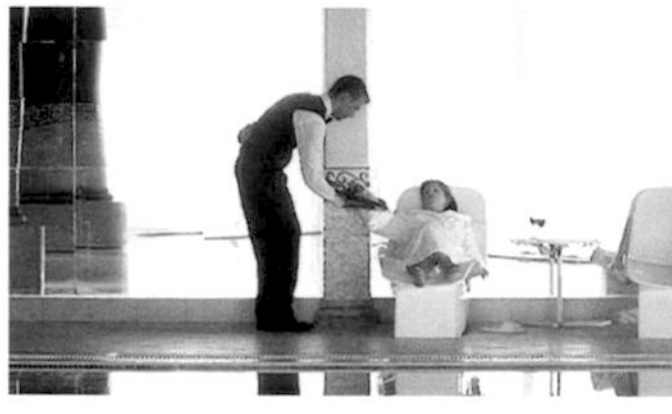

The Leisure Palace Company manufactured an immense city of interconnected glass bubbles, which was lowered down to Midnight's surface from orbiting spacecraft. Inside were all the luxuries necessary for an ultimate leisure world of spas, hotels, pools, sunloungers, shops and antigravity restaurants, all staffed by small armies of highly trained serving staff. For the first time since the planet's birth, life came to Midnight, surrounded and protected by 15-foot-thick Finitoglass.

CRUSADER TOURS

The Leisure Palace provided rest, relaxation and luxury, but it could not offer its visitors all the wonders of Midnight. Crusader Tours mapped a safe route from the Leisure Palace to the Multifaceted Coast and established Midnight's first and last tourist trail. An eight-hour round trip took the bored, the curious and the adventurous across 500 kliks of diamond plains to see the Sapphire Waterfall, from the safety of *Crusader 50*.

The *Crusader 50* was a large solid truck resembling a tank, with caterpillar treads and big headlights – a former explorer vehicle perfect for traversing Midnight's rocky terrain. Its box-like metal interior held seating for 24 passengers, with a TV screen sliding down in front of each seat. Toilets and a separate area for the tour Hostess were at the rear. At the front was the two-man driver's cabin, separated from the main part of the vehicle by an air-pressure seal. An entrance door and an emergency door consisted of two-hundredweight of hydraulics and toughened cast-iron, and both were also sealed. The windows that ran the length of each side and at the front of the driver's cabin were made from Finitoglass. This would give passengers a couple of minutes to view the Waterfall without risking sunburn when the bus reached the Waterfall Palace but, until then, all the windows were shielded with metal shutters. The engine ran on micropetrol and air was provided on a circular filter, theoretically sufficient to sustain the bus's passengers for up to ten years.

Onboard refreshments and facilities available from the Hostess

✦ Television (36 channels) ✦ Headphones
✦ Modem link for 3D vidgames
✦ Complimentary earplugs
✦ Complimentary slippers
✦ Complimentary juicepack (Peach & Clementine)
✦ Complimentary peanuts (warning: may contain nuts)

Crusader culture

✦ **Music Channel Retrovid**
Raffaella Carra – 'Do It, Do It Again' (Earth Classics)
✦ **Fine Art Projections**
Artistic Installations from Ludovic Klein
✦ **Children's Channel**
Betty Boop (Animation Archives)

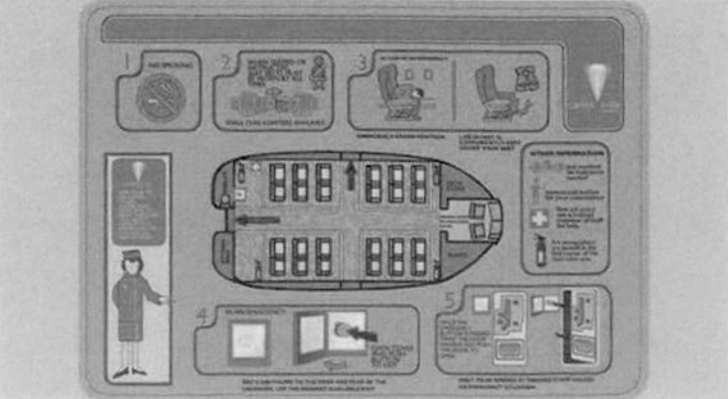

REPETITION

Crusader 50's final journey ended in the deaths of its driver, its mechanic, its Hostess and one of its passengers, Mrs Sky Silvestry. A diamondfall at the Winter Witch Canyon made a detour necessary, and the onboard computer automatically calculated a new course that took the bus 40 kliks west of its established route and into entirely uncharted territory. The bus was 251 kliks out from the Leisure Palace when it simply stopped – all the systems were operating properly, but *Crusader 50* would not move. The driver sent out a distress signal but then, impossibly, something started tapping on the exterior of the vehicle. Moments later, the entire driver's cabin was torn from the front of the bus.

Sky Silvestry began to repeat every single word that every other person said. Before long, she was repeating everything said by four or even six people at once, however complex. Then she started to catch up, synchronising with them and speaking identical words simultaneously with anyone who spoke; next she synchronised only with the Doctor. In the final stage, Sky began to speak before the Doctor – whatever had taken her over had stolen his voice and was now draining him and making him utterly powerless.

The terrified passengers turned on the Doctor, believing that, whatever the phenomenon was, it was now possessing him. They attempted to throw him out of the bus, having reasoned that six seconds would elapse after opening the door before the air-pressure wall that protected them would open and then reseal – enough time to open the door, eject the Doctor and close the door again. His life was saved by the Hostess, who realised that the unknown entity was still in Sky. She sacrificed herself and Sky as soon as the emergency door opened.

The nature of the entity that attacked the *Crusader 50* has never been determined.

THE LOST MOON OF POOSH

A small moon with its own gravity that was among the 27 planets transported to the Medusa Cascade by the Daleks to form part of their Reality Bomb in 2009. It was returned home by the Doctor.

POETRY

We must not look at Goblin Men
We must not buy their fruits
Who knows upon what soil they fed
Their hungry, thirsty roots?

– from Christina Rosetti, *Goblin Market* (1862), quoted by Dee Dee Blasco, on Sky's possession

THE SENSE-SPHERE

"The Ood-Sphere. I've been to this solar system before, years ago, ages! Close to the planet Sense-Sphere.

– The Doctor to Donna Noble (Ood-Sphere, 4126)

In the 28th century, this rich source of the mineral molybdenum was discovered by a small exploratory craft. The five-man crew attempted to trade with the Sense-Sphere 's inhabitants – the telepathic Sensorites. Trade was refused. When the Earth craft attempted to leave the planet, it blew up on take-off, but some of its crew survived and hid in cave systems near the Sensorites' city. They poisoned the water supply, causing a plague that made the creatures even more suspicious of visiting space travellers.

The crew of a second Earth craft were placed in suspended animation to prevent them from alerting other humans to the exploitation possibilities of the Sense-Sphere. The arrival of the First Doctor uncovered all this, and the 'plague' was cured. The Doctor acted as intermediary, persuading the Sensorites to release the humans and the men to return home without telling anyone about the Sense-Sphere.

The planet then remained undisturbed, although its neighbour, the Ood-Sphere, would be next to attract humanity's attentions a few centuries later...

40th Century

BALTAZAR

Scourge of the Galaxy and Corsair King of Triton, Baltazar attempted to attack the Earth. Having obliterated the planet's airborne defence forces, he was poised to unleash a field of plasma fire that would encase the Earth and superheat all its inhabitants – all carbon-based life forms would be super-compressed in the plasma field and turned into diamonds. The Doctor prevented the launch of the plasma field by destroying Baltazar's warship with a hydroxiding fungus, and Baltazar himself was incarcerated on the prison planet Volag-Noc.

In prison, Baltazar learned of the *Infinite*, a legendary starship lost centuries earlier that could give him his heart's desire.

Some years later, the apparently reformed Baltazar was released and immediately began to plot his revenge. Baltazar's companion, the metal bird Caw, tricked the Doctor and Martha Jones into going on a quest for the datachips that would lead to the *Infinite*. Baltazar tracked them through the seven galaxies, murdering various former inmates from Volag-Noc and relying on the Doctor to find the lost ship. When they reached it, Baltazar was shown an illusion of his heart's desire – enough treasure to construct a new battle fleet to once again terrorise the galaxy. The Doctor arranged for Baltazar to be taken back to Volag-Noc, where he was sentenced for the murders and imprisoned once more.

THE UNIVERSE

VOLAG-NOC

The coldest place in the galaxy. Beneath Volag-Noc's icy surface was an immense complex of prison cells – Volag-Noc was the Human Empire's foremost prison world. It was staffed by robot warders under the command of an android governor named Locke, and its erstwhile inmates included Baltazar, the pirate captain Kaliko and fraudster, blackmailer and thief Constantine Ethelred Gurney. At the end of his sentence, Gurney actually broke back into Volag-Noc, and used a computer program to convince the warders to accept him as governor. Gurney fitted Locke with an inhibitor and placed him in Cell 8447, then took over the prison. The Doctor was imprisoned on 3,005 counts of malfeasance, with a further 6,000 to be taken into consideration, ranging from 1,400 counts of traffic violation and 250 library fines to 18 counts of planetary demolition over the previous 3,000 years. Placed in Cell 8447, he quickly removed Locke's inhibitor and the pair escaped. They confronted Gurney, who fled to the surface. Locke concluded that the prisoners were all beyond redemption and ordered the warders to sterilise the prison cells. The Doctor countermanded the sterilisation order and corrected Locke's programming.

BOUKEN

This oil-rich desert world was taken over by OilCorp, and the company installed two artificial suns alongside the planet's original one to warm the planet up. Huge mobile oil rigs were then deployed to extract the planet's natural resources.

MYARR

The human colony that had settled on Myarr had spent generations establishing a viable agriculture. At a time when the expanding Human Empire was draining so many planets of their natural resources, Myarr became the last fertile planet in the galaxy and was vital to Earth's interests. When a vast swarm of Mantasphids invaded the planet, killing many colonists and driving the rest from their homes, Earth Command declared war. The Doctor and Martha landed on Myarr shortly before the final devastating assault, which was intended to effect complete spatial disintegration of the 100-mile vector in which the Mantasphid Hive was located. The attack was halted only when the Doctor claimed he was a pirate who had held the Mantasphid Queen hostage and the Mantasphids themselves were entirely blameless. He suggested that the Mantasphids could provide oil-replacing phosphorescence in exchange for plentiful supplies of dung.

PHEROS

The homeworld of a race of giant metal birds, powered by gold fusion – they ingested gold to feed their reactors. Baltazar's companion Caw hailed from Pheros, and the bird took the Doctor and Martha there to warn them that the Scourge of the Galaxy was at large and seeking the *Infinite*. Caw gave Martha a brooch that concealed a tracking device – actually his son, Squawk. The fully grown Squawk, bottle-fed on gold and with his engines pepped up to attain light speed, later provided the Doctor's means of following Baltazar from Volag-Noc to Asteroid 7574B.

THE INFINITE

A relic of the Dark Times, the *Infinite* was wrecked thousands of years earlier, its debris drifting through space. Amongst this space-borne flotsam were the remains of the ship's black box recorder, notably four data chips that could reveal the location of the *Infinite*. Each of these data chips ended up in the hands of former inmates of Volag-Noc and, when the Doctor retrieved them, the *Infinite*'s final resting place was revealed as Asteroid 7574B in the Ceres system of the Hesperus Galaxy. Baltazar hijacked the TARDIS and took Martha to Asteroid 7574B, leaving the Doctor stranded on Volag-Noc. When the Doctor managed to reach the asteroid, he used sonic vibrations to shake the gutted hull of the *Infinite* to pieces.

DATA CHIPS:
1. Held by Baltazar and given to the Doctor. It led to the planet Bouken.
2. Held by Kaliko. It led to the planet Myarr.
3. Held by Mergrass. It led to the planet Volag-Noc.
4. Held by Gurney. It led to Asteroid 7574B.

INDUSTRY AND PIRACY

OILCORP

The largest of the Human Empire's oil corporations was at the forefront of drilling operations across the galaxy. Petrol prices were at a record high and companies such as OilCorp took the profits while governments took the blame. Earth itself no longer had any oil at all, and the corporations were now sucking whole solar systems dry – entire colonies were dying out thanks to this unrestrained exploitation. OilCorp itself had developed huge, mobile robotic oil rigs that towered high above planet surfaces on long metal legs, walking across worlds and extracting every last drop of oil.

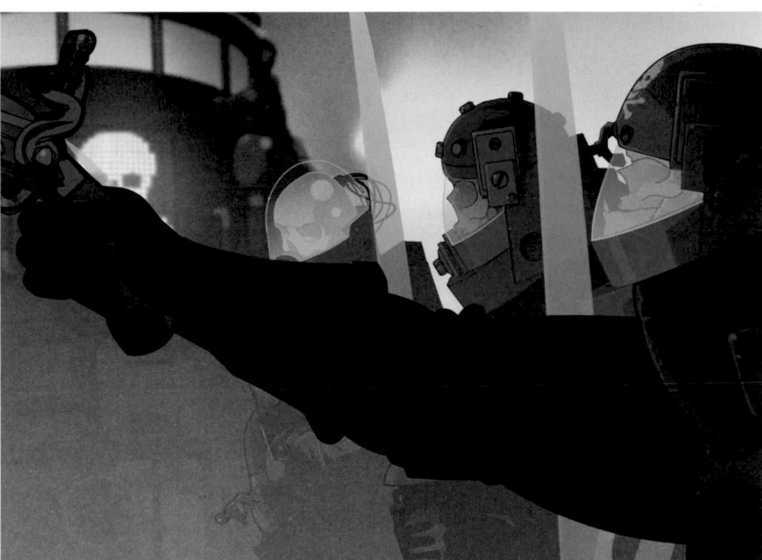

THE BLACK GOLD

The pirate captain Kaliko was one of those determined to prevent the oil companies being the sole beneficiaries of the natural resources of the galaxy. She used her ship, the *Black Gold*, to make raids on the mobile oil rigs, using heavy cables to drag them to the ground, then siphoning off all the oil they had collected. She then sold on the oil at less inflated prices – robbing the rich to fuel the poor. The *Black Gold* was crewed by the cheapest labour force available: an army of skeletons armed with laser weapons. Among them was an OilCorp spy, the First Mate Swabb. OilCorp had promised him a new body if he betrayed Kaliko, and the *Black Gold* was scuppered in an ambush by heavily armed oil rigs. One of the holders of the four *Infinite* data chips, Kaliko herself escaped but was murdered by Baltazar.

MANTASPHIDS

A race of giant flying insects that was attracted to the fertile world of Myarr and, especially, to its copious supplies of dung. The swarm, led by its Queen, forced out or killed all the human inhabitants of the planet and established a Hive. The gunrunner Ulysses Mergrass supplied weapons for the Mantasphids, who remained at war with the humans until the Doctor's intervention.

42nd Century

THE SECOND GREAT AND BOUNTIFUL HUMAN EMPIRE

Great advances in space-travel capabilities had gradually allowed the Human Empire to expand across three galaxies, with Galactic Central at its heart.

The Earth was full, but its Empire had expanded to encompass thousands of worlds and thousands of species. These formed an intergalactic network of trade and shared culture, connected by the Tri-Galactic broadcasting network and fleets of sleek rocket ships capable of reaching the deepest parts of space known to humanity. It was, though, an empire built on slavery...

K 37 GEM 5

Far out in the drifts of the universe, an extraordinary phenomenon awaited humanity's deep-space explorers. A black hole is an area of space where the collapsed mass of a dead star has become so concentrated that nothing in its vicinity can escape its gravitational pull. The black hole designated K 37 Gem 5 was much like any other – it pulled in and crushed nearby light, gravity, even time. It was surrounded by gas clouds, stars breaking up and entire solar systems being ripped apart and dragged in. One victim was the Scarlet System, home to the Pallushi, a civilisation that had existed for a billion years, completely destroyed as all its suns and planets burnt up into a red cloud of gas and debris that was sucked into the black hole. And yet, suspended in a perpetual geostationary orbit around it, a small nameless planet existed beyond the laws of physics.

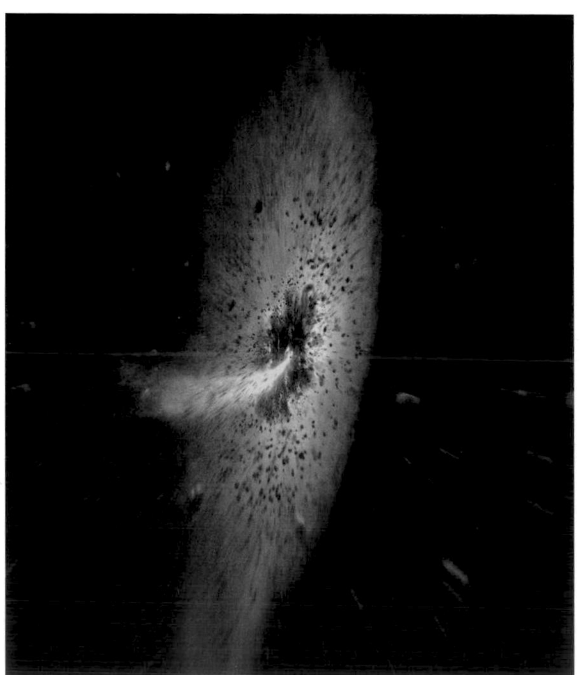

KROP TOR

In the scriptures of the Veltino, a mighty demon was tricked into devouring a small planet called Krop Tor ('the bitter pill'). It was poison, and the demon spat it out. The planet existed in a complete vacuum and had no atmosphere, but it was generating a gravity field, which held it in constant balance with the black hole and extended outwards from the planet in a funnel that reached into clear space. The generation of this gravity field and funnel required a power source with an inverted self-extrapolating reflex of six to the power of six every six seconds, and that power source, which measured 90 statts on the Blazen Scale, lay ten miles beneath the surface of the planet. Pottery fragments and examples of an untranslatable ancient language provided evidence that there had been life on the planet billions of years earlier.

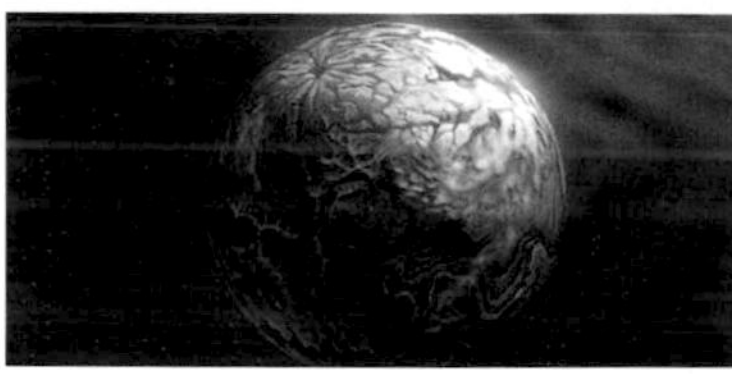

TORCHWOOD

Having discovered the existence of the black hole and the impossible orbiting planet, scientists from the Torchwood Archive spent two years calculating the energy requirements of the gravity field. Realising that acquiring the necessary power source could fuel the Human Empire and revolutionise modern science, an expedition was despatched to investigate the planet. When the Gedes expedition failed to return, the Torchwood Archive despatched a new team led by Captain Walker. Walker's team of eight officers, a security squad and 50 Ood used the unexplained gravity funnel to reach the nameless planet that orbited the black hole. The ship should have been torn apart – it survived, but its Captain lost his life during the approach.

SANCTUARY BASE 6

The Torchwood Archive team set up a Sanctuary Base – a deep-space exploration headquarters assembled from a kit – on the surface of the planet. Sanctuary Base 6 contained several Habitation areas for humans and, separately, Ood, plus extensive Storage areas, and a network of airless maintenance tunnels beneath the base, with routine repairs carried out by robotic drones. The base had its own generators and was airlock-sealed, and maintained its own internal oxygen field and gravity. Interior doors had either a basic frame or a security frame, and the computer systems monitored all entrances and exits. The entire base was monitored and controlled from a central Control Deck. There was a constant link to the rocket, their only means of escape from the planet, and the craft had an independent power source. The security personnel had weapons and limited stocks of ammunition – Firing Stock 15, which was only effective against organic matter.

Zachary Cross-Flane became Acting Captain in Walker's place. Soon after they had established themselves in the Sanctuary Base, the team lost two more crewmembers. Curt had been examining the personal effects of Captain Walker, including the artefacts and records recovered from the Gedes expedition, and was briefly possessed by the Beast before the artefacts spontaneously combusted.

His body was discovered moments later by Chenna but, by the time the rest of the crew discovered them, she too was dead.

These unexplained deaths were not the only challenge facing Sanctuary Base 6. The debris of collapsing star systems rained down and frequent earth tremors shook the whole planet and, as what sounded like a hurricane raged outside, surface cave-ins could destroy entire sections of the base. The crew became used to the regular alerts, strapping themselves down as the base shook around them, then emerging to assess the damage – on a single occasion, they lost Storage areas 5 to 8, which included the Habitation area where the TARDIS had landed. A hull breach that claimed the life of Scooti Manista also destroyed Sections 11 to 13 of SB6 before the systems could automatically seal and repair the breach. The crew logged out spacesuits to venture outside SB6 to conduct routine maintenance, but were not allowed through the airlocks during the nightshift, when exterior conditions were impossible to survive. As each nightshift began, the crew checked the rocket link, the airlock seals and the base lockdown. All crewmembers had implanted biochips so their whereabouts could be constantly monitored.

SB6 Officers

✦ Zachary Cross Flane (Acting Captain)
✦ Ida Scott (Science Officer)
✦ Daniel Bartock (Ethics Committee)

Deceased with honours

✦ Captain Walker ✦ Chenna
✦ Curt ✦ John Maynard Jefferson (Head of Security) ✦ Scootori Manista (Trainee Maintenance)
✦ Tobias Zed (Archaeology Officer)

FOOD

Nutrition on SB6 was provided by the Ood, with payment charged to each crew member's Designation Code. Refreshments on offer included:

✦ Protein One (flavour: milk)
✦ Protein Two (flavour: salt)
✦ Protein Three (flavour: sugar)

A popular choice was Protein One with just a dash of Three.

A balanced diet of carbohydrates, fats, vitamins and fibre was served by colour, with optional sauces.

ARTS

POETRY

And how can man die better
Than facing fearful odds
For the ashes of his father
And the temples of his gods.

— from Thomas Babington Macaulay, *Horatius* (1842), quoted by John Jefferson at the death of Scooti Manista

MUSIC

As the nightshift began on SB6, the computer played music chosen by the crew throughout the base, including Ravel's *Boléro* (1928).

42nd Century

SOCIETY AND RELIGION

There were countless religions practised throughout the galaxies, among them:

✦ The Arkiphets ✦ Quoldonity ✦ Christianity
✦ Pash Pash ✦ Neo-Classic Congregational
✦ Neo-Judaism ✦ San Claar
✦ The Church of the Tin Vagabond

Many religious groups, like the Neo-Classics, had no devil figure. Most did though, and the horned beast was an image that cropped up in the myths and legends of a million worlds across the universe, including:

✦ Dæmos, whose people – the Dæmons – were twin-horned and cloven-hoofed and once travelled the cosmos attempting to aid nascent civilisations
✦ Draconia, whose reptilian inhabitants had forged an empire to rival Earth's centuries earlier
✦ Earth, itself a beneficiary of the Dæmons
✦ Skaro, birthplace of the Daleks and, much earlier, homeworld of the Thals and the Kaleds, who numbered the Kaled God of War among their pantheon of deities
✦ Vel Consadine

POINT 0

The main purpose of the expedition was to drill through ten miles (16,093 metres) of solid rock to reach Point 0, the location of the power source. Their resources allowed them to bore only one central shaft, keeping the drill head at point 16 and pressure at 60, although the drill speed seemed to increase as the shaft neared Point 0. When the drilling was completed, a capsule was dropped down the shaft on a steel cable, lowering the Doctor and Ida Scott into a gigantic, airless subterranean cavern. At the same time, possessed Ood began to attack the crew, killing the two remaining security personnel with their interface devices, and Condition Red was declared. This gave Security Head Jefferson the authority to execute Toby Zed who had also been possessed, although Rose Tyler interceded on his behalf, since the Beast seemed to have released him.

Ten miles beneath the base, the Doctor and Ida Scott explored the cavern, lighting it with a gravity globe and discovering that the interior of the planet was apparently so vast that it had its own weather system. They found the remains of a large temple or shrine and then, north north-west from their position, the power source, located beneath a huge trapdoor. This metal seal was some nine metres in diameter and covered in symbols from the mysterious ancient language. As the Ood attacked in the base up above, the seal opened to reveal a dark chasm and the whole planet began to shake. Its gravity field was weakening as it moved fractionally out of its orbit and threatened to plunge into the black hole. Just as suddenly, the planet stabilised and settled back into its orbit. The Doctor and Ida attempted to return to the base, but the capsule cable snapped, leaving them trapped with enough oxygen for just 55 minutes. The Doctor used the cable to abseil down into the pit below, and found that below a crust some six metres down there was a seemingly endless black nothingness.

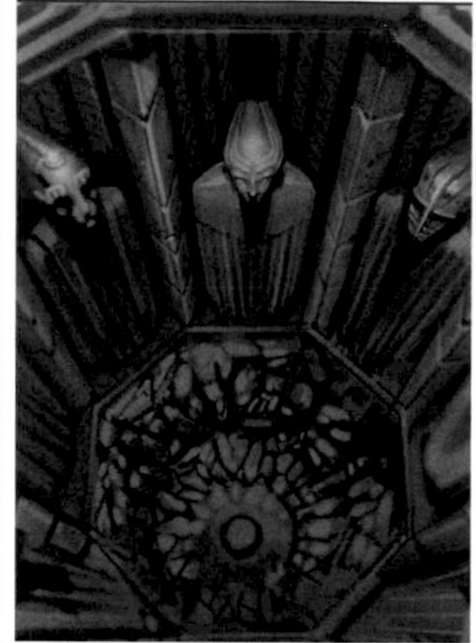

Falling to the bottom of this dark pit, the Doctor was saved by an air cushion that both broke his fall and allowed him to breathe. He was in another cave system, this one decorated with wall paintings depicting the defeat and imprisonment of a mighty beast. And then he encountered the Beast itself.

THE BEAST

> **Rose:** What do you think it was though? Really?
> **The Doctor:** I think... we beat it. That's good enough for me.

An enormous horned creature, chained at the bottom of the pit, the Beast had been influencing events on SB6 for some time. He had telepathically possessed the Ood, causing the slave race to turn on the humans, and transferred his mind to Toby Zed. He was able to read people's thoughts and memories, probing their minds until he found a weakness or fear that he could play on to undermine them – Jefferson's wife had never forgiven him; Zach had no confidence in his ability to lead; Ida was afraid of her father; Toby was a virgin; Danny had lied about something; the Doctor was the killer of this own people; and Rose Tyler would soon die in battle.

Claiming to pre-date the universe itself, the Beast had been imprisoned for eternity beneath Krop Tor billions of years earlier by the Disciples of the Light and may have been the original template for the ideas, myths and legends of the devil that permeated every society. He had described himself as sin, temptation, desire, pain, loss, death of hope, rage, bile, ferocity, agony, fear, the prince and the fool, and the darkness in every sentient being's mind. But the creature the Doctor encountered showed no sign of intelligence and seemed unable to talk.

The Beast's prison was the equilibrium between the planet and the black hole – if he broke free from his chains, the gravity field would shut down and the planet would crash into the black hole, taking the Beast with it. Two urns stood on pedestals in front of the chained creature and, when he smashed them, the Doctor condemned the Beast's body to death.

Names for the Beast

✦ Abbadon ✦ Bringer of Night ✦ Deathless Prince ✦ Devil ✦ King of Despair ✦ Krop Tor ✦ Lucifer ✦ Satan

SCIENCE AND TECHNOLOGY

The Ood uprising on SB6 convinced Zach to initiate Strategy Nine – a base lockdown procedure that would ensure the safety of the human crew while the airlocks were opened and the belligerent Ood sucked out into the vacuum. Strategy Nine required full power, however, and SB6 was by this point operating on limited power leached from the rocket ship after the Ood gutted the base's generators. By opening the bypass conduits and overriding the safety controls, they were able to channel the rocket feed into the base. This gave them enough power to disable the Ood by broadcasting a flare from the central monitor in Ood Habitation that disrupted their telepathic field and temporarily knocked them out.

Zach then decided to abandon SB6 and attempt to escape in the rocket with the few survivors, hoping to ensure that no one would ever revisit K 37 Gem 5. They closed down the feed-links between the base and the rocket, put the retroscopes online and fled to the rocket. Having cleared the Negapact feed-line, raised Blu-Nitro levels to maximum and disconnected all three docking clamps, the rocket was ready to lift off. Zach set the coordinates for Earth and, with Toby monitoring the hull pressure (constant), the gravity funnel (stable at 66.5) and the Statts (53) they attempted to make the first-ever rocket flight away from a black hole.

With just seconds until the rocket would emerge from the gravity funnel into clear space, the Doctor smashed the urns in the Pit below, instantly deactivating the gravity field. Both the planet and the rocket were heading straight for the black hole when the Beast revealed that its mind was still inside Toby. Rose used the last bolt in a bolt gun to smash the forward viewscreen of the rocket and Toby was sucked out into the airless vacuum around them. Emergency shields activated immediately, but the rocket remained out of control, still heading for the black hole. They were saved by the Doctor who towed the rocket back out into clear space with the TARDIS. He had rescued Ida Scott from Point 0, although he had not had enough time to save the Ood, who perished with the planet and the Beast inside the black hole.

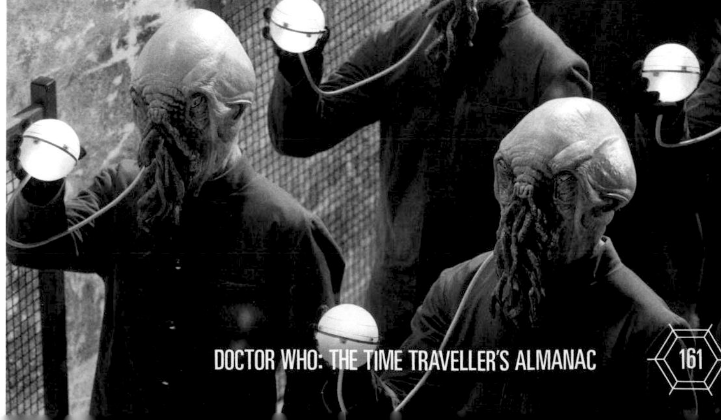

42nd Century

TECHNOLOGY

UNIVERSAL ROAMING

The Doctor used his sonic screwdriver to give Martha's mobile phone access to Universal Roaming, so that she could call anywhere in time and space. Over the next 45 minutes, she called her mother Francine in London on Election Day 2008 three times.

THE TORAJII SYSTEM

Half a universe away from Earth, the Torajii System lay in the remotest reaches of the Human Empire territories. Its largest planet was Torajii Alpha, and the SS *Pentallian* recruited coffee-shop manager Erina Lissak to its crew when it stopped there briefly. The outer worlds of the system provided a tourist trail for rich kids on backpacking holidays. Until the *Pentallian*'s near-impact, no one had realised that the heart of the system was a living sun, which, the Doctor pointed out, needed care and protection like any other living thing.

A space freighter that transported cargo across the galaxy. Everything aboard the ship was fully automated, so its seven-strong crew's only duty was to keep the engines going. They illegally used fusion scoops to collect energy, and their last refuelling stop had been at the Torajii system's living sun. Since fusion scoops were illegal, they mined it and stripped its surface for cheap fuel without first scanning for life, which would have taken too long – they would have risked being caught. Once the *Pentallian* was on its way, the sun particles in the fuel started to drag the cargo ship back towards the sun, and a sun-possessed member of the crew was used to sabotage the engines and deadlock-seal the 29 internal doors between the Engine Room and the auxiliary engines. These doors were password protected, and the passwords were randomly generated from questions set by the crew nine tours earlier. The first question asked for the date of SS *Pentallian*'s first flight. Inputting the correct answer sent a remote pulse to a clamp which would open the door, although there was only one chance and a mistake would seal the entire system.

Sample door security protocols

✦ 28. Find the next number in the sequence: 313, 331, 367, ...? (379, the fourth in a sequence of happy primes. Any number that reduces to one when you take the sum of the square of its digits and continue iterating is a happy number; a happy prime is a number that's both happy and prime.)

✦ 27. Classical music: Who had the most pre-download Number Ones, Elvis Presley or The Beatles? (Elvis)

✦ 10. What is Riley Vashtee's favourite colour? (Purple. Or orange...)

Crew

✦ Captain Kath McDonnell ✦ Korwin McDonnell ✦ Dev Ashton ✦ Orin Scannell ✦ Riley Vashtee ✦ Abi Lerner ✦ Erina Lissak

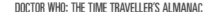

SS PENTALLIAN

Impact projections

46:27 The *Pentallian*'s engines are sabotaged by Korwin, who sends a heat pulse to melt the controls.

45:48 Erina transmits an automated distress signal.

43:11 Korwin initiates Secure Closure. The TARDIS lands in the Vent Chamber.

42:43 The Doctor and Martha meet McDonnell, Riley, Scannell and Erina in Area 30. All the ship's connecting doors close.

42:27 The Doctor and Martha are told that the *Pentallian* is about to crash into the sun.

40:26 Temperatures in the Vent Chamber have risen 3,000 degrees in ten seconds. They discover the sabotaged engines. Riley and Martha set out to open the password-sealed doors and access the auxiliary engines.

34:31 Ashton calls McDonnell to the Med Centre. The Doctor sedates Korwin and places him in a Stasis Chamber to regulate his body temp. Abi runs a bio-scan, a tissue profile and a metabolic detail.

32:50 Heat shields are failing at 25 per cent. Martha and Riley begin to answer the door-code questions.

30:50 The Doctor suggests jumpstarting the ship using power from its generator.

29:46 Martha calls her mother.

28:50 Abi discovers that Korwin's biological make-up is changing. He gets out of the Stasis Chamber and kills her by endothermic vaporisation.

27:06 The Doctor tells McDonnell that Korwin now has an internal temperature of 100 degrees, and his body oxygen has been replaced by hydrogen. Korwin kills Erina.

24:51 Korwin shares the sun-possession with Ashton. Heat shields are failing at 20 per cent. Ashton attacks Martha and Riley, who hide in an escape pod in Area 17. Korwin tells McDonnell that the situation is her fault. Ashton initiates escape pod jettison, which Riley counters with override codes and a Sierpinski sequence, but Ashton crushes the controls and the pod is jettisoned. Scannell freezes Korwin using the ship's ice vents. Ashton collapses at the same time.

17:05 McDonnell forces Ashton into the Stasis Chamber, reducing the temperature to minus 273 degrees. The Doctor prepares to go outside the ship, and starts decompression of the Area 17 airlock.

12:55 Martha calls Francine again.

11:15 Heat shields are failing at 10 per cent. The Doctor boosts the magnetic lock on the ship's exterior, re-magnetising the escape pod. As it returns to the ship, the Doctor realises the sun is alive.

08:57 Airlock recompression is completed. Martha and Riley find that the Doctor has been infected by the sun. He tells McDonnell that the sun is screaming and is now living in him but he is resisting sun-possession.

07:30 Riley and Scannell continue to open the sealed doors. McDonnell and Martha take the Doctor to the Med Centre and place him in the Stasis Chamber intending to lower his temperature to minus 200 degrees to freeze the sun particles out of him. Heat shields are failing at 5 per cent. Korwin revives in the Engine Room and shuts down the power to the Stasis Chamber. The Doctor's temperature is down to only minus 70 degrees. McDonnell heads down to the Engine Room.

04:47 Scannell and Riley have reached Area 3. The Doctor sends Martha to vent the ship's engines and return the sun particles.

04:08 McDonnell lures Korwin towards an airlock.

03:43 Korwin finds McDonnell in the airlock chamber. She activates an airlock override and the exterior airlock opens. The two are sucked out into space. Riley and Scannell reach the final door.

02:17 The Doctor emerges from the Stasis Chamber. Primary engines are critical. Survival estimate projection is 0 per cent. The Doctor succumbs to sun-possession.

01:21 Riley and Scannell open the final door to the auxiliary engines. Life-support systems are reaching critical.

01:06 Collision alert.

00:58 Fatal impact imminent. Martha reaches Riley and Scannell and orders them to vent the fuel and get rid of the sun particles. The sun leaves the Doctor. The engines fire and the Pentallian pulls away.

00:02 Impact averted.

42nd Century

NEW WORLDS

KURHAN

Having survived their experiences on the *Pentallian*, the Doctor offered to take Martha ice-skating on the Mineral Lakes of Kurhan.

THE OOD-SPHERE

Located in Galactic Sector 242.16 in the same solar system as the Sense-Sphere, the Ood-Sphere is a planet of ice and wind and snow, populated by the Oodkind. The Ood managed to avoid attention for some 12 centuries after the disastrous first encounter between humans and Sensorites in the 28th century, but the early years of the 40th century brought humans to the Ood-Sphere in the shape of a businessman named Halpen. His exploration teams discovered a giant brain beneath the planet's Northern Glacier. Having established that the brain actually connected all the Ood that were roaming freely on the ice, Halpen suppressed the telepathic field around the brain to gain control over the Oodkind. The brain was chained inside a circular electrical psycho-barrier, which dampened the telepathic field it generated. The Ood were rounded up and placed in Breeding Farms, with batches of 2,000 removed for experimentation until a compliant race of slaves was successfully developed. Halpen began to sell the Ood as servants throughout the Human Empire, establishing his primary Ood Distribution Centre and headquarters on the Ood-Sphere to form the heart of a new business empire.

If your Ood is happy, then you'll be happy

Halpen's venture into slavery opened for business in 3914, and for the next 212 years the family-run firm profited from the exploitation of the Ood. The creatures were modified and sold to private users, commercial concerns and even the military. The company claimed that the Ood were born to serve, and fostered the myth that without orders the creatures had no purpose and would shrivel up and die. Meanwhile, experiments continued to refine and adapt the Ood, with the Halpen family always alert to new marketing opportunities. Ood Operations – 'the Double O' – eventually passed to Klineman Halpen, grandson of the company founder.

With distribution centres across three galaxies, Ood Operations expanded its headquarters on the Ood-Sphere. The Ood Brain, surrounded by the pylons that generated the telepathic barrier, was kept in Warehouse 15. Batches of Ood were brought in cages from the Breeding Farms to the Experimentation Labs in the Ood Conversion section, where the flesh tubes connecting them to their hind-brains were severed and replaced with plastic pipes stitched to their heads and linked to spherical interface devices. These translator balls channelled the Ood's thoughts and lit up as the Ood spoke. Processed Ood were taken from Ood Conversion along the West Ridge of the complex to Ood Cargo, where they were packed into large containers, 100 to a crate, then taken out to the rocket sheds to be distributed around the Human Empire.

By 4126, sales of Ood were not as strong as they had been, and Halpen combined aggressive marketing with

OOD OPERATIONS

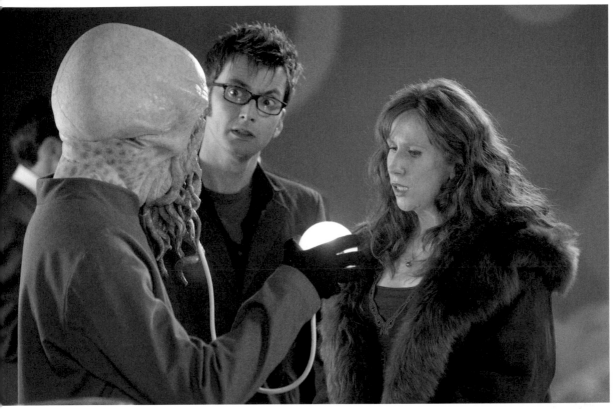

cost-cutting, intending to drop the price of a basic Ood to just 50 credits. At the same time, the range of Ood continued to expand, with added features and even a range of voices. Ood Operations seemed sensitive to the demands of pressure groups like Friends Of The Ood, and company advertising maintained that the Ood were treated with care and respect, wanted for nothing and were always happy. The creatures were trusted friends, ran the sales pitch, well fed and educated and kept in facilities of the highest quality.

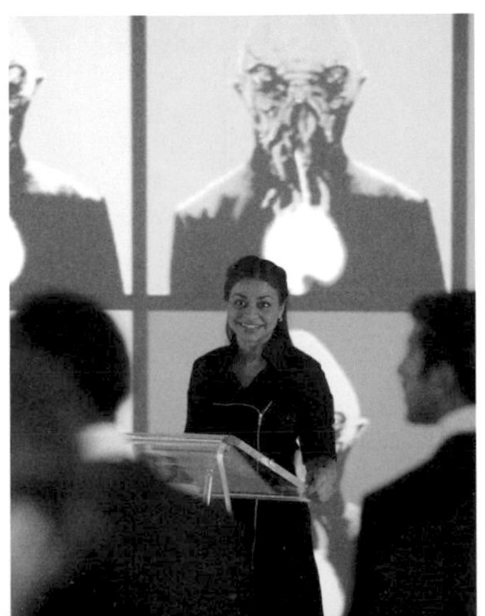

Commercial buyers were regularly invited to the Ood-Sphere. The visitors were given Information Packs containing vouchers, 3-D tickets and a map of the Double O complex, before being escorted to the Executive Suites and Reception Rooms for alcohol-free refreshments and presentations. At the last such meeting, the reps were shown the new variety package of male and female voices that the latest translator balls could supply, including 'something for the gentlemen' and the 'comedy classic'. All available for only five extra credits.

The Ood range

✦ Household Ood ✦ Pilot Ood
✦ Personal Trainer Ood
✦ Military Ood

Company personnel

✦ **Chief Executive Officer**
Klineman Halpen
✦ **Head of Ood Management**
Doctor Ryder
✦ **Head of Marketing and Galactic Liaison**
Solana Mercurio
✦ **Sales and Marketing Manager**
Mr Bartle
✦ **Guard Commander**
Mr Kess

42nd Century

THE OOD

A species born to serve could never have evolved. Each natural Ood is born with a hind-brain in its hand, a secondary brain that processes emotions and memory. The hind-brain is covered by a membrane that holds a sustaining fluid, and a thin tube of flesh connects it to the Ood's mouth. However, no life form could have survived with separate hind-brain and forebrain. All of Oodkind is connected by a low-level telepathic field generated by the huge Ood Brain, which links each Ood's forebrain and hind-brain with every other Ood. Undisturbed, they roam their ice planet joining in the collective Song of the Ood and they are an instinctively peaceful and trusting race that could never kill or cause harm to others.

The intrusion of Ood Operations changed all this. As the ideal slave race, the Ood replaced more expensive robots as the servant of choice in every sphere of human activity. The Krop Tor expedition included a complement of 50 Ood, of Class Alpha One and Class Gamma Server. Their duties included catering, mineshaft and drilling supervision and maintenance on Sanctuary Base 6. They had no rights, and even the base's computer system failed to recognise them as proper life forms. Pressure from Friends Of The Ood had forced the Ethics Committee representative on any Human Empire mission to include the Ood among his responsibilities. For SB6's Danny Bartock this essentially meant no more than monitoring their telepathic field, which usually measured at around Basic 5. When the Beast awoke in the Pit below the base and his stronger mind took over the Ood, the field quickly rose to Basic 30 – either they were screaming at each other or something else was shouting inside their heads. By now the wary humans had confined all non-essential Ood to their Habitation. From Basic 30, the field shot up to Basic 100, as the Beast took full possession. Basic 100 should have brought on brain death for every Ood – instead they moved through the base killing humans with their interface devices. Although the Ood were susceptible to certain viruses, SB6 was not equipped to deal with the revolt. But Danny was able to knock the Ood out by broadcasting a flare from the central monitor which cut the telepathic field from Basic 100 to Basic 0, although it quickly

PLANET OF ORIGIN
The Ood-Sphere

APPEARANCE
Humanoid; albino; fronds hanging from face; tubes connecting hand-held brains/translator balls to heads

ABILITIES
Low-level telepathy; song

WEAPONS
Grafted interface devices

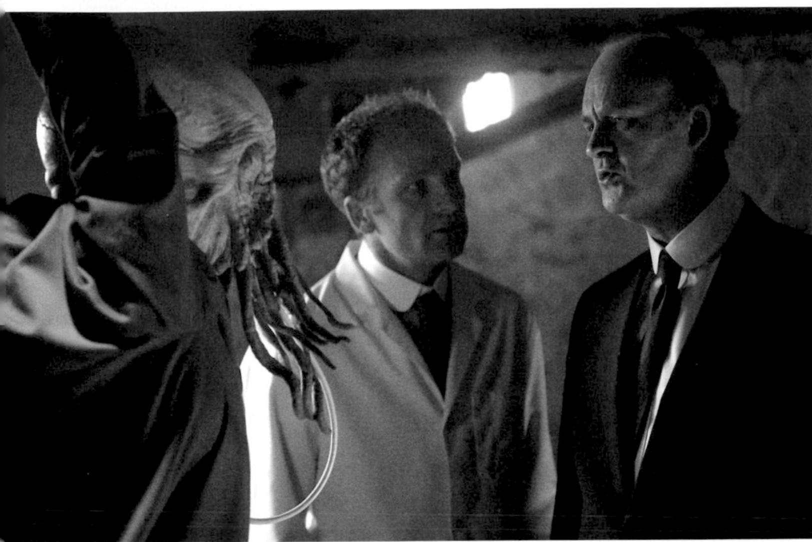

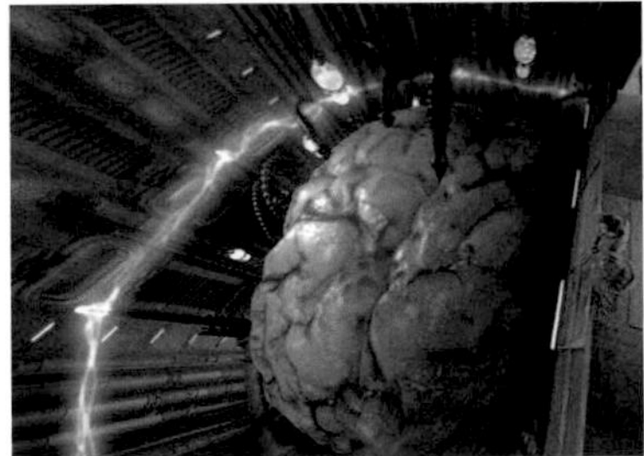

reasserted itself. The creatures began to stir again as the remaining crew abandoned the base. All Ood that had not been shot as the humans defended themselves then perished when the planet crashed into the black hole.

Back on the Ood-Sphere, another Ood uprising began in 4126. In the space of three months, three Double O employees died, seemingly from heart attacks or industrial accidents. But the death of marketing manager Bartle was caught on camera, and he had been murdered by an Ood. As on SB6, the Ood's translator ball had been converted into a weapon, emitting a buzzing noise and discharging lethal electrical energy. Several of the Ood were developing Red Eye, which the Double O scientists assumed was an infection, although they were unable to trace any bacterial source. The affected Ood became violent and aggressive and their eyes glowed red. At the same time, other Ood were becoming rabid. Klineman Halpen concluded that an entire batch of 2,000 Ood had been contaminated and ordered them confined and gassed to death. The company was insured, so he would not lose out financially. Canisters were primed with a 200-second countdown until their cores would heat up and release the deadly gas, killing the infected livestock. By now, however, the Ood had broken free from their containers and were rampaging across the complex – heavily armed security guards machine-gunned some, but there were at least as many human deaths.

FRIENDS OF THE OOD

A ten-year infiltration operation eventually enabled FOTO activist Doctor Ryder to gain access to the pycho-barrier in Warehouse 15. The Ood Brain had been adapting over the preceding two centuries, gradually managing to reach out to some of the captive Ood and causing their Red Eye. When Ryder lowered the barrier to its minimum level, the Brain was at last able to reach out and influence all of Oodkind on the planet. As the Ood revolution spread through the complex, Halpen implemented an emergency strategy devised by his grandfather – he placed detonation packs around the circumference of the barrier, intending to blow up the Brain and kill all the Ood.

Halpen was unable to complete his plan. His personal Ood, Ood Sigma, had for several years been secretly giving him Ood graft in a biological compound. Standing so close to the Brain, Halpen felt its full telepathic force as his body began to change and he became an Ood. Ood Sigma pledged that Ood Halpen would be cared for by his people as the Doctor deactivated the detonators and turned off the psycho-barrier.

As the electricity died on the pylons surrounding the Brain, the Song of the Ood was heard for the first time in 212 years. It resonated across three galaxies, ensuring that everyone heard it and understood what had happened on the Ood-Sphere. Soon the Human Empire's fleets of rockets were carrying the Ood back home.

51st Century

NEW WORLDS

✦ **Asgard** Good place for a picnic
✦ **Boeshane Peninsula** A human colony city of interconnected dwellings surrounded by seas and sand dunes
✦ **Dagmar Cluster** Two-and-a-half galaxies away from the Earth
✦ **Darillium** Noted for its singing towers
✦ **Karras Don Kazra Don Slava** Beaches of intelligent sand and seas full of talking fish

CAPTAIN JACK HARKNESS

REPORTED SIGHTING #1

ESTIMATED AGE: 15–20

LOCATION: Boeshane Peninsula, 51st century

AVAILABLE INFORMATION: The first ever citizen of the Boeshane Peninsula to be recruited by the Time Agency became a local celebrity and was nicknamed the Face of Boe...

SS MADAME DE POMPADOUR

Flying through the Dagmar Cluster, the SS *Madame de Pompadour* was struck without warning by an ion storm. The crew instituted a systems lockdown and attempted to send a mayday, but there was an immediate 82 per cent systems failure. The ship's clockwork repair robots promptly went to work but did not have sufficient spare parts to complete their work. Following their programming, which had failed to make a distinction between technology and organic life, the robots killed all 50 crewmembers and adapted their bodies to patch up the spaceship – eyes were used to replace shattered camera lenses; a human heart could be wired into the machinery to maintain the flow of power. The combination of human flesh and the intense heat of the systems filled the ship with the stench of burning meat. The repair work continued for over a year.

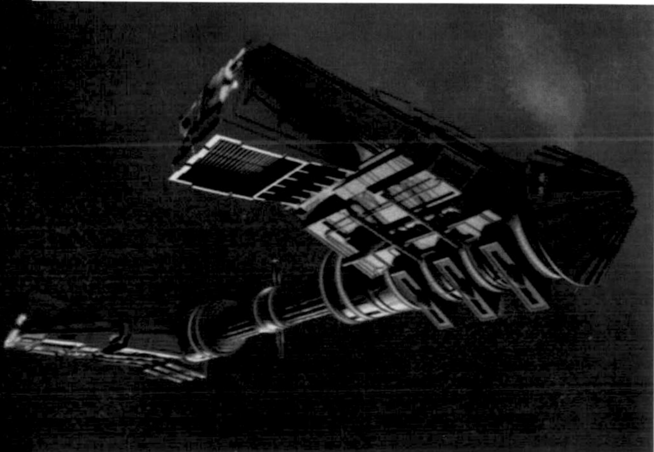

The onboard computer's command circuit and memory decks had been destroyed and needed replacing before the ship could move again. The robots reasoned that a human brain could fulfil its functions and that just one specific brain would be compatible with the 37-year-old SS *Madame de Pompadour*. They ran the warp engines at full capacity and opened spatio-temporal hyperlinks between the unmoving ship and pre-Revolutionary France, arranging them along the timeline of Reinette Poisson. Their camouflage protocols led them to create elaborate disguises – parodies of the wigs and costumes of 18th-century French aristocrats, and they used short-range teleports to visit Reinette at various points in her life until they located her in 1758 Versailles when she was 37.

SCIENCE AND TECHNOLOGY

CLOCKWORK ROBOTS

The SS *Madame de Pompadour* carried a quota of nine repair androids, which operated independently of the ship's main power supplies and continued to function after the ion storm struck. They had been programmed to repair the ship by any possible means using any available material, which they interpreted literally. They were equipped with a range of built-in tools and blades and were able to inject tranquillising chemicals. They were susceptible to extreme cold and multi-grade anti-oil, both of which temporarily suspended their mechanisms.

TIME PORTALS

✦ **1727 Paris** *Revolving double-sided fireplace into Reinette's bedroom*
✦ **1740 Paris** *Revolving double-sided fireplace into Reinette's bedroom*
✦ **1744 Paris** *Ornate doorway into gardens*
✦ **1745 Versailles** *Wall-length mirror into Palace chamber*
✦ **1753 Versailles** *Floor-to-ceiling tapestry into Madame de Pompadour's private sitting room*
✦ **1758 Versailles** *Wall-mounted mirror into Palace ballroom*
✦ **1764 Versailles** *Revolving double-sided fireplace into Reinette's bedroom*

CAPTAIN JACK HARKNESS

REPORTED SIGHTINGS #2, 3 & 4

ESTIMATED AGE: 20–35

LOCATION: Unknown, various eras

AVAILABLE INFORMATION: Still working as a Time Agent, Captain Jack discovered that the Agency had removed two years of his memories. He left the Time Agency and became a time-travelling intergalactic conman. Sentenced to death for unknown crimes, Captain Jack's last request was four hyper-vodkas for his final breakfast. The next morning he woke up in bed with both his executioners, and kept in touch with them for years afterwards. While operating as a conman, Captain Jack met a gorgeous woman from whom he stole the Chula warship he later used to travel to London in 1941.

VASHTA NERADA

"Almost every species in the universe has an irrational fear of the dark. But they're wrong. Cos it's not irrational. It's Vashta Nerada.

– *The Doctor*

A flesh-eating swarm that exists in the dark, the Vashta Nerada could be in any shadow on any of a billion worlds where there is meat. They generally swarm in small clusters and can sometimes be glimpsed as dust particles in sunbeams. They hunt by latching onto a possible food source as a second shadow, keeping its meat fresh until they are ready to consume it. They eat at incredible speed, stripping away the flesh and leaving nothing but dried-out bone in an instant. They can live off roadkill, but sometimes they take people. There is no defence against them – the only option is to run. The Vashta Nerada hatch from micro-spores in trees. Establishing the biggest library in the universe, the Lux Corporation unwittingly pulped their breeding forests to make the paper for a million million books. An aggressive swarm hatched inside The Library. CAL saved all The Library's occupants as soon as the hatching cycle began, and the Vashta Nerada waited in silence for a century before a Lux expedition managed to gain access to the planet again. One by one, the members of the expedition were killed and their spacesuits animated by the shadows. The Doctor offered to seal The Library and leave them to swarm there and the creatures retreated when they discovered who it was they were facing.

THE LIBRARY

The biggest library in the universe was a whole world. Specially printed, mint-condition editions of every book ever written could be found somewhere on the vast continents of towers full of carved wooden bookshelves that covered its entire surface. The Library ran on fission cells that would outlast the sun and was arranged geographically – the Biography section, for example, was found near the planet's equator. Inside each tower were chambers and rooms and corridors, all crammed with shelves. The separate towers were linked by gantries and walkways, and each tower held colour-coded index rooms, book-lined corridors, anterooms, enquiry desks and a little shop. A teleport terminal in each shop beamed visitors between areas of The Library.

Beneath the surface, the planet's whole core was The Library's central computer processor, a glowing red globe known as the Data Core, the biggest hard drive ever constructed. This contained back-up copies of every book. The computer monitored The Library with floating security cameras housed in carved wooden spheres and could be accessed from terminals in every colour-coded index room. The Under-Library chamber holding the central computer was accessed via a gravity platform concealed beneath a six-metre circular hatch in Yellow Index.

The Library was built by the Felman Lux Corporation when Lux discovered that his daughter – ten-year-old Charlotte Abigail Lux – was dying. Charlotte loved books more than anything, and her father placed her living mind inside the Data Core as its main command node, CAL. There she could access all of human history through every book from every era, and dream of a normal life with her father.

THE LIBRARY

As the Vashta Nerada hatching cycle began, CAL activated all the teleports to remove 4,022 people from The Library. But there was nowhere to send them, and they all remained inside the system. CAL saved them to the Data Core hard drive, storing their physical forms as energy signatures that could one day be actualised again. CAL allowed

them all to share in the virtual reality she inhabited, living make-believe lives as perfect reproductions of their real selves in a fantasy world. She then sealed The Library, which fell silent for a hundred years. The last message received from The Library stated that the lights were going out, and an accompanying data extract read: '4,022 saved. No survivors.'

After a century, Felman Lux's grandson, Strackman, finally managed to decode the seals and led a small expedition to The Library. They found no bodies but did meet the Doctor and Donna, just as the Vashta Nerada began to attack. As the Doctor attempted to break through security protocols, while Donna – trapped inside the Data Core – learnt the truth about the fantasy world, CAL panicked and triggered an auto-destruct mechanism. The Library would erase its Data Core in just 20 minutes. Having warned off the Vashta Nerada, the Doctor's solution was to beam everyone out of the Data Core – the computer would then reset and the self-destruct countdown would abort. Since CAL's memory space was insufficient to achieve this, he planned to connect himself to the computer. Professor River Song took his place, however, and physically died during the transfer as her heart was burnt out by the strain. Thanks to the Doctor, however, she lived on inside the Data Core fantasy world, accompanied by virtual versions of the Vashta Nerada's victims, and by Charlotte and Doctor Moon.

SCIENCE AND TECHNOLOGY

COURTESY NODES

Node: This flesh aspect was donated by Mark Chambers on the occasion of his death ... It has been actualised individually for you, from the many facial aspects saved to our extensive flesh banks. Please enjoy.

The Library's Courtesy Nodes were revolving statue-like information points for visitors. All Nodes displayed genuine human faces, donated to the Flesh Banks by former Library users. The Nodes reminded visitors of Library rules and relayed messages, which were rated for content and sometimes censored by an Automated Decency Filter.

DATA GHOSTING

The spacesuits worn by the members of the Lux expedition all had collar-fitted communicators that incorporated a neural relay device for the transmission of thought-mails. A technical quirk meant that these neural relays could retain a temporary impression of a living consciousness after death, the result of which was that the communicator could continue to broadcast a dead person's brainwaves as speech, for minutes and sometimes hours. The initially coherent speech of the Data Ghost would gradually deteriorate into looped phrases or words and then fall silent.

DOCTOR MOON

The moon orbiting the planet was an artificially constructed virus-checker built to support and maintain the Data Core. Signals were transmitted between The Library and the Doctor Moon as the two communicated. There was also a manifestation of Doctor Moon inside CAL's virtual reality, who helped to preserve the fantasy world and integrate its 4,022 guests.

RIVER SONG'S TIMELINE

[Spoilers omitted]

- River Song meets the Doctor for the first time
- River Song and the Doctor picnic at Asgard
- River Song and the Doctor are present at the Crash of the *Byzantium*
- River Song and the Doctor travel to the end of the universe
- The Doctor, with a new haircut and a suit, visits River Song and takes her to see the singing towers at Darillium. He gives her his sonic screwdriver
- River Song sends the Doctor a message on the psychic paper, asking him to come to The Library
- The Doctor meets River Song for the first time. She knows his name
- River Song sacrifices herself to save the Doctor and The Library
- The Doctor beams River Song from a neural relay in her sonic screwdriver into The Library's Data Core

VILLENGARD

I like bananas. Bananas are good.
– *The Doctor to Jack Harkness (London, 1941)*

The Banana Groves of Villengard mark a site which once hosted famous weapon factories that supplied armies and time agents throughout the galaxy. The last-known weapon produced at Villengard – before the factories were vaporised in an explosion as the main reactor went critical – was a sonic blaster carried by Captain Jack Harkness. The blaster could remove precisely square areas of anything it targeted, and was fitted with a digital rewind to exactly replace the same square area. Also functioning as a sonic cannon or a triple-enfolded sonic disruptor, the blaster's chief limitation was its reliance on batteries obtainable only from Villengard. Jack left the blaster aboard the TARDIS in 200,100. Some time before her visit to The Library, in her own timeline, River Song retrieved the same blaster from the TARDIS.

6012

MESSALINE

The planet Messaline was an inhospitable and infertile world of bleak, windswept moors and dark, wet bogs. Nitrogen constituted 80 per cent of its atmosphere with the remaining 20 per cent oxygen, which made the air breathable for human-type life forms, although its ozone and radiation levels were high. On 11 July 6012 (60120711 in the New Byzantine Calendar), a crew of humans and Hath landed a fusion-drive spaceship equipped with terraforming technology on Messaline's surface. This huge red cylinder, *Messaline Leader One*, dominated the landscape for two weeks while its colonisation programme got under way.

FIRST-WAVE HUMAN-HATH CO-COLONISATION PROGRAMME

Subterranean Deployment: The lower parts of the spaceship bored into the planet's surface

Phase One: **Construction Drones activated**

- Sections 1A, 1B, 2A, 2B, 3C and 3D completed 12 July
- Sections 1C, 1D, 2C, 2D, 3A and 3B completed 13 July
- Sections 4A, 4B, 4C and 4D completed 14 July
- Sections 5A, 5B, 6A, 6C, 7B and 7D completed 15 July
- Sections 5C, 5D, 6B, 6D, 7A and 7C completed 16 July
- Sections 8A, 8B, 8C and 8D completed 17 July

Robotic drones worked their way out from the ship, constructing tunnel sections and then civic buildings, auditoriums and what would become holding pens. As each section was completed it was date-stamped, and the western quadrant of the city was finished in six days, preserved below ground to await the terraforming of the surface.

Phase Two: **Progenation initiated**

Designated pioneers provided tissue samples for the generation of a new wave of colonists

At this point, the third phase – terraforming the surface – should have begun, but the mission commander was diagnosed with Byzantine fever and quarantined. When he died, there was no agreement on who should replace him, the humans and Hath split into factions and began fighting. This quickly developed into an all-out war that claimed thousands of lives in just seven days.

HATH

The creatures that accompanied the humans on their co-colonisation missions at this time were humanoid but with piscine heads. Each Hath had a translucent, liquid-filled tube on his face in place of a mouth, and they communicated with burbles and gurgles.

SCIENCE AND TECHNOLOGY

PROGENATION

Messaline Leader One brought only a small number of humans and Hath to begin the colonisation programme. Once construction of the first quadrant of their new city was completed, they used progenation machines to increase their numbers. A progenation machine took a tissue sample from an individual's hand, extracting diploid cells containing a pair of each type of chromosome. The diploid cells were divided into haploid cells, containing one member of each chromosome pair, and then recombined into a new arrangement and grown. This growth was accelerated, and a new life was generated by the machine. What emerged from the machine a matter of moments after the initial tissue extraction was a fully grown human or Hath in optimum physical condition.

The progenation process also provided an instant mental download, but the war led both humans and Hath to reprogram the machines to instil only strategic and military protocols. Both sides were able to produce 20 generations of fully trained combat-ready soldiers in a single day.

THE SEVEN-DAY WAR

With the progenation machines producing 20 new generations of soldiers every day, making them fit to fight but not implanting any knowledge of their history or purpose, both Hath and humans quickly forgot how and why the war had started and what they were doing on Messaline. With countless generations dying in battle every day, it took just days for both sides to mythologise their story, not realising that the buildings they were fighting in were the brand new basis for a whole new civilisation. All movement was regulated: the humans took over an auditorium as their encampment, while the Hath based themselves in a civic building, filling them with makeshift shelters and lighting campfires. Early on the final day of the war – three generations back – a group of humans in what was designated the Eastern Zone suffered what the rest described as an outbreak of pacifism, but this was the only sign of people managing to think beyond the conflict and they lost all contact with the rest of the colonists. The legends of both sides told of a lost Temple that held something called the Source – the breath of life that would allow the victors to control the planet.

SCIENCE AND TECHNOLOGY

TERRAFORMING

Messaline Leader One brought third-generation terraforming technology that would rejuvenate the planet's ecosystem, transforming it from barren wasteland to fertile paradise, changing the atmosphere and filling the land with lush plant life. At the heart of the process was the Source, a spherical glass container kept stable in the spaceship and filled with a gaseous compound of ammonia, methane, hydrogen, amino acids, proteins and nucleic acids. The release of the gases from this orb triggered the terraforming process, accelerating evolution and plant growth on the surface and stripping away the top layers of polluted earth to uncover the new city.

THE DOCTOR'S DAUGHTER

When the Doctor described her as a 'generated anomaly', Donna suggested that the latest child of the progenation machine should call herself Jenny. She had been progenated in moments after a tissue sample was taken from the Doctor. She was in peak physical condition, like all the human soldiers, but had also gained at least some elements of a Time Lord's biology which the machine had extrapolated from the Doctor. Although she had two hearts, however, she was not actually a Time Lord, and she was unable to regenerate when she was shot. But an unforeseen side effect of her death in proximity to the activation of the terraforming was that her body was revived by the gaseous compound from the Source. The Doctor, Martha and Donna had already left Messaline when Jenny revived, so she took the colonists' shuttle and left Messaline to save planets, rescue civilisations, defeat creatures and do an awful lot of running.

85th–372nd Centuries

SHAN SHEN

The Chino-planet Shan Shen lies millions of light years from Earth, a distant outpost of street markets and alleyways, pagodas and kites, peasants and stallholders. Every street is decorated with long red banners adorned with Chinese inscriptions and symbols. When the Doctor and Donna visited the markets of Shan Shen, Donna came across a Fortune Teller who offered to reveal her future. Instead, she asked about her past...

TRICKSTER'S BEETLE

As Donna talked about her first meeting with the Doctor, the Fortune Teller's incense caused her to briefly re-experience the events of Christmas 2007. Disoriented, she was aware of something dark and insectoid leaping onto her back. It had a shiny black carapace, spindly black legs and huge mandibles. This was a large, beetle-like creature that fed off time itself by changing tiny but significant events in someone's life. It was one of the Trickster's Brigade, which delighted in disrupting timelines and destroying lives. Taking Donna back to the day that she accepted a job at H.C. Clements, the Beetle and the Fortune Teller compelled her to make a different choice to the one that had led her to the Doctor. A whole new parallel world was created around her as, one morning in 2007, Donna's car turned right at a road junction instead of left.

In this world, Donna Noble never met the Doctor, who died saving the Earth from the Racnoss. Without the Doctor to save it, the Earth suffered again and again throughout 2008 and 2009. Millions of lives were lost, making the planet even more vulnerable to the Dalek attack that was to come. As the walls between the universes crumbled, Rose Tyler was pulled into this new reality. She identified the turning point and persuaded this version of Donna to travel back to that day in 2007 and sacrifice herself to save the universe.

Back on Shan Shen, the Beetle fell from Donna's back, denied the time energy it needed. The Fortune Teller recoiled from the glimpse she suddenly had of Donna's future and what she would soon become.

BAD WOLF

Rose told Donna to warn the Doctor: Bad Wolf. As Donna repeated the two words to the Doctor, every banner and sign on Shan Shen, even the police box notice above the TARDIS doors, seemed to change to read Bad Wolf too. It meant, the Doctor told her, the end of the universe.

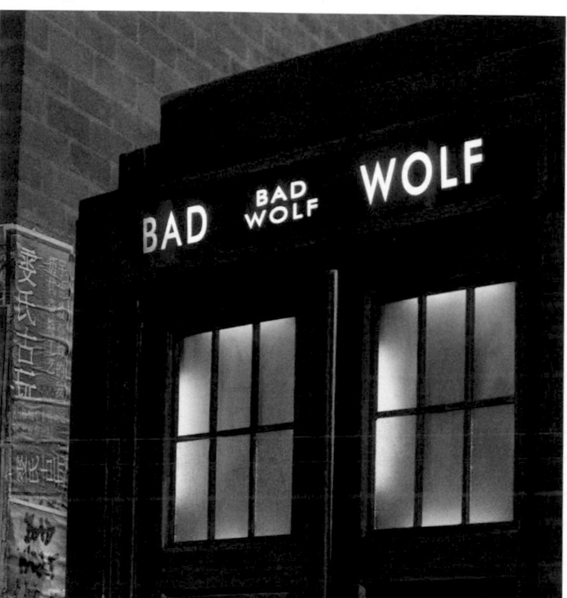

THE NEW ROMAN EMPIRE

> **The Doctor:** Ten thousand years in the future. Step outside, it's twelve thousand and five. The New Roman Empire.
> **Rose Tyler:** You think you're so impressive.
> **The Doctor:** I am so impressive!

ZETA MINOR

> **Sarah Jane Smith:** I saw things you wouldn't believe.
> **Rose Tyler:** Try me.
> **... Sarah:** Anti-matter monsters! *(London, 2007)*

In 37,166, a geological expedition to Zeta Minor and the military mission sent to help were all but wiped out by creatures composed of anti-matter that were attempting to prevent the removal of mineral samples from the planet. The Fourth Doctor and Sarah returned the samples, which also contained anti-matter, and the survivors of the expeditions were allowed to leave.

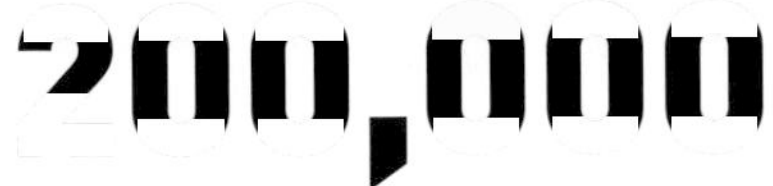

THE FOURTH GREAT AND BOUNTIFUL HUMAN EMPIRE

By now, Earth was at the centre of a galactic empire that encompassed a million species on a million planets. The Earth was covered with mega-cities that reached up into space and housed a population of 96 billion in hundreds of independent republics, and elaborate metal crests circled the globe. The poles had long since melted away, and the increased gravity of a planet that bristled with technology had attracted four additional moons, which orbited the Earth alongside huge satellites and a constant stream of spaceships.

The human race at this time should have been at its most intelligent and inquisitive, its culture, art, politics, philosophy and cuisine at a creative peak. But something had set Earth back by about 90 years, stalling its technological advances and slowly isolating it from other civilisations – the Daleks were hidden in space, quietly influencing mankind's development. Ninety-one years earlier, they had placed an agent aboard the news-transmitting space station Satellite Five and had been affecting and influencing Earth's development ever since. A burgeoning climate of fear led to tighter immigration laws that prevented alien species from coming to Earth, while an acquiescent population and news media unquestioningly accepted a series of flimsy explanations for their increasing remoteness from the rest of the Empire – the price of spacewarp had doubled, the collapse of the government on Chavic Fice had stopped visitors from that sector, and so on. Meanwhile, all citizens were registered, and Satellite Five kept census records for the entire Empire. The Daleks, through the Jagrafess, were breeding a human race that didn't ask questions.

JAGRAFESS

The Mighty Jagrafess of the Holy Hadrojassic Maxarodenfoe was installed on the top floor of Satellite Five by a Syndicate of bankers represented by the Editor and working, perhaps unknowingly, for the Daleks. A great slab of raw meat and white fat, with sharp teeth in massive snapping jaws, it formed the ceiling of Floor 500, from where it monitored everything that happened and acted as Editor-in-Chief for the Human Empire's news broadcasts, controlling information and guiding and shaping mankind.

The Jagrafess's metabolism generated immense quantities of heat, and Satellite Five was designed to pump this heat away from the creature and down through the space station – the creature had to stay cold to stay alive.

Although Floor 500's temperature was kept below zero, water constantly dripped from the Jagrafess onto the icy floor below it. It was destroyed when a news journalist, Cathica Santini Khadeni, reversed the satellite's heating systems to pump heat up to Floor 500. The Jagrafess exploded.

SATELLITE FIVE

A vertical tube ringed with hoops and covered in transmitters and pylons, Satellite Five orbited the Earth and broadcast a constant stream of news from 600 television channels. Its 500 floors were linked by key-coded high-velocity lifts, and all contained series of Observation Decks and Spike Rooms, linked by corridors and constantly monitored by thousands of security cameras. Each floor provided fast-food booths selling Kronkburgers (with cheese or pajatos) and synthesised drinks like Zaffic (which tasted of beef), paid for with credit bars. Loudspeaker announcements and alarm klaxons reminded workers of station rules and regulated the work periods.

Here, hundreds of human journalists, but no aliens, devoted their lives to gathering, processing and distributing the news. On arrival on the satellite, each employee first visited Floor 016, the medical section, then went to their allocated Floor to work, eat and sleep. On the news floors like Floor 139, those who had been given the full info-spike had the news streamed directly into their brains in the Spike Rooms. Every employee hoped to be promoted to Editorial on Floor 500 where, it was said, the walls were made of gold – with 15 different menus, marble toilets and double beds, the staff on Floor 500 made all the big decisions. Once someone went up to Floor 500, they never returned.

This was actually because Floor 500 was kept at sub-zero temperatures and staffed by pallid, black-eyed Drones. These were the reanimated corpses of former employees, controlled like puppets via their chip implants by the Editor. When the Drones' flesh eventually rotted away, their skeletons were abandoned in disused Spike Rooms.

The final addition to the ranks of the Editor's Drones was Eva Saint Julienne, last surviving member of the Freedom Fifteen. A dissident organisation called the Freedom Foundation had been monitoring Satellite Five's broadcasts and had evidence that the news reports were being altered and manipulated. Eva was placed on the station, a genetic graft disguising her as Suki Macrae Cantrell, but her identity was uncovered by the Editor, and the Jagrafess killed her.

SCIENCE AND TECHNOLOGY

INFO-SPIKES

Every worker on Satellite Five had a chip implanted that allowed them to access and control the computer systems. Most had the Type One head-chip (100 credits) inserted into the back of the skull, which enabled them to interface with computers. The Type Two info-spike (10,000 credits) was inserted by a picosurgeon in a painless ten-minute procedure, and effectively turned the brain into part of the computer. A small door opened in the forehead so that a compressed stream of information could be beamed directly into the brain. It was activated by a personally selected signal with its default setting a simple click of the fingers, and it allowed access to the entire Satellite Five archive – the entire history of the human race.

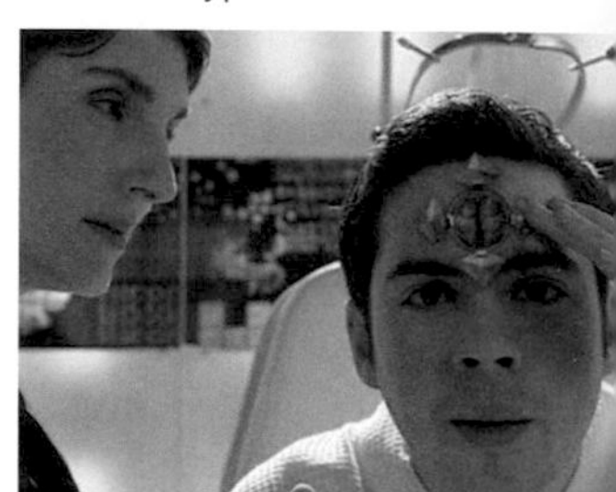

VOMIT-O-MATIC

Installed free as part of the info-spiking process, nano-termites were placed in the lining of the throat. In the event of sickness, the waste product was frozen into a small lozenge.

SMT

Single Molecule Transcription was developed by the Butler Corporation in Cincinnati, Ohio, and replaced microprocessors in 2019. It indents the wall of a hydrogen molecule with code that responds to the physical excitation of surrounding space.

FINAL BROADCASTS

✦ **Channel ☺+1**: Solar flare activity was increasing across Space Lane 556, and Space Lane 77 had been closed by sunspot activity. Solar flares were raging at 5.9, and all commercial flights were advised to avoid these routes.

✦ **Bad WolfTV**: Sandstorms on the New Venus Archipelago had left 200 dead and were causing chaos.

✦ The Face of Boe announced that he was pregnant with Baby Boemina.

✦ **Channel McB:** On Caledonia Prime, the Glasgow water riots had just entered their third day.

100 YEARS OF HELL

After the death of the Jagrafess, the news channels were immediately closed down. With no replacements available, however, Earth and its Empire were left without information, which soon led to the collapse of Earth's governments and economy. Within 80 years, planet-wide pollution had become so bad that the Great Atlantic Smog Storm began, and bulletins had to be issued to let people know when it was safe to venture into the open air. Half the world was starving, and the other half was watching game shows on TV...

EMPEROR DALEK

> I cultivated pure and blessed Daleks.
>
> *– The Emperor Dalek*

Just one Dalek saucer had survived the devastation that ended the Time War – the command ship fell through time and the Emperor Dalek escaped the annihilation of his race. For centuries the Emperor hid in the dark space on the edge of Earth's solar system, rebuilding his forces while watching and then shaping Earth's development. Then he began to harvest the humans, at first taking their imprisoned criminals, refugees and dispossessed. Each body was filleted, its flesh crushed and sorted to separate out the one cell in a billion that could be used to nurture a new Dalek mutant. The Emperor created a new breed of semi-human Daleks, though he claimed that everything human had been purged. Now insane, the Emperor Dalek had come to believe that he was immortal, the God of all Daleks.

DALEKS (2)

> You hate your own existence.
>
> *– The Doctor*

The human race had seen nothing of the Daleks since the Tenth Dalek Occupation, when they vanished from space and time and became embroiled in the Time War. The Emperor's new force of half a million Daleks had, like their creator, been driven insane, both by the centuries spent hiding in silence and by the non-Dalek source of their own flesh. Now the Dalek Stratagem was reaching its conclusion – they had manipulated Earth for centuries, installing first the Jagrafess and then a Controller aboard Satellite Five and using the station's television transmissions not just to influence mankind's development but also to mask their presence in the solar system. The Dalek Fleet was ready to attack by the time the Doctor uncovered their existence. Before long, 200 ships, each carrying over 2,000 Daleks, were heading for the Earth and the orbiting space station. The Dalek Fleet attacked the Earth and bombed whole continents. It took just 15 seconds for their saucers to devastate Europa, Pacifica and the New American Alliance and entirely obliterate Australasia.

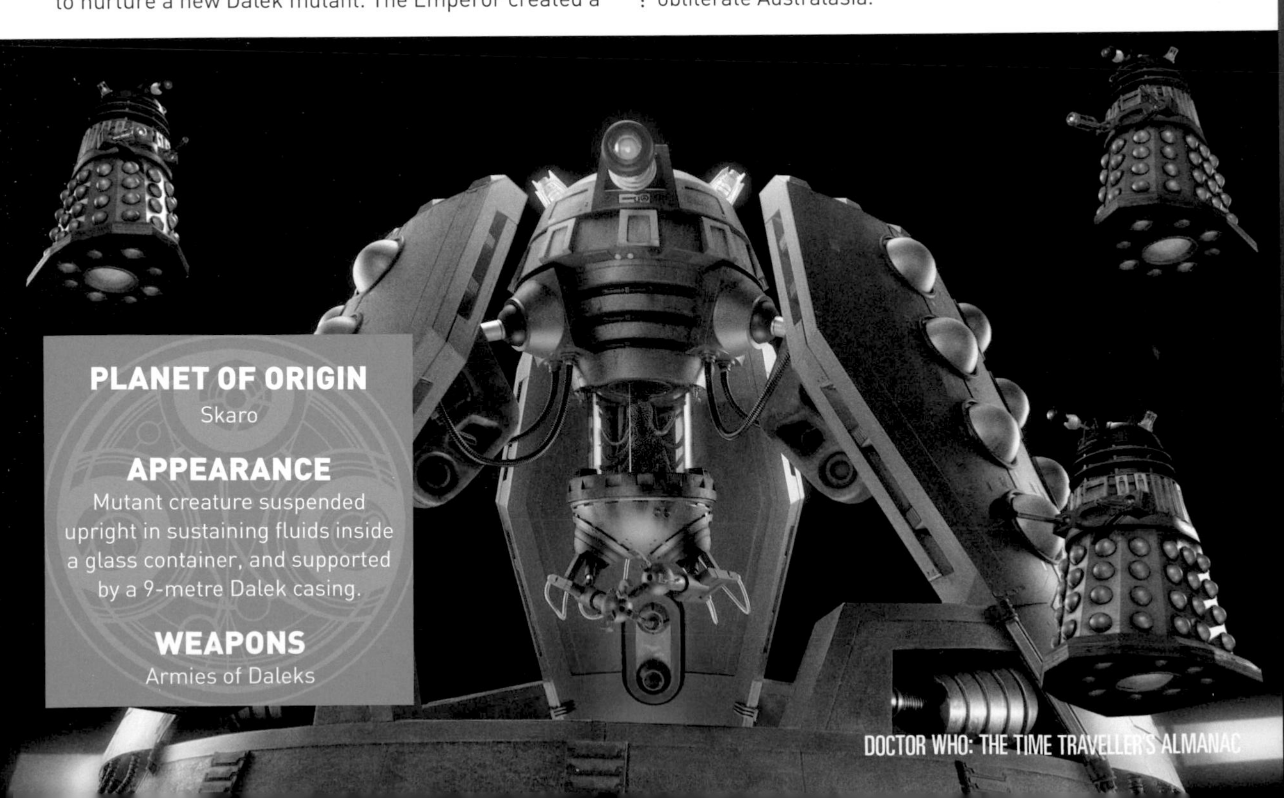

PLANET OF ORIGIN
Skaro

APPEARANCE
Mutant creature suspended upright in sustaining fluids inside a glass container, and supported by a 9-metre Dalek casing.

WEAPONS
Armies of Daleks

GAME STATION

When news transmissions ceased in 200,000, the Bad Wolf Corporation reopened Satellite Five as the Game Station. The Game Station Syndicate it established to control the station's output was – intentionally or not – working for the Daleks. The satellite now operated under its own private legislation, and was powerful enough to convict criminals and despatch them to the Earth's Lunar Penal Colony. The Game Station was broadcasting a powerful encrypted signal that masked the Dalek Fleet from all sonars, radars and scanners. That signal was hidden by the constant transmission of hundreds of game shows. This was interrupted only by solar flare activity, when the Game Station powered down and viewers were shown repeats. Although all channels carried adverts, it was illegal not to purchase a television licence, and the penalty for evasion was execution. A transmat beam randomly selected contestants for brutal versions of game shows. The losers were apparently disintegrated, although the disintegrator was actually a secondary transmat system that transported people onto the Dalek command ship.

A human Controller was wired into the Game Station systems on Floor 500 to monitor the satellite's entire output, which was channelled through her brain. She responded only to authorised Game Station personnel and, of course, to her Dalek masters. Each programme was overseen by one of the Programmers working on Floor 500. Below that were the television studios of Floors 1 to 499 where the shows were made. Shuttles docked with the satellite at Floor 000. When the Doctor ordered the evacuation of the satellite ahead of the Dalek Fleet's attack, there were not enough shuttles to take everyone, and 108 people were stranded there.

The Game Station's exterior was reinforced against meteors, and its viewscreens were Exoglass. Shielded rooms were accessed via deadlock-sealed doors constructed from Hydra Combination. The Daleks overrode the station's internal laser codes and took all defences offline, entering the Game Station at Floor 494. They fought their way up, pausing only to use the station's ventilation shafts to descend to Floor 000 and exterminate the trapped humans. The Anne-Droid was deployed on Floor 495, and it destroyed a three-Dalek advance guard before it was obliterated. The Daleks located and exterminated Lynda, who was monitoring everything from the Observation Deck on Floor 056. They then climbed the western duct to Floor 499.

BROADCASTING

BEAR WITH ME

Format: Three people had to live with a bear *Trivia:* During a celebrity edition, the bear got into the bath

BIG BROTHER

Broadcast: Channel 44,000 on Floor 056 *Host:* Davina-Droid *Final contestants:* Linda-with-an-i, Crosbie, Strood, Lynda-with-a-y Moss, the Doctor *Format:* Contestants were selected for eviction one by one; they were disintegrated as they left the House *Trivia:* All *Big Brother* houses were deadlock sealed after a walkout by contestants during *Big Brother* 504; there were ten Floors broadcasting different *Big Brother* shows

CALL MY BLUFF

Format: Played with real guns

COUNTDOWN

Format: Stop a bomb exploding in thirty seconds

GROUND FORCE

Format: Runners-up were turned into compost

STARS IN THEIR EYES

Format: Sing, or be blinded

THE WEAKEST LINK

Broadcast: Game Room 6 on Floor 407 *Host:* Anne-Droid *Final contestants:* Agorax, Fitch, Rose, Rodrick, Colleen, Broff *Format:* After each round of questions from the Anne-Droid, one contestant was voted off by their rivals; they were then disintegrated by the Anne-Droid *Trivia:* The winner collected 1,600 credits

WHAT NOT TO WEAR

Broadcast: Floor 299 *Hosts:* Trin-E and Zu-Zana *Final contestant:* Captain Jack Harkness *Format:* The two androids suggested outfits for the contestants, then removed their faces with chainsaws and scissors ('the face-off')

WIPEOUT

Format: The title speaks for itself

CAPTAIN JACK HARKNESS

REPORTED SIGHTING #9 CONFIRMED

ESTIMATED AGE: 35

LOCATION: Game Station, 200,100

AVAILABLE INFORMATION: Transmatted aboard the Game Station from the TARDIS, Captain Jack recruited a small band of volunteers to delay the Daleks while the Doctor constructed a Delta Wave. He was the last man standing when the Daleks reached Floor 500 and was exterminated, but Rose resurrected him using the power of the Time Vortex. The Doctor immediately sensed that Jack would now always come back to life when killed and abandoned him on the Game Station.

SCIENCE AND TECHNOLOGY

DEFABRICATOR

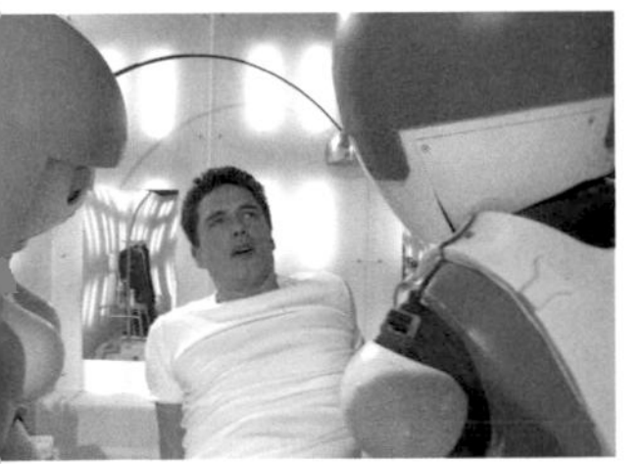

Used by Trin-E and Zu-Zana to dissolve and remove contestants' clothing, Captain Jack adapted this to create a weapon to fight the Daleks, here and in 2009. Firing a single shot drained its power supply, however.

EXTRAPOLATOR FORCE FIELD

The Doctor and Captain Jack converted the tribophysical waveform macro-kinetic extrapolator that they'd taken from the Slitheen in 2006 into a force field to protect the TARDIS against the Dalek Fleet. Captain Jack then linked it to the Game Station's defences to protect the top six Floors and force the Daleks to enter at Floor 494.

DELTA WAVE

The Doctor rewired the Game Station's systems to change, fold back and sequence the transmission signal and create a wave of Van Cassadyne energy. This Delta Wave would burn up the brain cells of every living thing in its path. He completed it just as the Daleks reached Floor 500. But, with the Game Station's transmitter covering the whole of the Earth, the Doctor could not bring himself to activate the signal.

BAD WOLF

> I did nothing ... They are not part of my design.
> – *The Emperor Dalek*

That the Game Station was owned by the mysterious Bad Wolf Corporation was part of a stranger phenomenon that echoed throughout space and time. When the Doctor sent Rose Tyler home to the Powell Estate in South London using TARDIS Emergency Programme One, the phrase 'Bad Wolf' seemed to be everywhere: on a poster in a fast-food café, on playground walls, on the tarmacked ground. Until now, Rose and the Doctor had assumed that Bad Wolf was a warning, or perhaps part of a scheme to draw them into the Daleks' trap. Now Rose realised that it was a message to her, a link between herself and the Doctor. She and Mickey forced open the TARDIS console and the energy of the Time Vortex flowed into her, giving her extraordinary power. Returning to the Game Station to save the Doctor, she took the phrase from a Bad Wolf Corporation sign and scattered the words throughout time and space – she had left the message for herself. She was the Bad Wolf, and she had created herself. With the Vortex still running through her head, she divided the Daleks, their Fleet and their Emperor into their constituent particles. The power was killing her though, so the Doctor drew it out of her and returned it to the TARDIS, healing Rose as he did so. The Vortex energy had the same damaging effect on him as it had on Rose, and he was forced to regenerate...

EVERYTHING
HAS ITS TIME

THE END OF THE WORLD

The expansion of the star Sol as it blossomed into a red giant in the year officially designated 5.5/apple/26 finally destroyed the planet Earth. For several centuries, the owners of the Earth – the National Trust – had staved off the inevitable, installing gravity satellites to combat continental shift and maintaining a Classic Earth. Meanwhile, humanity had gradually abandoned its home world, first during millennia of colonisation as mankind explored the galaxies, and then in waves of space arks that had eventually evacuated the planet completely. By the year five billion, the Earth was empty, while the galaxies were full of New Humans, Proto-Humans and Digi-Humans.

On the day of the world's destruction, the galaxy's richest people gathered on a heavily shielded orbiting space station to witness the spectacle. Earthdeath was scheduled for 15:39. But when it came, no one was watching...

PLATFORM ONE

One of 15 viewing platforms owned by The Corporation, Platform One was a three-mile-long structure centred on the Luxury Area – a maximum hospitality zone of private viewing galleries, hospitality suites and guest rooms, linked by corridors and threaded with maintenance ducts and junctions, with staff offices, engine rooms and a ventilation chamber supporting the infrastructure. The entire station was controlled by a central computer, which regulated the temperature and the Platform's shielding and SunFilter Technology, as well as making regular information announcements. There was a small complement of diminutive waiting staff and maintenance engineers, headed by a Steward. The staff were all recruited from Crespallion, part of the Jaggit Brocade affiliated to the Scarlet Junction Convex 56. Only the Steward was permitted to talk to the guests without permission, and the idents of all machines and robotic devices had to be registered on the controlling computer.

Attendance at the Earthdeath event, sponsored by the Face of Boe, was by invitation only. Specially commissioned shuttles brought guests to Platform One, and visitors were allowed anywhere on the station, but the use of weapons, teleportation and religion was forbidden under Peace Treaty 5.4/cup/16. Each guest was allocated a private suite, protected by a code wall. The event began with the introduction of each of the guests and an exchange of gifts representing peace. This took place in the Manchester Suite, where refreshments were to be served after Earthdeath.

Platform One was sabotaged by the Lady Cassandra using robot spiders concealed in stainless-steel orbs brought on board as gifts by the Adherents of the Repeated Meme. The spider devices infiltrated the whole of Platform One, taking control of the computer mainframe and disabling the safety systems. This caused the engines to pitch up by about 30 hertz, while all the sun filters descended and allowed the sun's rays to bombard the unprotected space station. With the force fields gone, the Exoglass viewing windows fractured, allowing the 5,000-degree heat to penetrate the viewing galleries and hospitality suites. The systems that weren't melting were failing, and could only be reset by a switch in the ventilation chamber, blocked by the enormous fans that were meant to keep the temperatures down. The fans were controlled by a wall-mounted lever, and Jabe of the Forest of Cheem sacrificed herself in the extreme temperature attempting to slow the fans so the Doctor could access the reset switch. He raised the Platform's safety shield just three seconds before the Earth exploded. The computer systems then regained control and initiated automatic repairs. As the surviving guests departed, Platform One was closed for maintenance.

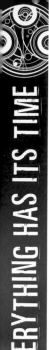

SCIENCE AND TECHNOLOGY

PSYCHIC PAPER

Rose first saw the Doctor use this on Platform One. It shows people whatever he wants them to see and has, occasionally, received messages.

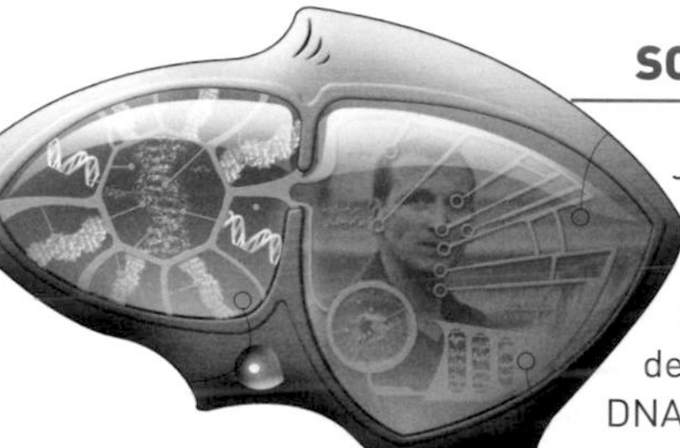

SCANNER

Jabe's handheld device scanned and photographed a subject and could detect and identify DNA.

EARTH CLASSICS

ON DISPLAY

- ✦ J.K. Rowling, *Harry Potter and the Philosopher's Stone* (1997)
- ✦ An Underwood typewriter
- ✦ Spools of reel-to-reel audiotape
- ✦ A Santa Claus ornament

ON CASSANDRA'S 'iPOD'

- ✦ Soft Cell – Tainted Love
- ✦ Britney Spears – Toxic
- ✦ The Police – Roxanne/Peanuts
- ✦ The Tubes – Prime Time/No Way Out
- ✦ Supertramp – The Logical Song/Another Nervous Wreck
- ✦ Edwin Starr – H.A.P.P.Y. Radio
- ✦ Donna Summer – Bad Girls/On My Honor
- ✦ Earth Wind & Fire – Boogie Wonderland (with The Emotions)
- ✦ The Knack – My Sharona/Let Me Out
- ✦ Spyro Gyra – Morning Dance/Jubilee

THE DOCTOR AND ROSE TYLER

The Doctor brought the gift of air from his lungs. The Forest of Cheem's Jabe was highly appreciative, but the Adherents of the Repeated Meme appeared indifferent.

THE FOREST OF CHEEM

Jabe, Lute and Coffa represented this collective of sentient treeforms on Platform One, and brought cuttings of their forebears as peace offerings. They were humanoid but made of wood, with bark for skin and twigs and leaves growing from them. Their ancestors had been transplanted from Earth during its Middle Blue Period, and Jabe was directly descended from the tropical rainforests. They claimed to have no understanding of machinery or computers, but were considered wise and peaceful, and were numbered among the Higher Species of the universe – those who were aware of or affected by the Last Great Time War. With forests on planets throughout the universe, these Trees owned large amounts of land and were extremely wealthy. Their liana were not intended for public display.

THE MOXX OF BALHOON

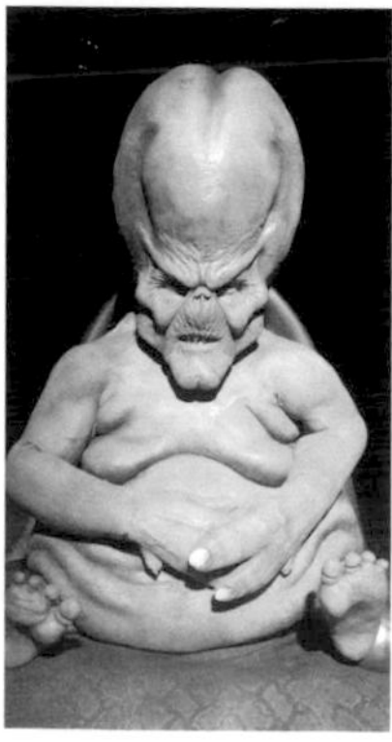

Representing the solicitors Jolco and Jolco, the Moxx was a small, blue-skinned creature that travelled on an anti-gravity chair. His gift to fellow guests was bodily saliva, which carried a standard health warning (he could sweat glaxic acids if his bodily fluids were not renewed regularly). He perished when the Manchester Suite's Exoglass windows fractured.

HONOURED GUESTS

THE ADHERENTS OF THE REPEATED MEME

Arriving as representatives of Financial Family Seven, these remote-controlled, part-organic, cowled androids were Cassandra's agents and brought her robot spiders onto Platform One in the orbs they gave as gifts. They recited their meme at 30-minute intervals. The Doctor deactivated them by snapping the ganglia in their arms.

AMBASSADORS FROM THE CITY STATE OF BINDING LIGHT

Mildly oxygen-averse, so air composition had to be strictly monitored in their presence.

THE FACE OF BOE

The sponsor of the Earthdeath event.

(See also 200,000; 5,000,000,023; and 5,000,000,053)

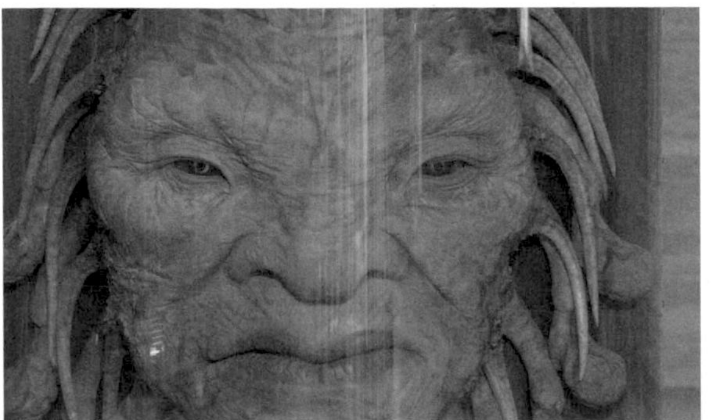

THE BROTHERS HOP PYLEEN

The inventors and copyright holders of hyposlip travel systems, from the clifftops of Rex Vox Jax.

CAL 'SPARK PLUG' MACNANNOVICH

The cybernetic hyperstar (and entourage).

MR AND MRS PACKOO

Two-metre-tall bird people.

THE CHOSEN SCHOLARS OF CLASS FIFTY-FIVE

Selected to attend by the University of Rago Rago Five Six Rago.

THE LADY CASSANDRA O'BRIEN DOT DELTA SEVENTEEN

The Last Human – at least in her own view.

(See also 5,000,000,023)

5,000,000,023

NEW EARTH

The planet Earth's destruction in 5,000,000,000 quickly aroused feelings of nostalgia among humans across the cosmos and, when a similar planet was discovered 50,000 light years from Earth in the galaxy M87, a full-scale revival movement soon got under way. This planet was the same size as the Earth, with the same atmosphere and the same orbit. Its discoverers named it New Earth, and its colonisation began. After just a few years, New Earth was a viable world, with a population of millions.

The pioneers who established New Earth as the latest human home world mimicked millennia of tradition when they came to name its continents and cities. New New York was typical – the fifteenth city in the cosmos to be named after Old Earth's New York. It was situated on the coast of the New Atlantic Ocean, and the surrounding land was more verdant than had been seen for billions of years around the original. The scent of apple grass was a novelty, but in most other respects New New York's skyline was a faithful replica. Recreations of most of the famous landmarks, including the Statue of Liberty, could be seen from the flying shuttle cars that constantly streamed through the airways around the city. The Senate rose high above the Overcity, from which New New York's administration governed the population of ten million. Some enjoyed the cocktails and glitter of the levels above ground, but there was also an extensive subterranean Undercity. At the lowest level was Pharmacytown, where street traders sold mood patches to the desperate and the poor.

NEW NEW YORK HOSPITAL

Situated on an island in New New York's bay area was a large building with a green crescent-moon on its walls. The moon was the universal symbol for hospitals, the building the New New York Hospital. It was run by the Sisters of Plenitude, who claimed that their charitable institution could cure anything except old age.

Inside the tall and gleaming complex were many floors of wards and operating theatres, post-op centres and nanodentistry clinics (but no shop). Computer-controlled announcements informed visitors and patients of hospital regulations and when they could visit the hospital's pleasure gardens, and reminded them of the motto adopted by the Sisters: Hope, Harmony and Health. The hospital's ambient temperature was also broadcast regularly – this was kept at 14 degrees cohezic, which had been evaluated as the ideal temperature to promote healing and well-being. Voice-controlled lifts carried them between the complex's many floors. A three-stage disinfection process was carried out for each new entrant to the hospital as the lift carried them between floors.

The hospital had an astonishing success rate, providing cures for incurable diseases using a cell-washing cascade of solutions developed in the hospital's own laboratories. The secret of this success lay in a vast, hidden and sterile chamber at the heart of the complex. This was Intensive Care, a farm for human plague carriers, where thousands of specially bred 'patients' were simultaneously subjected to a thousand different diseases. They were held individually in dark cells, where they were fed through tubes and subjected to a top-up of bacteria and viruses every ten minutes, as well as regular blood-washing cascades. A thousand died each day, but there were always thousands more. In theory, these patients were not in any way sentient and were kept in an unconscious state, but they eventually developed independent thought, speech and vocabulary,

becoming aware of what had been done to them and starting to construct logical arguments. Whenever any of the patients showed signs of consciousness, standard procedure was to incinerate them in their cells. Sister Corvin had theorised that migration of sentience was bringing about this change, and Matron Casp, the leader of the Sisterhood, suggested reviewing the hospital's brainstem policies to prevent this development.

Before she could act on this, the patients were released from their cells by Cassandra. They smashed the equipment that had held and regulated them and began to move through the hospital, spreading disease and instantly killing everyone they touched. They were reaching out simply to touch and hold others, sensations that had been denied to them throughout their lives. The hospital was sealed off, its lifts quarantined and all incoming shuttle flights diverted, and no one was permitted to leave the premises. The Doctor mixed a cocktail of the Sisters' remedies and used the lifts' disinfection process to spread the cure among the patients, a new sub-species – New Humans. The New New York Police Department entered the hospital and arrested its staff, taking statements from visitors, while the new life forms were catalogued.

Miracle Cures

✦ Hawtrey's Syndrome ✦ Petrifold Regression
✦ Marconi's Disease ✦ Pallidome Pancrosis

Hospital Staff

✦ Sister Jatt ✦ Novice Hame
✦ Matron Casp ✦ Sister Corvin

Celebrity Patients

✦ The Duke of Manhattan ✦ The Face of Boe

CASSANDRA

The self-proclaimed Last Human was the Lady Cassandra O'Brien Dot Delta Seventeen. She claimed that her father was Texan and her mother was from the Arctic Desert, making her the last Pure Human, and seems to have survived for hundreds, perhaps thousands of years. When she attended the Earthdeath event on Platform One, she joked that she didn't look a day over 2,000. This was thanks to 708 operations to have herself reduced to a thin layer of skin, which was taken from the front of her body and stretched across a metal frame. Her eyes and mouth were at the centre of the skin, and her brain was suspended in a case of sustaining fluids at the base of the frame. The rest of her body was apparently preserved at a secret location. She was attended by a pair of masked surgeons, who regularly moisturised her skin to prevent her drying out.

She used robot spiders to sabotage Platform One's systems, hoping to fake a hostage situation and collect a fortune in insurance. This did not go according to plan and she instead teleported off the space station leaving the other guests to die – she would still profit, having invested in shares in all their businesses. The Doctor, having reset Platform One's systems, reversed her teleportation device and brought her back to the Manchester Suite. There, the intense heat caused her skin to tighten and snap. Cassandra had apparently perished. Her brain survived, however, which her servant Chip recovered, along with her frame and her eyes. Chip secretly took Cassandra's remains to New New York's hospital, hiding her in the basement and stealing medicine for her. A new piece of skin was taken from the back of her body, stretched across her rusting frame, and reconnected with her brain. She continued to hide in the basement, attempting to learn the Sisterhood's secrets, watching ancient film reels of her past glories, and devising a plan to return to humanoid form and remake her fortune.

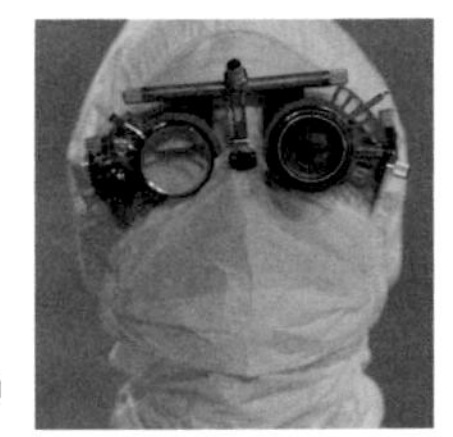

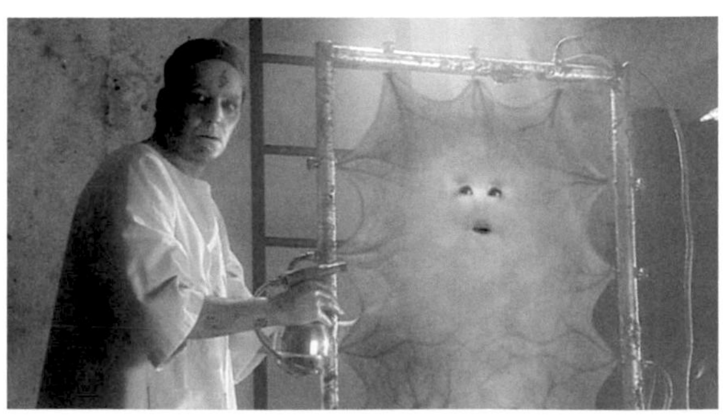

SCIENCE AND TECHNOLOGY

PSYCHO-GRAFT

A device for transferring the intelligence and consciousness of a living being from its own brain into the mind of another, the psycho-graft had been banned on every civilised world because it worked by compressing the recipient's consciousness to nothing. Cassandra had concealed a psycho-graft machine in the hospital basement and used it to transfer herself into Rose Tyler. In the process, Cassandra's original brain-meat finally expired, and her old skin evaporated. The psycho-graft allowed Cassandra to exhale her consciousness into a series of new victims, and she variously inhabited Rose, the Doctor, an infected hospital patient and, finally, Chip.

FORCE-GROWN CLONES

Many years earlier, when she was still humanoid, Cassandra had attended a reception for the Ambassador of Thrace. A stranger with henna tattoos across his skin approached her and told her she was beautiful, then collapsed and died in her arms. The henna tattoos became her favourite pattern, and she modelled a force-grown clone on the strange man, calling it Chip. She treated him as her pet, but he remained constantly faithful to her. He volunteered to have his mistress's mind transferred into his body, but the effort was too much for his heart, which quickly failed. The Doctor took Cassandra in the TARDIS back to the reception for the Thracian Ambassador, where, in Chip's form, she was able to tell herself that she was beautiful before she died at last.

CATKIND

This race of felines was native to New Earth and quickly became a fully integrated part of the new society that developed there – Catkind and humans would sometimes marry and have litters of kittens. Among the best known of the Catkind were the Sisters of Plenitude, an order of nuns devoted to the goddess Santori. They had sworn to help and heal the sick and ran the New New York Hospital, but the arrival on New Earth of the human race brought so many new illnesses that the Sisterhood could not cope. At first they experimented with clone-meat and bio-cattle in their attempts to find cures, but eventually they resorted to growing human flesh, perhaps unaware initially that they were creating a whole new life form. When their experiments were uncovered and the hospital was closed, the surviving Sisters were all arrested. Among their number was Novice Hame, whose penance was to nurse the Face of Boe through his lingering death from old age. She had previously nursed him for several years in the hospital. When disaster came to New Earth six years later, the Face of Boe shrouded her in his smoke, keeping her alive to help save millions of people in the New New York Undercity.

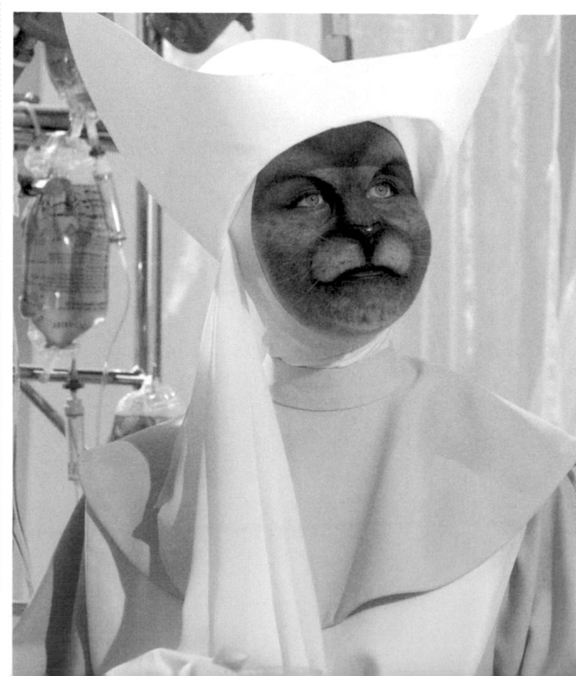

AUTOMATIC QUARANTINE

The people of New Earth had for many years used mood patches to enhance, stimulate and regulate their emotional highs and lows, using the patches as a legal drug. In 5,000,000,029 a new mood called Bliss was developed, and it was quickly taken up throughout New Earth society. But when a virus mutated inside the Bliss compound and became airborne, it killed everyone on the planet's surface in just seven minutes. The last act of the NNY Senate was to declare New Earth unsafe, and the planet was placed in automatic quarantine for 100 years. Alone in the Overcity, the Face of Boe and Novice Hame managed to close the walkways and flyovers to the Undercity, saving the poorer population but leaving them trapped below ground.

Over the next 24 years, more and more of the people sealed in beneath the surface took to their cars and attempted to escape via the motorway. They were tempted by stories of open skies, the scent of

apple grass and plentiful jobs in the areas beyond the city, and soon there were millions of cars gridlocked on the hundreds of motorway lanes. Every exit from New New York was blocked, and the cars could only inch their way along the enclosed routes. Before long, the drivers had come to expect a journey of five miles to take twelve years, with lay-bys reached every six months – people started to live in their cars. As a fuel-saving measure, the automated systems that regulated the motorway still allowed any car with three or more passengers to descend to the lowest level, the fast lane, where they could supposedly reach 30 miles per hour, but there were Macra at the bottom of the motorway, and those cars were never seen again. With no one in the Overcity, there were no ambulances or rescue services, and callers to the NNYPD were automatically placed on hold.

Hoping to prevent widespread despair and panic, the Face of Boe and Novice Hame provided a televised hologram, Sally Calypso, whose image was beamed directly into each car, giving optimistic traffic and weather reports telling of blue skies, 36-degree temperatures in the open air and extra lanes opening on the New New Jersey Expressway. The hologram also led a Daily Contemplation, during which all the drivers sang hymns.

Traditional Hymns for the Daily Contemplation

✦ The Old Rugged Cross
✦ Abide With Me

SCIENCE AND TECHNOLOGY

MOOD PATCHES

Every mood could be bought, and a range of strengths from 1 to 50 were available for as little as two credits. Among the most popular were:

✦ Happy 27 ✦ Forget 43 ✦ Fury 10 ✦ Angry 16 ✦ Honesty 28 ✦ Sleep 14 ✦ Witty 19 ✦ Rage 05 ✦ Mellow 19

CARS

New Earth's cars floated on anti-gravs and ran on self-replicating fuel, producing an enormous quantity of exhaust fumes in the enclosed space of the motorway. Each vehicle had an onboard computer linked directly into the NNY network which provided navigation, traffic system instruction and a connection to Sally Calypso's broadcasts. Some drivers had worked out how to convince these computers that their cars were carrying three passengers and could therefore join the fast lane; others resorted to car-jacking – kidnapping people to make up the numbers.

Each car had its individual call sign, such as Car 1-0-hot-5 or Car 4-6-5-diamond-6. Externally the same, every car was different on the inside, as drivers and families adapted their surroundings to give themselves miniature homes. Muscle stimulants replaced exercise, and waste products were recycled as food.

5,000,000,053

MACRA

It is now widely believed that the Macra that inhabited the bottom of the NNY motorway had escaped from a zoo when the Bliss virus wiped out the Overcity. Once, billions of years earlier, the gas-eating Macra had been an intelligent race, if unpleasant. They were the scourge of Galaxy M87, building an empire of enslaved humans to mine the gas that they consumed as food. But they had devolved over the millennia, becoming nothing more than gigantic, unthinking beasts, living off the exhaust fumes from the cars and blindly attacking any vehicle that made it into the fast lane. They perished when the motorway roof was reopened and the fumes cleared.

PLANET OF ORIGIN
Unknown

APPEARANCE
Immense crabs with huge claws

WEAKNESS
Dependency on gas, the filthier the better

BAD WOLF

The Doctor made his way down towards the fast lane, clambering through the cars until he reached the bottom layer of vehicles. On his way, he passed through a car driven by a Japanese couple, who had decorated the car interior with posters. One of these displayed the word 悪狼 (*akuro*), which means Bad Wolf.

GREAT LIVES

THE FACE OF BOE

A legendary being, who survived the extinction of Boekind during the Fourth Great and Bountiful Human Empire and lived on for billions of years. He was the sponsor of Platform One's Earthdeath event, by which time he was living in the Silver Devastation. Twenty-three years later he was a patient in the New New York hospital, dying of old age and watched over by Novice Hame. He sent a message to the Doctor's psychic paper, asking him to visit, and was apparently revived by the successful cure of the infected New Humans. He teleported himself out of the hospital, promising that he and the Doctor would meet one last time. When the Doctor returned to New Earth with Martha Jones, he learned of the Face of Boe and Novice Hame's attempt to save the population of the New New York Undercity. The Face of Boe had wired himself into the city's mainframe, donating his life force to maintain the motorway system and keep millions of people alive. Attempting to open the motorway roof, the Doctor pushed the city's residual energy up to maximum, inverted it and fed it through the electricity grid, but the transformers were blocked and he couldn't get a signal through. The Face of Boe boosted it with the last of his own energy, and the cars were finally free to escape the motorway into the open air and reclaim the city. This final effort proved too much, and the glass in the Face of Boe's tank shattered. The Doctor and Hame placed him on the floor of the Senate, and were with him as he died.

Superstitions and legends had surrounded the Face of Boe for millennia. One was that the sky would crack asunder at the time of his death; another was that, before he died, he would tell a great secret to a traveller, a lonely god like himself. The first came true when the roof of the motorway was opened. The second prediction was fulfilled when the Face of Boe told the Doctor: You Are Not Alone...

PLANET OF ORIGIN
Unknown

APPEARANCE
Gigantic head in a 1.5-metre steam-driven, glass-fronted tank filled with fluids and smoke

OTHER SIGHTINGS
200,000; 5,000,000,000; 5,000,000,023

100,000,000,000,000

GREAT LIVES

PROFESSOR YANA

When an abandoned naked child was discovered on the coast of the Silver Devastation, there was nothing to identify him, and the only thing he had with him was an old fob watch. He was given the name Yana and, as he grew up, he became a scientist. There were no longer any universities to work for, but he took the title Professor. Professor Yana was an unnoticed genius, who spent his life moving from one refugee ship to another, helping his fellow humans in their efforts to escape the end of the universe. Eventually, he ended up in a laboratory in the Silo on the planet Malcassairo, surrounded by machinery that he had assembled from the most basic materials to hand – gluten extract, even string and staples. He was attempting to create a working means of rocket propulsion: the Footprint Impeller System.

All his life, Yana had been plagued through every waking moment by the constant sound of drumming in his head. The arrival of the TARDIS on Malcassairo began to stir memories hidden deep inside his mind – memories of time travel and Time Lords, Daleks and a great Time War. Although it had never worked, he had always kept his fob watch with him and, when Martha Jones recognised it as part of the Chameleon Arch process, Yana finally began to overcome its inbuilt perception filter. Strange yet familiar voices raged in his head, demanding that he open the watch and free what was contained within it...

MALCASSAIRO

By this time, the surviving humans were scattered across the galaxies, small clusters of refugees fleeing from one haven to another. One group ended up on Malcassairo, a barren world of mountains and moorlands, protected by an atmospheric shell that prevented its inhabitants from freezing to death. Before the humans arrived, there was another great civilisation, which had left behind it the remains of a great city, resembling a hive or a nest, its pathways and roads carved through rock.

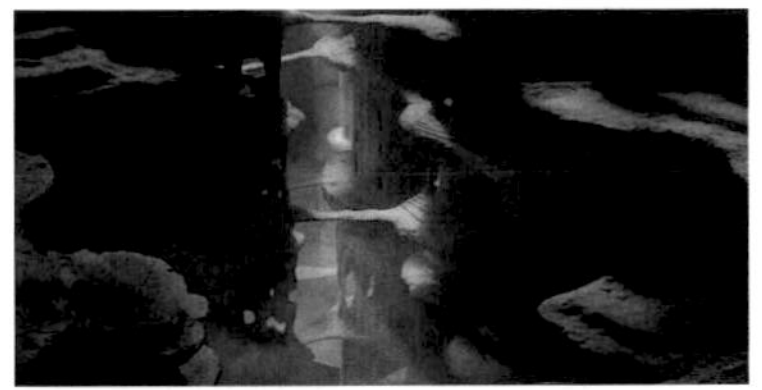

MALMOOTH

There had been indigenous life on Malcassairo before the arrival of the humans. The abandoned city was once home to the Malmooth Conglomeration, a race of blue-skinned bipedal 1.5-metre insects that fed on their own internal milk. The Malmooth had been a sophisticated and technologically advanced race, with strict behavioural codes. These included a requirement to begin each sentence with the first syllable of their own name and end it with the second syllable – not to do so would be rude. The last of the Malmooth, Chantho, joined the human effort to find a way off the planet. A devoted assistant to Professor Yana, she refused to leave without him.

100,000,000,000,000

FUTUREKIND

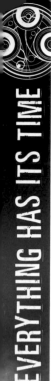

Malcassairo was also home to a tribe of primitive scavengers. They wore tattoos and piercings and had sharp pointed teeth and only rudimentary language skills. Constantly hungry, they hunted any *humani* that strayed across the surface of the planet,and feasted on those they caught. The humans feared that this was what they would themselves become, and named them Futurekind. The humans kept the gates of their Silo base chained, allowing fellow-humans in only once their teeth had been examined.

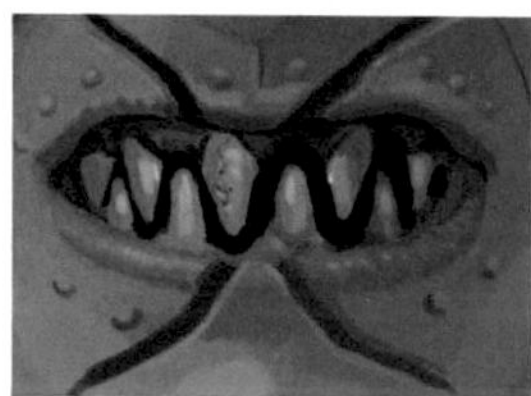

SCIENCE AND TECHNOLOGY

FOOTPRINT IMPELLER SYSTEM

The humans established a base on Malcassairo, not far from the remains of the Malmooth city. This was the Silo, at the heart of which was an enormous rocket in which they hoped to fly everyone to Utopia. They had developed a Gravitational Field Navigation System, a matrix that would enable them to travel without the stars to guide them. Professor Yana developed a rocket propulsion system based on end-time gravity mechanics. Using a gravitissimal accelerator to harmonise the five impact patterns of a gravity pulse and unify them into a single, stable 'footprint', it was theoretically possible for a rocket to achieve escape velocity and be propelled into space as the gravity pulse stamped down. Yana had been unable to harmonise the impact patterns, but the Doctor used a boost reversal circuit to generate the power needed to activate the impeller system. With the system finally operational and the TARDIS supplying extra power, the human refugees boarded the rocket. All that was needed was to connect the couplings in a chamber below the rocket itself, but the chamber was flooded with stet radiation, which instantly evaporated any human it touched.

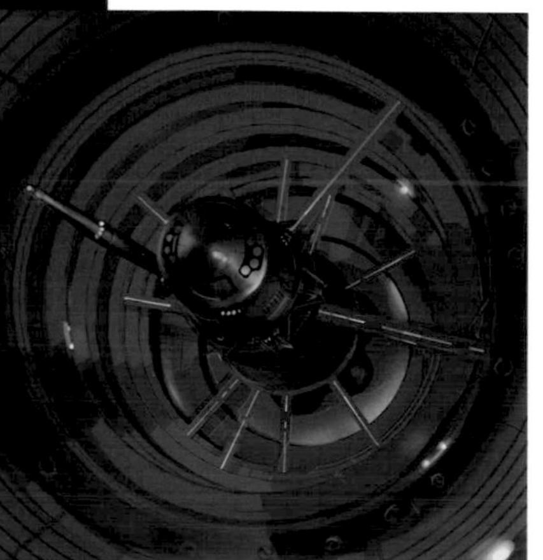

CAPTAIN JACK HARKNESS

REPORTED SIGHTING #14 CONFIRMED

ESTIMATED AGE: 174

LOCATION: Malcassairo, 100 trillion

AVAILABLE INFORMATION: Clinging to the TARDIS exterior as it plunged through the Vortex, Captain Jack actually caused the TARDIS to race 100 trillion years through time to Malcassairo as it tried to shake him off. Like his TARDIS, the Doctor instinctively felt that Jack's deathless status as a fixed point in time was wrong. But Jack's ability to come back from the dead made him the one man who could survive stet radiation and connect the couplings so that the rocket could launch.

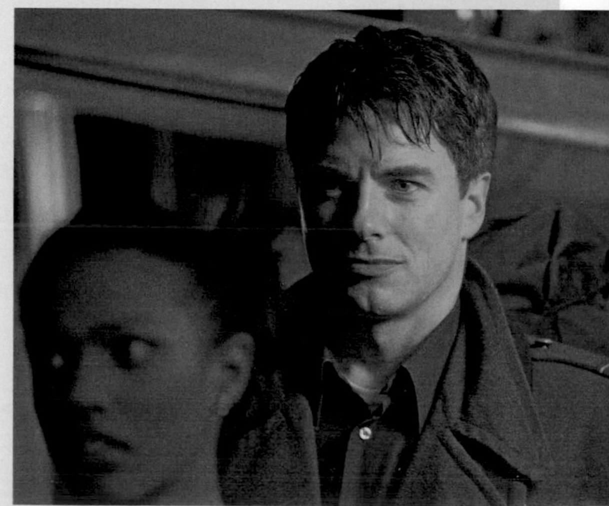

THE MASTER

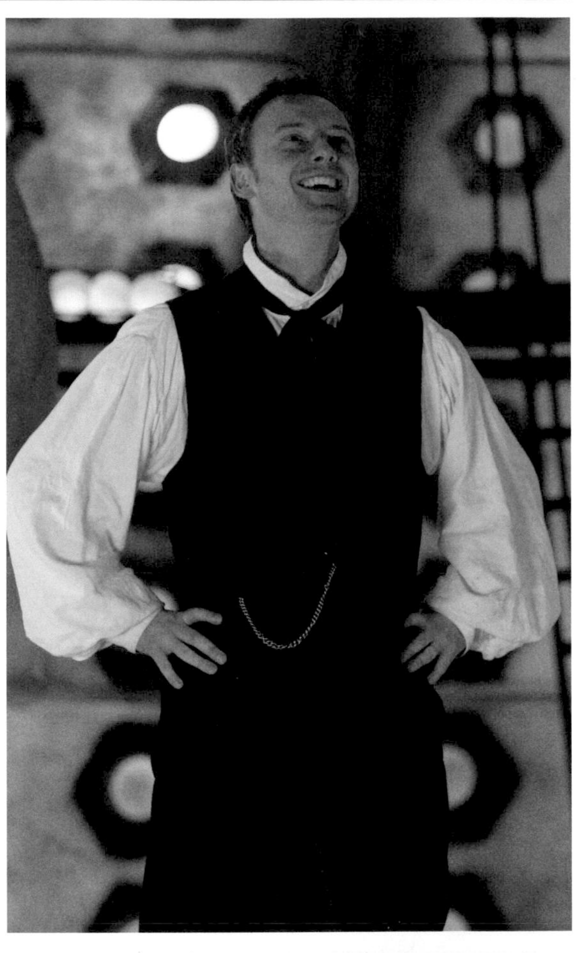

The Chameleon Arch was a device on board every TARDIS that rewrote the biology of a Time Lord and changed him into a human with no knowledge of what he had been – his Time Lord consciousness was stored inside a fob watch protected by a perception filter. The Doctor had used this process to hide from the Family of Blood in 1913. When Yana overcame the perception field and opened the watch, he discovered that his whole life as the Professor had been an invention: he was the Master, who had taken human form to escape the Time War.

The Master's first act was to attack Chantho with a live electrical cable, before trapping the Doctor, Martha and Jack in the Silo and lowering the base's defences to let the Futurekind in to hunt them down. The dying Chantho shot him just as the Doctor broke back into the lab. The Master retreated into the Doctor's TARDIS, where he began to regenerate. As the new Master prepared to leave Malcassairo, the Doctor managed to fuse the ship's coordinates so it could only travel between the end of the universe and 21st-century Earth. Taking data about Utopia and the Doctor's original right hand – the hand he had lost fighting the Sycorax in 2006, which Jack had preserved in a jar and used as a Doctor-detector – the Master departed for Earth.

THE END OF THE UNIVERSE

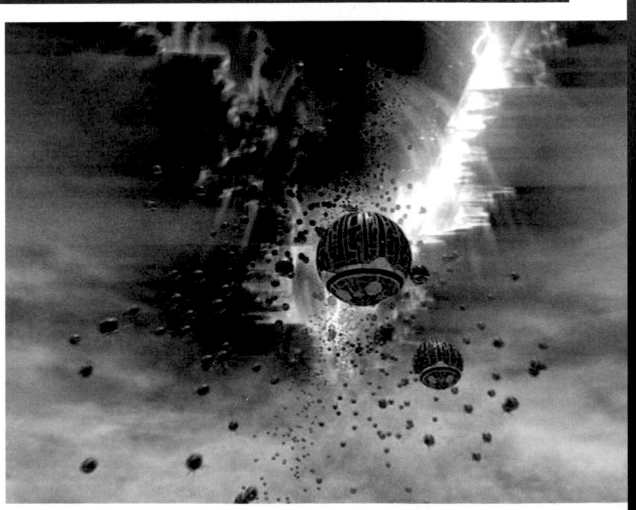

The Master later returned to the end of the universe, where he showed Lucy Saxon the fate of the human race among the burning furnaces of Utopia. Over the millennia, humans had spent a million years evolving into clouds of gas and another million years as digital downloads called Digi-Humans. Now, still struggling to outlast creation, the remnants of the human race had cannibalised themselves, reducing their organic existence to shrunken heads transported in heavily armed, magnetically sealed floating spheres. The Master named them Toclafane, and offered them a new 100 trillion-year future – in the past. Six billion Toclafane abandoned Utopia and passed through a tear in reality to the Earth of 2008.

Moments later, they reappeared in Utopia, the last, insane vestiges of humanity, destined to watch as the universe finally ended.

For my son,
and invaluable research assistant,
Kieran

Acknowledgements

Huge thanks to:
Russell T Davies, for late-night emails on dating the future, Weetabix and the unpasteurised economy of the planet Sto. And – most of all – for transforming my favourite TV programme in the world into the world's best TV programme.
Albert DePetrillo, for thinking up the whole idea of a book *something* like this, and for being endlessly encouraging and enthusiastic.
Gary Russell, for this opportunity, and many others.
Paul Lang, for inspired and inspiring design, and limitless patience and energy.
Justin Richards, for wisdom and pedantry.
Lee Binding, for a storming cover, as always.
Nick Payne, for support and assistance.
Edward Russell, Ian Grutchfield, Matt Nicholls and all the other tireless people in Cardiff, for their relentless commitment to quality.
Clayton Hickman, for saying nice things.
Ian Farrington, for a hugely important break.
Glenn Ogden, without whom I definitely wouldn't be here, now, doing this.
And Kari, for everything.

Illustration and Photo Credits

BBC Books would like to thank the following for providing photographs and for permission to reproduce copyright material. While every effort has been made to trace and acknowledge all copyright holders, we would like to apologise should there have been any errors or omissions.